Third Grade Math with Confidence

Student Workbook

Part B

Third Grade Math with Confidence

Student Workbook

Part B

KATE SNOW

WELL-TRAINED MIND PRESS

Names: Snow, Kate (Teacher), author.

Title: Third grade math with confidence. Student workbook part B / Kate Snow.

Other titles: Student workbook part B

Description: [Charles City, Virginia] : Well-Trained Mind Press, [2023] | Series: Math with confidence | Interest age level: 007-009.

Identifiers: ISBN: 978-1-944481-31-5 (paperback)

Subjects: LCSH: Mathematics--Study and teaching (Elementary) | LCGFT: Problems and exercises. | BISAC: JUVENILE NONFICTION / MATHEMATICS / Arithmetic.

Classification: LCC: QA107.2 .S663 2023 | DDC: 372.7--dc23

Reprinted November 2025 by Versa Press, Inc.

#J25-09670

Table of Contents

Author's Note

You'll need three books to teach *Third Grade Math with Confidence.* All three books are essential for the program.

- The Instructor Guide contains the scripted lesson plans for the entire year (Units 1-16).
- Student Workbook Part A contains the workbook pages for the first half of the year (Units 1-8).
- Student Workbook Part B contains the workbook pages for the second half of the year (Units 9-16).

The Student Workbooks are not meant to be used as stand-alone workbooks. The hands-on teaching activities in the Instructor Guide are an essential part of the program. You'll need the directions in the Instructor Guide to guide your child through the Lesson Activities pages. The icon with two heads means that your child should complete these pages with you, and that she is not expected to complete these pages on her own.

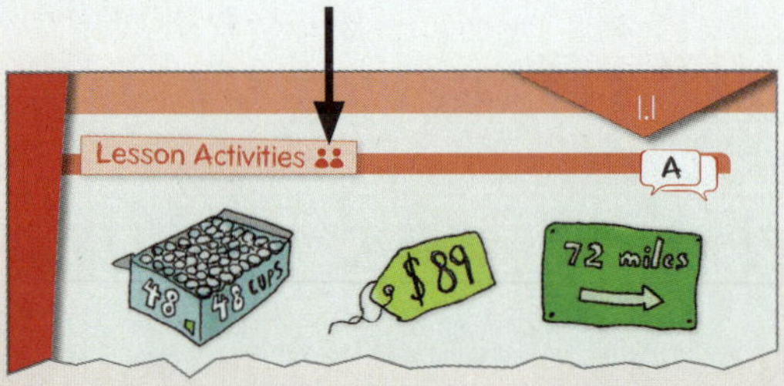

The Practice and Review pages give your child practice with new concepts and review previously-learned skills. The icon with one head means that your child may complete these pages on his own. Most third-graders will be able to complete these workbook pages independently, but some may need help reading and interpreting the directions.

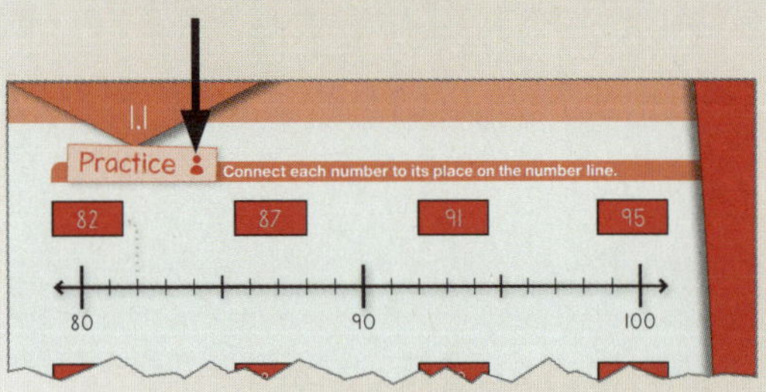

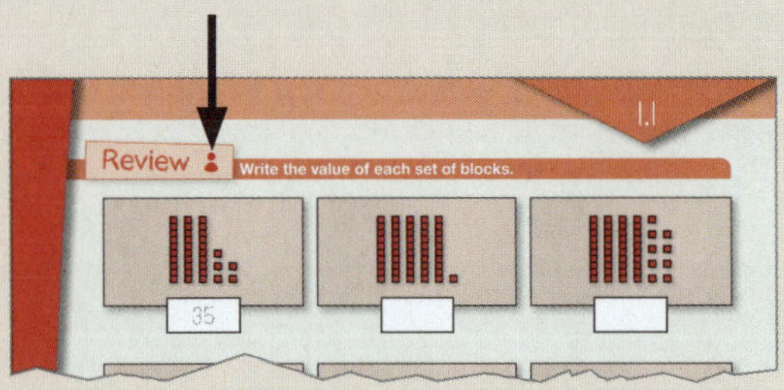

Lesson Activities

A

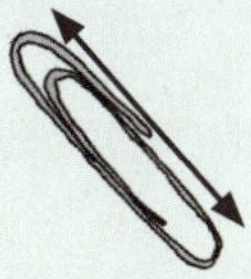

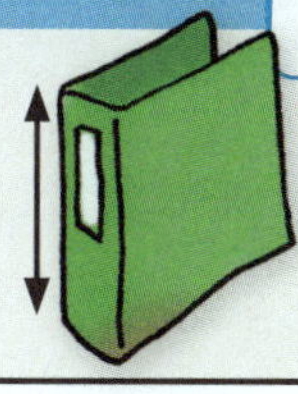

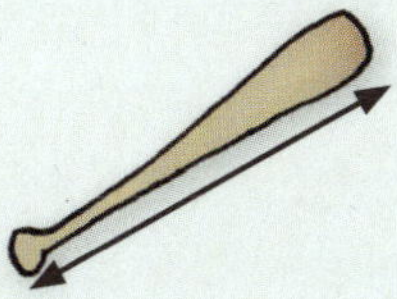

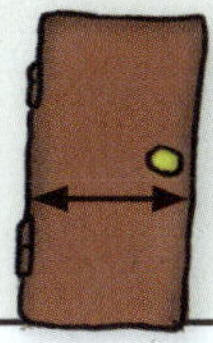

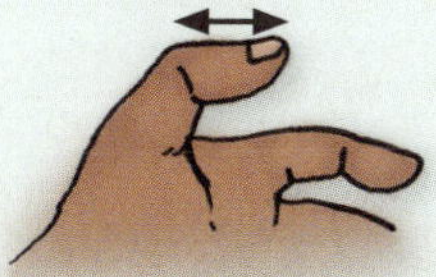

B

inches

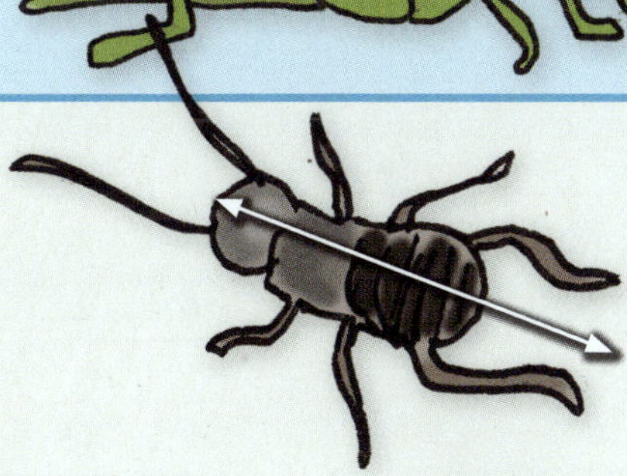

inches

inch

inches

C

$3\frac{1}{2}$ inches

$2\frac{1}{2}$ inches

$4\frac{1}{2}$ inches

Practice

Circle the more sensible measurement for each item.

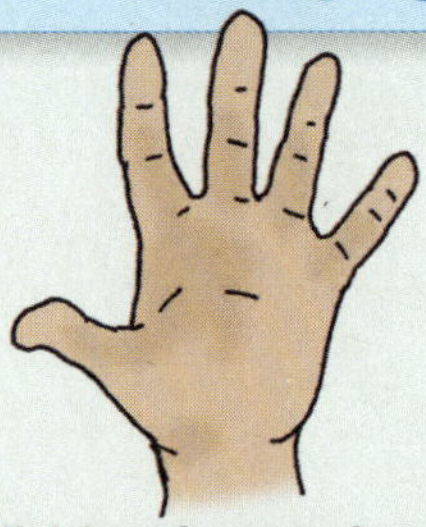

Width of your hand

5 inches	5 feet

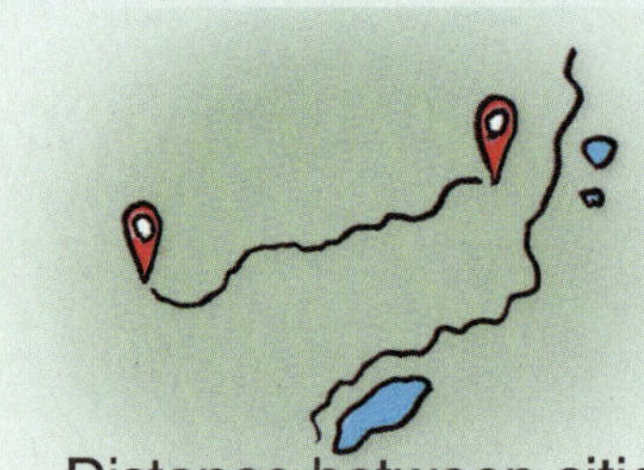

Distance between cities

100 yards	100 miles

Length of a river

150 miles	150 feet

Height of a flagpole

35 feet	35 inches

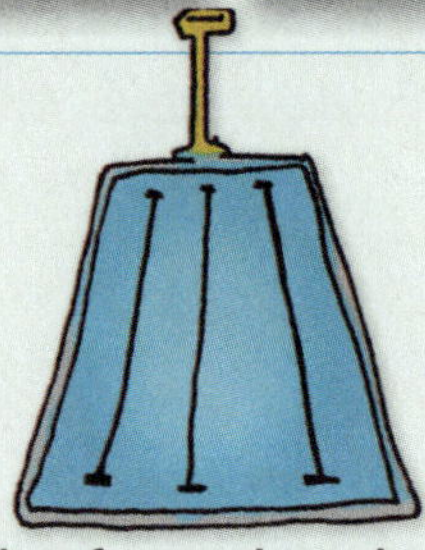

Length of a swimming pool

25 yards	25 miles

Length of a pencil

7 inches	7 feet

Use a ruler to measure the school supplies to the nearest half-inch.

inches

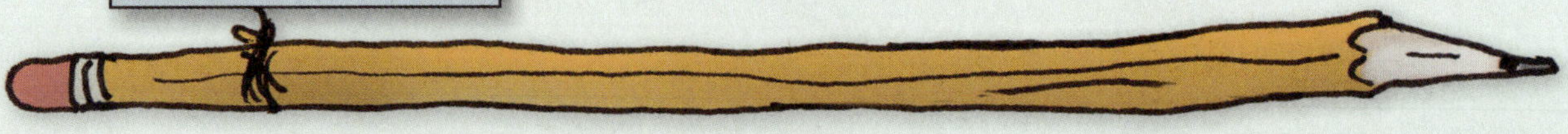

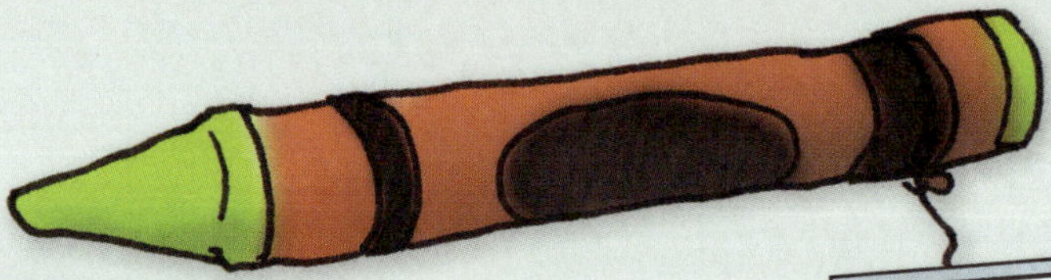

inches

inches

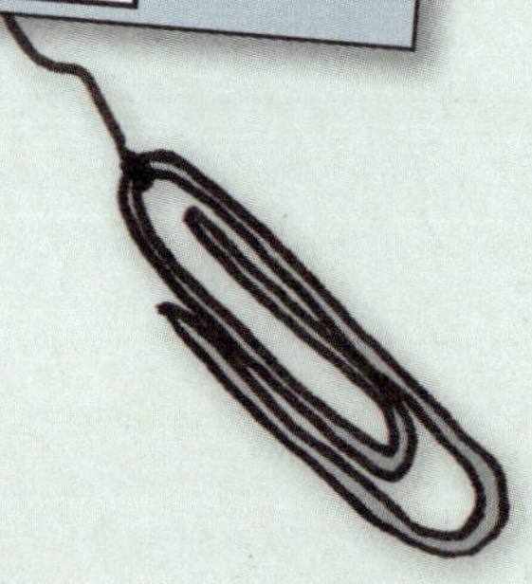

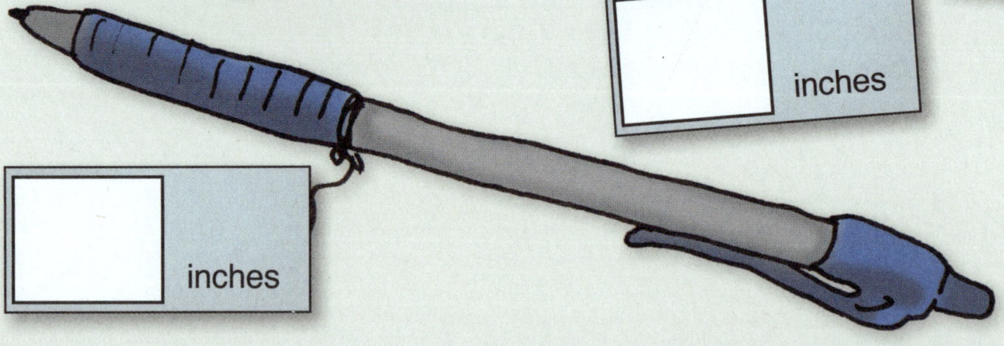

inches

Review

Complete.

6×8

8×7

9×6

7×6

10×9

8×9

7×7

8×8

6×6

10×10

Write the time.

Solve. Write the equations you use.

Calvin packed 9 bags of pretzels for a picnic. He put 7 pretzels in each bag. How many pretzels did he use?

Cora bought cocoa mix for $3.59 and marshmallows for $1.79. How much did she spend?

Lesson Activities

A

Unit	inch	foot	yard	mile
Abbreviation	in.	ft.	yd.	mi.

B

in.

in.

in.

in.

in.

C

	Height (in.)	Width (in.)
Book 1		
Book 2		
Book 3		

Practice

Use a ruler to measure the sticks to the nearest quarter-inch.

Use a ruler to draw a line that matches each length.

$2\frac{1}{4}$ in.

$2\frac{3}{4}$ in.

$3\frac{1}{2}$ in.

4 in.

$4\frac{3}{4}$ in.

Review

Complete the multiplication chart.

×	5	6	7	8	9	10
5	25	30	35	40	45	50
6	30					60
7	35					70
8	40					80
9	45					90
10	50	60	70	80	90	100

Wesley asked his friends and family about their favorite winter activities. Use the chart to complete the bar graph.

Activity	Number of People
Sledding	17
Ice Skating	12
Skiing	6

Complete.

$94 - 36 = \square$

$58 + 27 = \square$

$75 - 68 = \square$

$90 + 40 = \square$

$30 \times 4 = \square$

$80 \times 6 = \square$

$50 \times 7 = \square$

$9 \times 40 = \square$

Lesson Activities

A

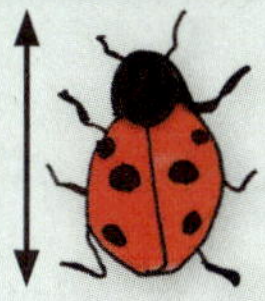

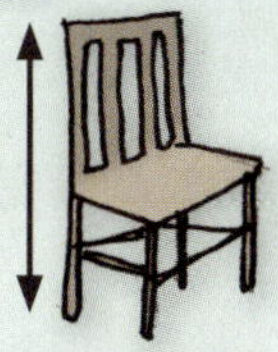

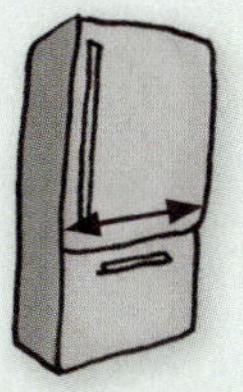

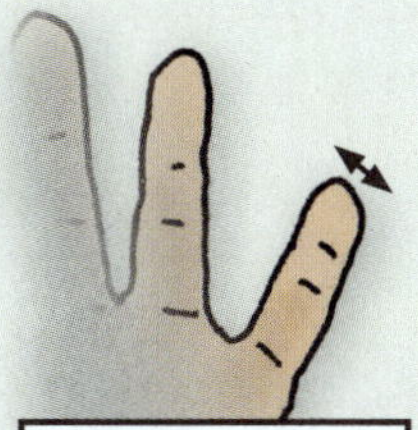

Unit	Abbreviation
centimeter	cm
meter	m
kilometer	km

B

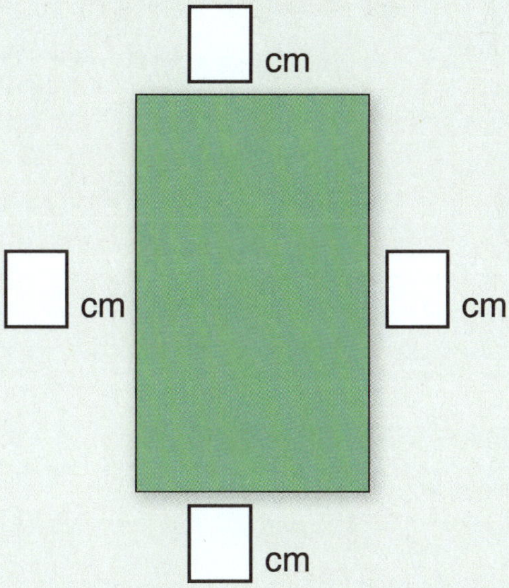

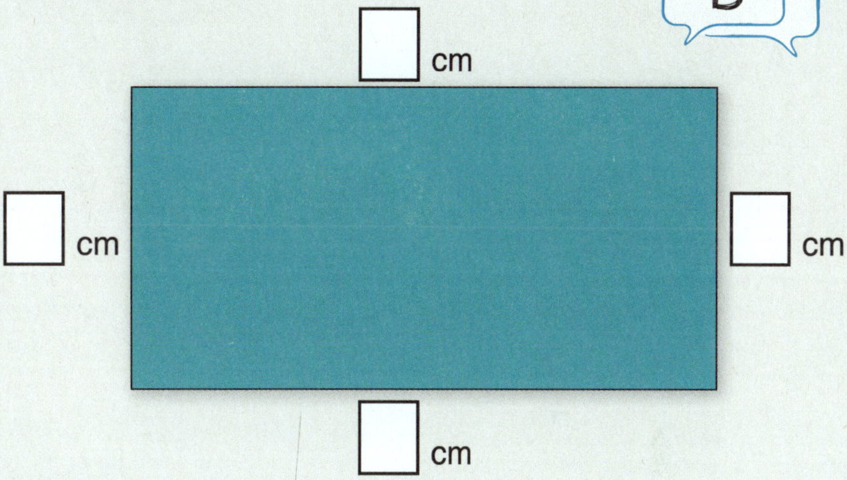

C

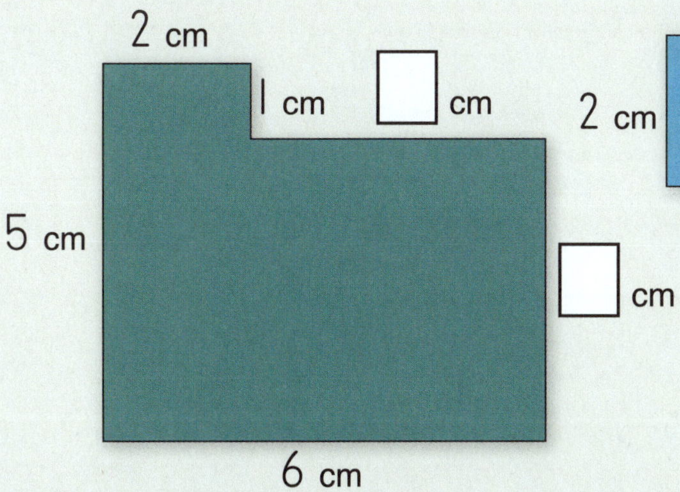

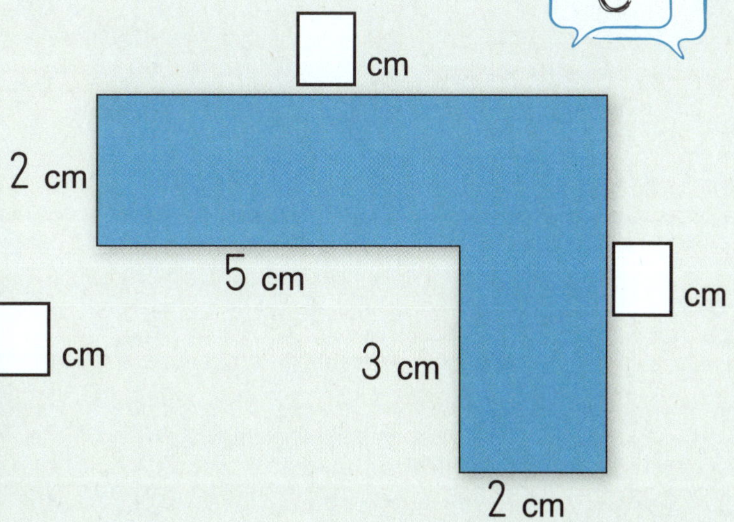

9.3

Practice

Circle the more sensible measurement for each item.

Distance between cities

100 meters | 100 kilometers

Height of an elephant

3 meters | 3 kilometers

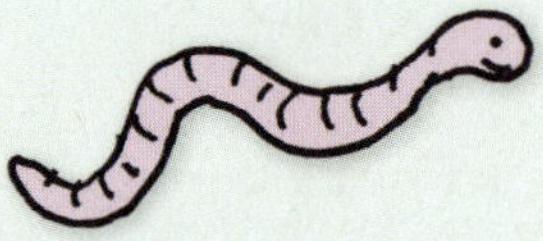

Length of a worm

10 meters | 10 centimeters

Height of a book

25 centimeters | 25 meters

Length of a hike

6 meters | 6 kilometers

Length of a bus

11 meters | 11 centimeters

Use logical thinking to label the missing sides of the shapes.

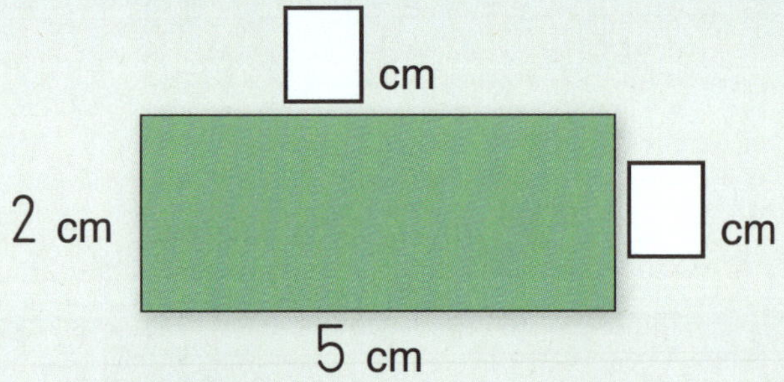

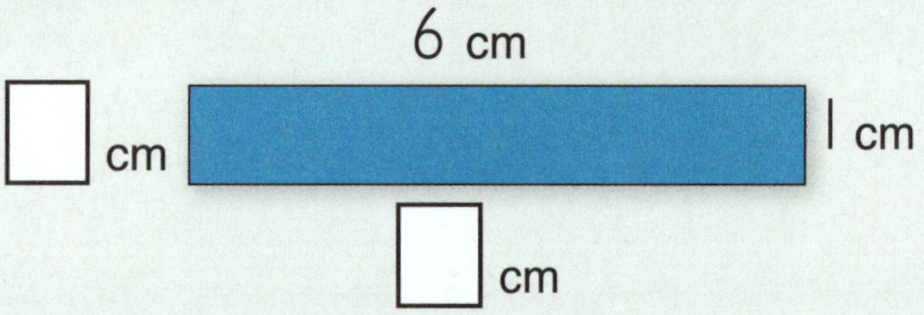

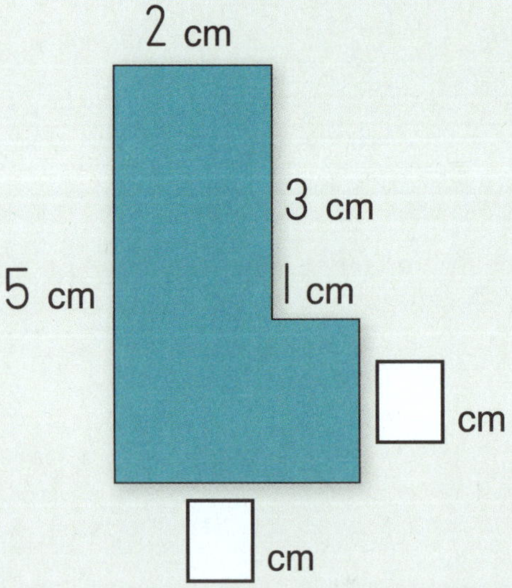

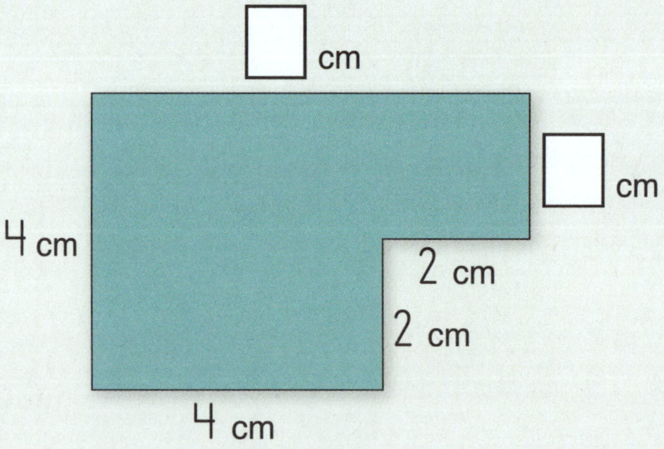

Review

Use a ruler to draw a line that matches each length.

$2\frac{1}{2}$ in.

$3\frac{3}{4}$ in.

Complete the sequences.

Count by 100s				600	700			

Count by 50s				650	700			

Count by 25s				675	700			

Complete.

	7.	4	2
−	3.	0	8
$			

	5.	3	8
+	2.	9	9
$			

Complete.

		6
×		7

		8
×		6

		7
×		8

		7
×		9

		6
×		9

		9
×		9

Lesson Activities

A

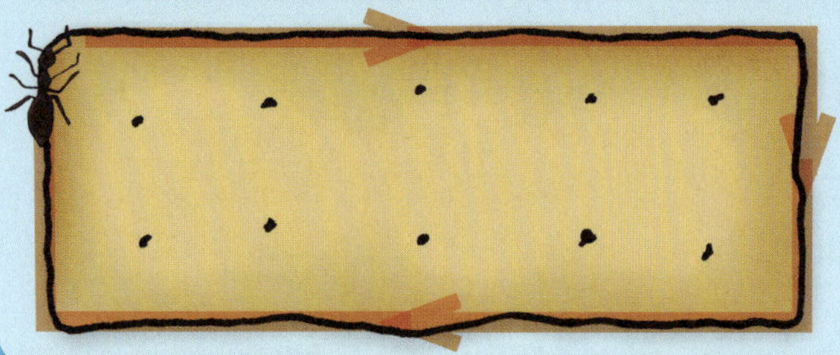

Perimeter

The distance around the outside edge

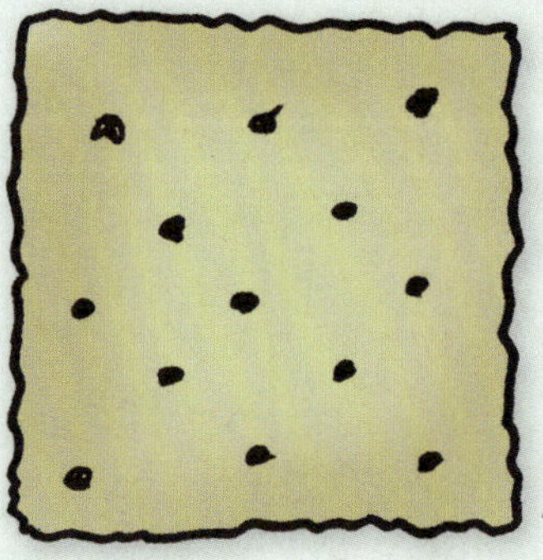

Perimeter: ☐ cm

Perimeter: ☐ cm

Perimeter: ☐ cm

B

What is the perimeter of the yard?

Perimeter: ☐ in.

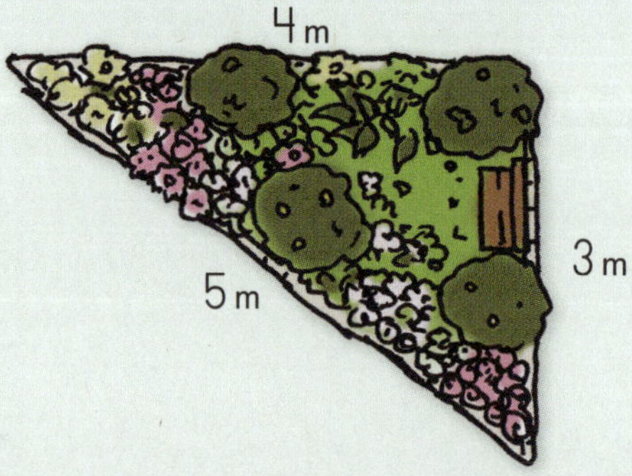

Perimeter: ☐ m

C

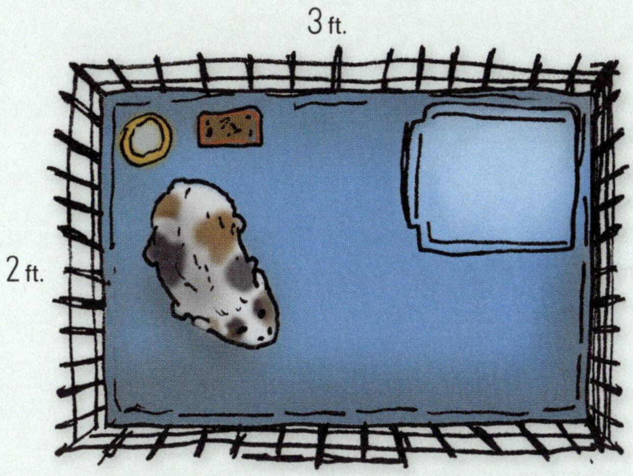

Perimeter: ☐ ft.

Perimeter: ☐ km

Practice

Find the perimeter of each shape.

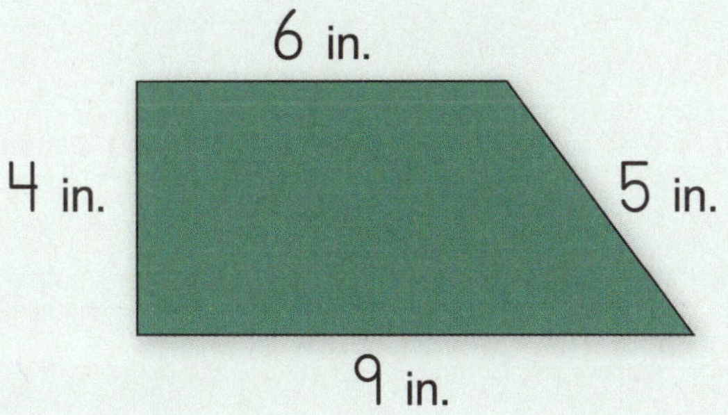

Perimeter: ☐ in.

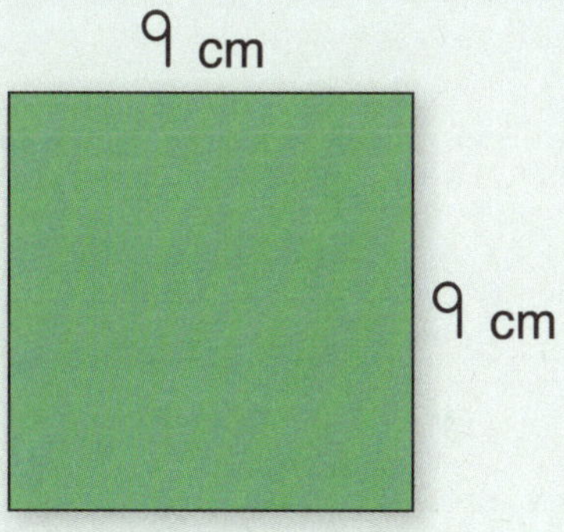

Perimeter: ☐ cm

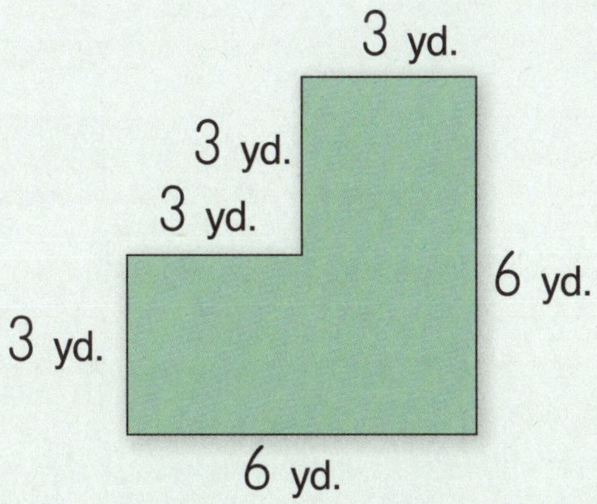

Perimeter: ☐ yd.

★

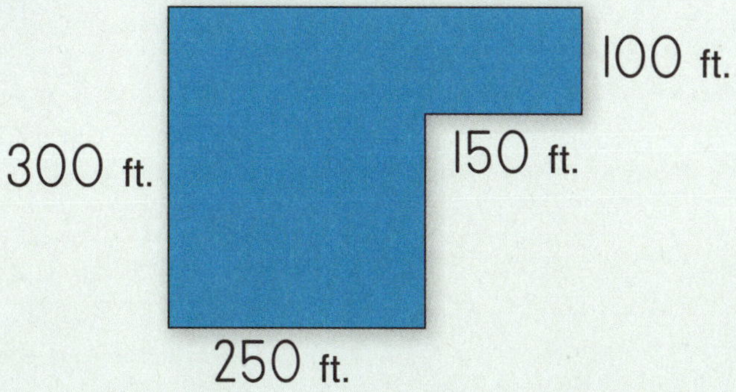

Perimeter: ☐ ft.

Review

Circle the more sensible measurement for each item.

Length of an aquarium

1 yard	1 mile

Height of a cereal box

13 inches	13 yards

Length of a bathtub

5 yards	5 feet

Complete.

$\frac{6}{8} - \frac{1}{8} = \frac{\square}{\square}$

$\frac{2}{6} + \frac{3}{6} = \frac{\square}{\square}$

$\frac{2}{4} + \frac{1}{4} = \frac{\square}{\square}$

$\frac{2}{3} - \frac{1}{3} = \frac{\square}{\square}$

Complete.

$3 \times 5 + 4 = \square$

$6 \times 2 + 1 = \square$

$10 \times 5 + 4 = \square$

$8 \times 4 + 2 = \square$

$5 \times 5 + 3 = \square$

Match.

6×8	45
8×7	48
9×6	49
7×7	54
9×5	56

Lesson Activities

A

What is the perimeter of the room?

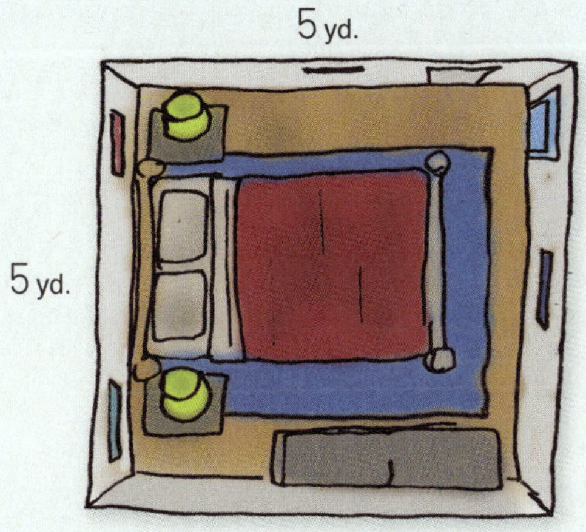

Perimeter: ☐ yd.

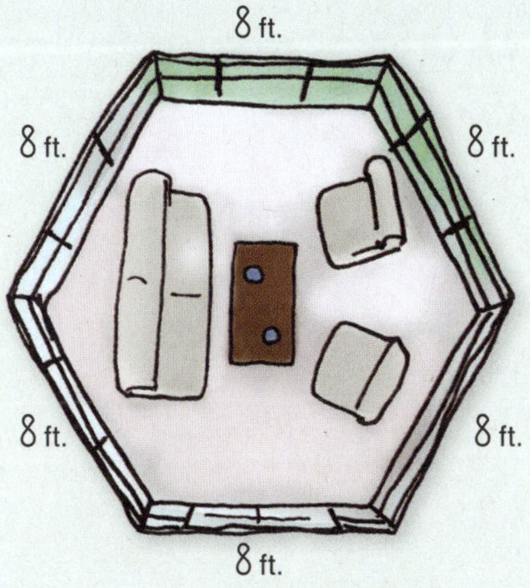

Perimeter: ☐ ft.

B

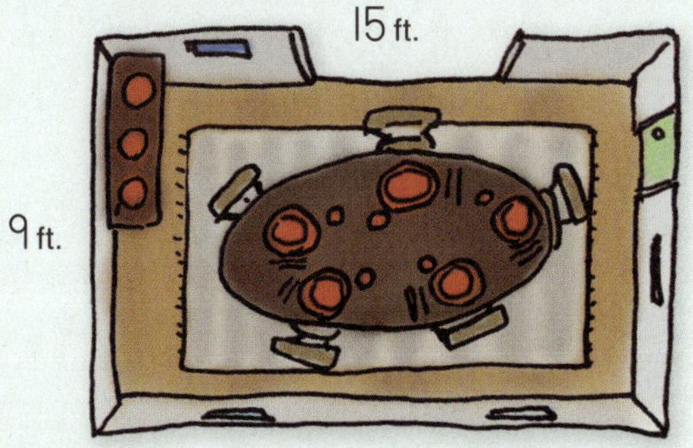

Perimeter: ☐ ft.

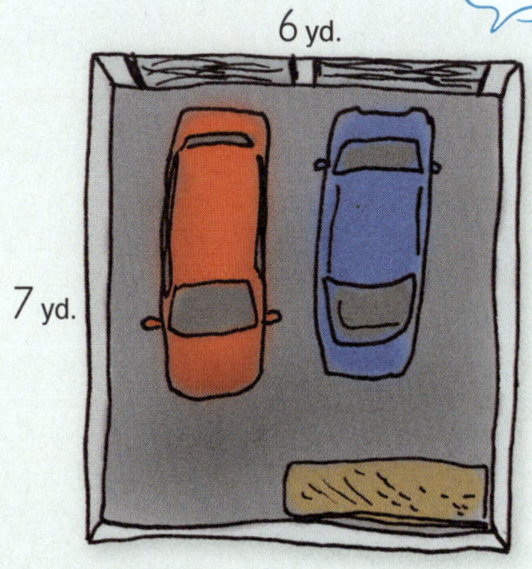

Perimeter: ☐ yd.

Practice

Find the perimeter of each shape.

All sides are 20 yd. long.

Perimeter: ☐ yd.

All sides are 5 ft. long.

Perimeter: ☐ ft.

All sides are 9 cm long.

Perimeter: ☐ cm

★ All sides are 2 in. long.

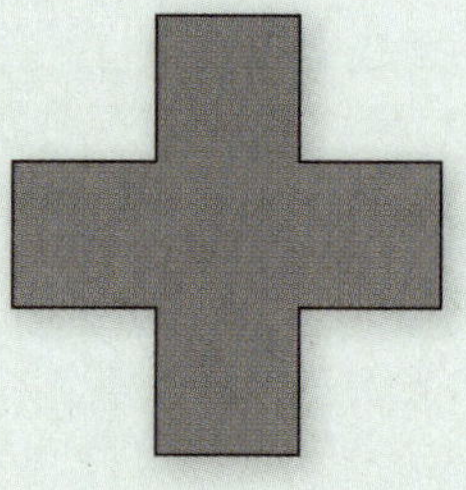

Perimeter: ☐ in.

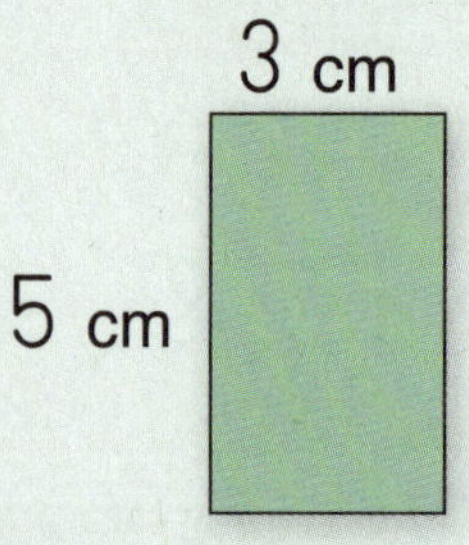

Perimeter: ☐ cm

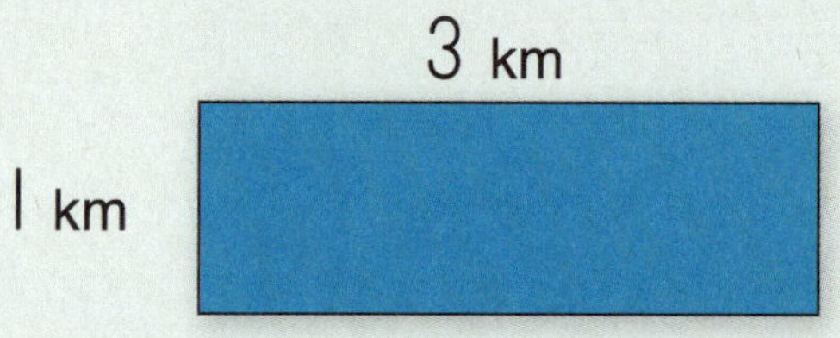

Perimeter: ☐ km

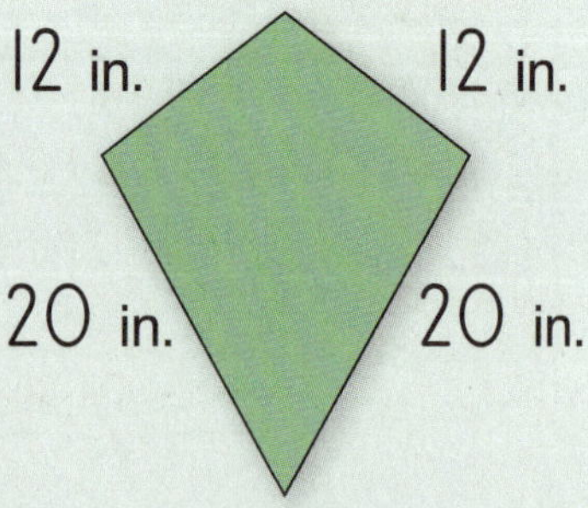

Perimeter: ☐ in.

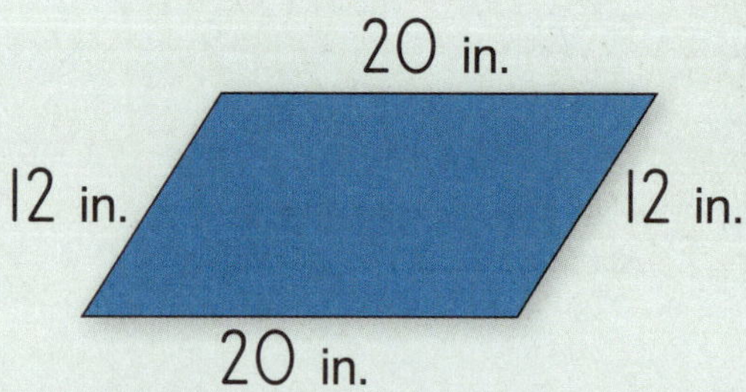

Perimeter: ☐ in.

Review

Circle the more sensible unit for each item.

Length of a fork

20 centimeters	20 meters

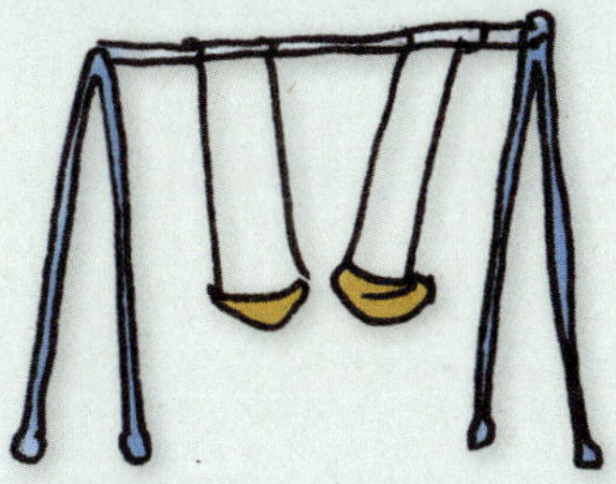

Length of a playground

50 meters	50 kilometers

Length of a baby

50 meters	50 centimeters

Complete.

2 weeks = ☐ days

4 weeks = ☐ days

5 weeks = ☐ days

6 weeks = ☐ days

9 weeks = ☐ days

Match.

9 × 7	56
9 × 8	63
8 × 7	64
9 × 9	72
8 × 8	81

Solve. Write the equations you use.

A box of chocolates costs $6.29.
A box of valentines costs $1.35 less than a box of chocolates.
How much does a box of valentines cost?

Marco played outside for 60 minutes. He spent 15 minutes making a snowman, 20 minutes building a snow fort, and the rest of the time throwing snowballs. How much time did he spend throwing snowballs?

Lesson Activities

A

Kaya made a poster 20 inches long and 15 inches wide. What is the perimeter of the poster?

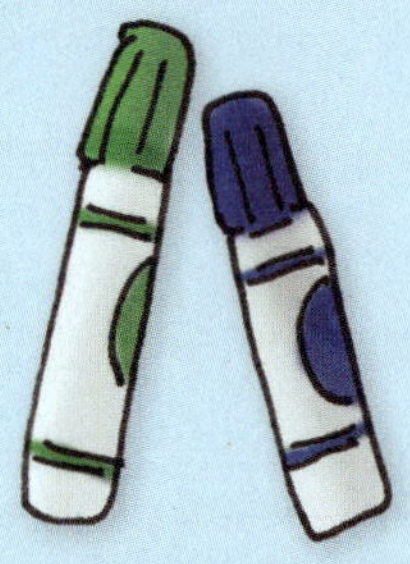

Ja'shon helps his parents build a chicken coop with 6 sides. Each side is 4 feet long. What is the perimeter of the chicken coop?

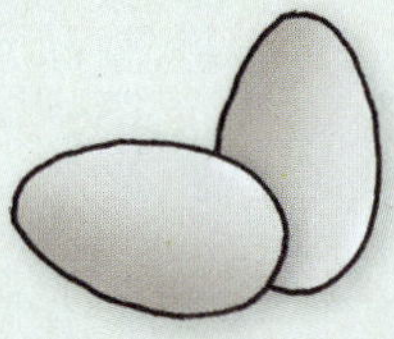

B

Kelsey and her dad use 30 feet of fence to enclose this garden. How long is the shortest side of the garden?

Jonah's yard has a perimeter of 115 meters. How long is the unlabeled side of the yard?

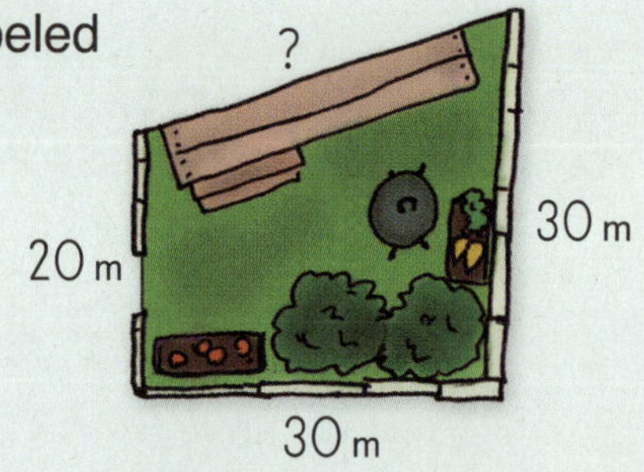

Practice

Solve. Write the equations you use.

Caroline's bedroom is shaped like a rectangle. It is 12 feet long and 10 feet wide. What is the perimeter of her bedroom?

Zayne used craft sticks to make a pentagon with 5 sides. Each craft stick is 4 inches long. What is the perimeter of the pentagon?

The perimeter of this triangle is 20 meters. How long is the unlabeled side?

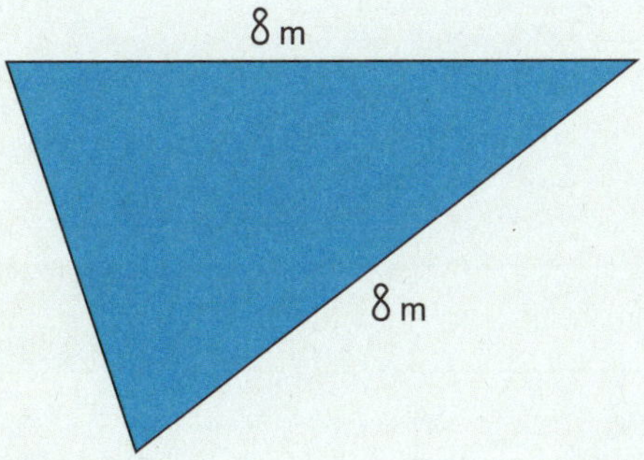

★ Lucas built this rectangle with blocks. The perimeter of the rectangle is 54 inches. The longer sides are 15 inches long. How long are the shorter sides?

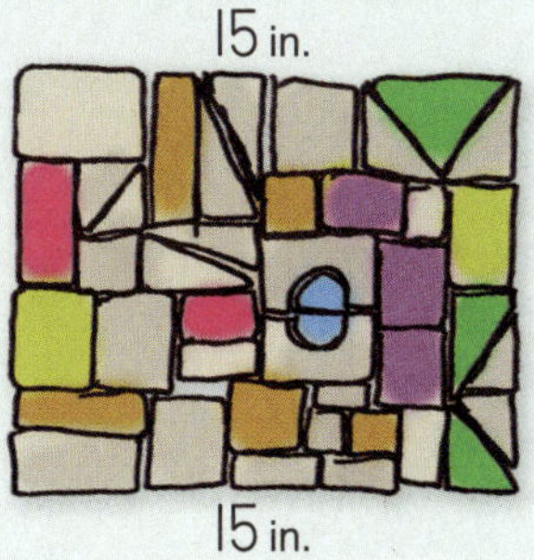

9.6

Review

Connect each number to its dot on the number line.

507 525 548 589 593

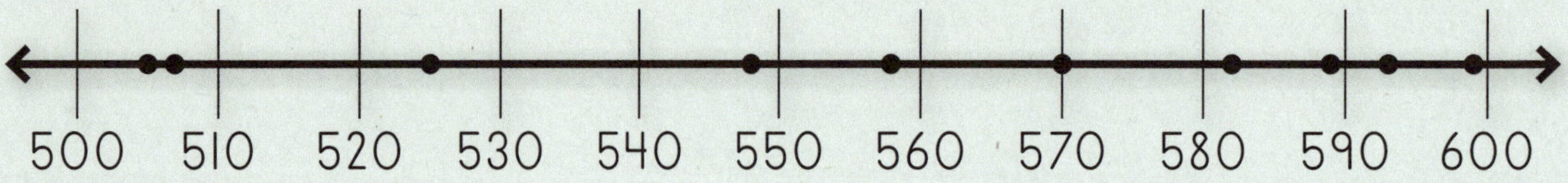

505 558 570 599 582

Complete.

$9.01 = ☐ ¢

$5.75 = ☐ ¢

$ ☐ = 250 ¢

$ ☐ = 800 ¢

Round to the nearest dollar.

$9.78	
$0.95	
$6.07	
$4.55	

Match.

6 × 7	42
9 × 7	56
8 × 8	63
7 × 8	64

8 × 9	48
7 × 7	49
9 × 9	72
8 × 6	81

Lesson Activities

A

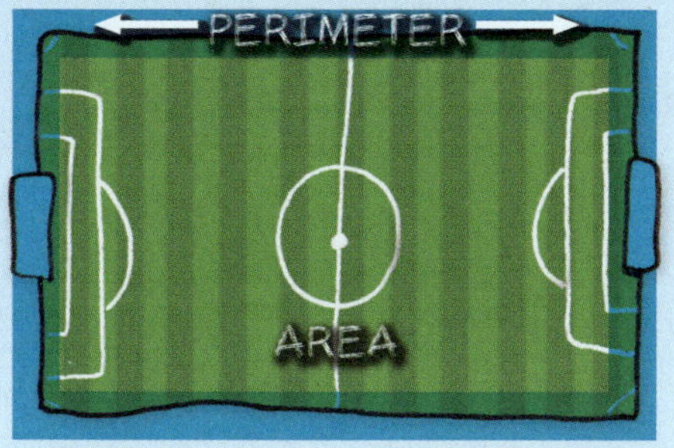

Perimeter
The distance around the outside edge of a shape

Area
The amount of space the shape covers.

B

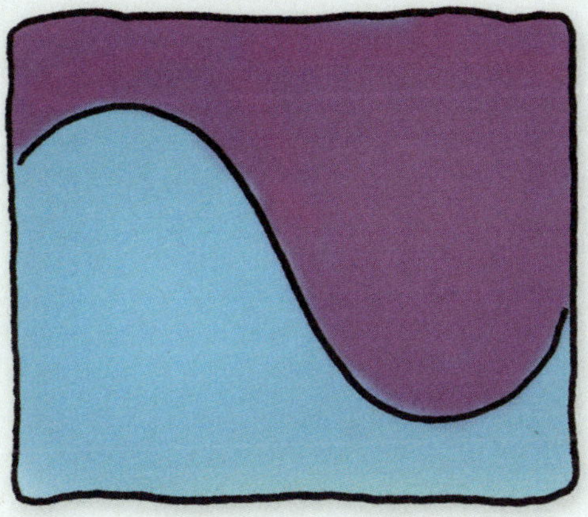

Perimeter: ☐ cm

☐ square cm

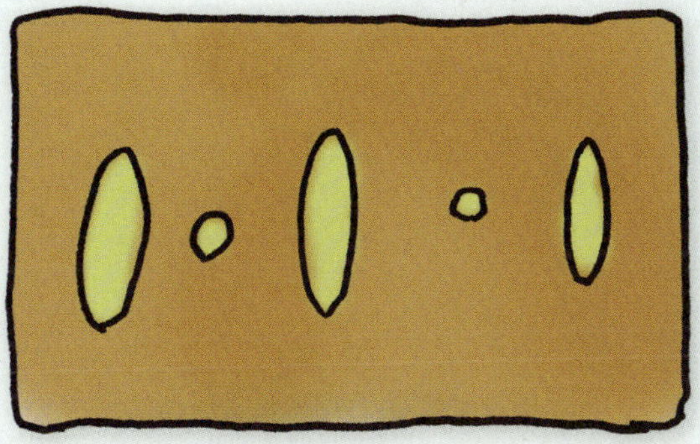

Perimeter: ☐ cm

☐ square cm

Perimeter: ☐ cm

☐ square cm

Perimeter: ☐ cm

☐ square cm

Practice

Find the perimeter and area of each shape.

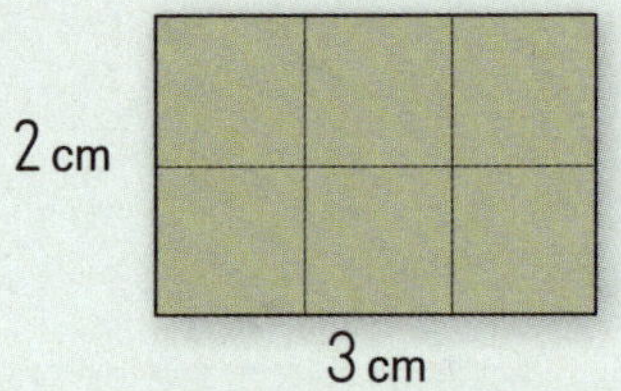

Perimeter: ☐ cm

☐ square cm

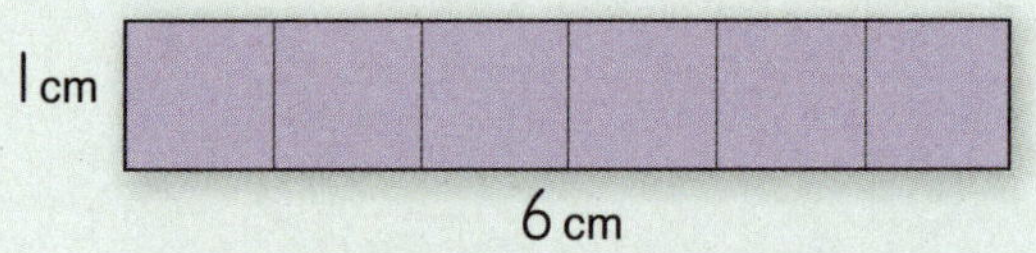

Perimeter: ☐ cm

☐ square cm

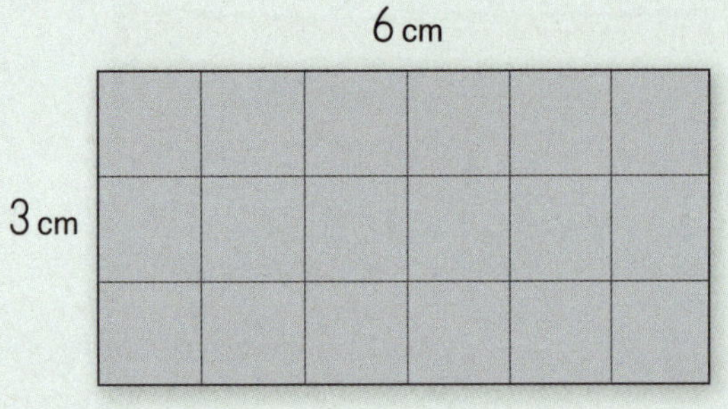

Perimeter: ☐ cm

☐ square cm

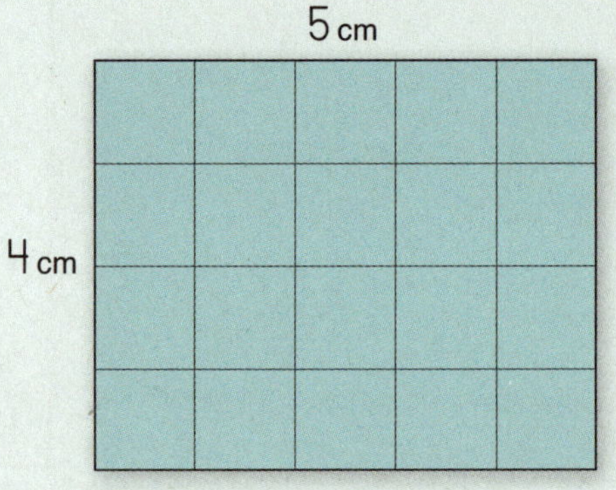

Perimeter: ☐ cm

☐ square cm

★

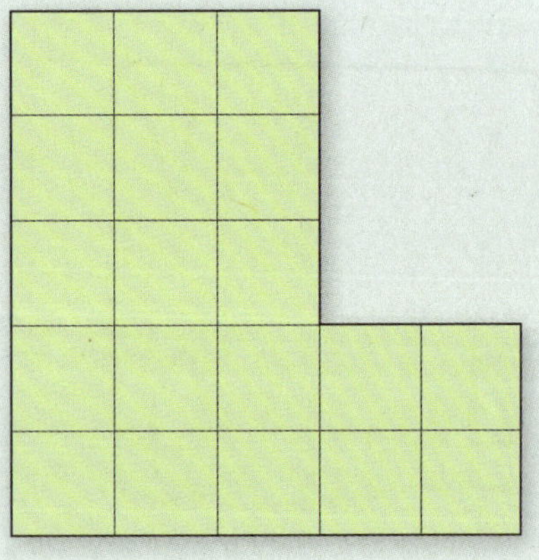

Perimeter: ☐ cm

☐ square cm

★

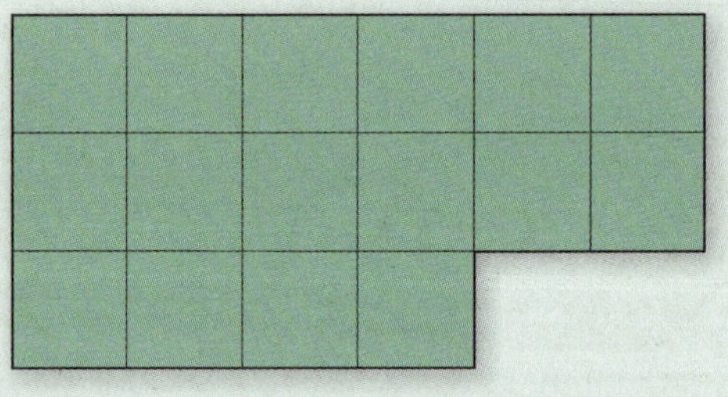

Perimeter: ☐ cm

☐ square cm

Review

Use a ruler to measure the straws to the nearest quarter-inch.

Complete.

5 weeks, 1 day = ☐ days

4 weeks, 2 days = ☐ days

5 weeks, 5 days = ☐ days

10 weeks, 3 days = ☐ days

Match.

8 × 8	36
6 × 6	49
9 × 9	64
10 × 10	81
7 × 7	100

Solve. Write the equations you use.

Madelyn organized her stuffed animals. She has 3 shelves, and she put 7 animals on each shelf. She had 2 stuffed animals left, so she put them on her bed. How many stuffed animals does she have?

The chocolate chip cookie box has 4 rows of 9 cookies. The lemon cookie box has 6 rows of 7 cookies. How many cookies are there in all?

Lesson Activities

A

Perimeter: ☐ cm

Area: ☐ sq. cm

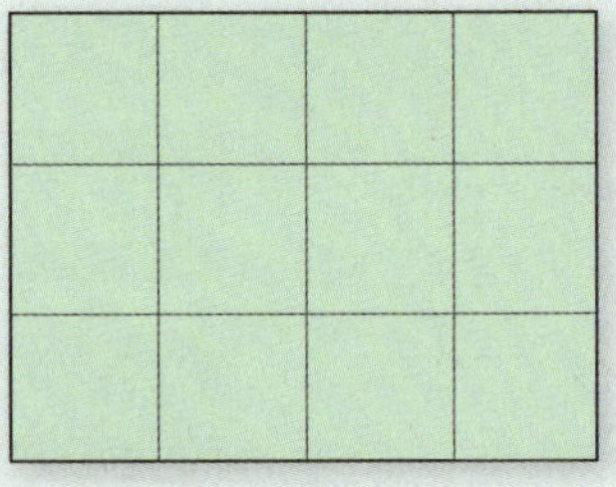

Perimeter: ☐ cm

☐ sq. cm

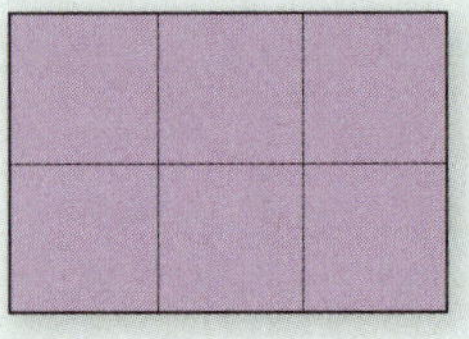

Perimeter: ☐ cm

☐ sq. cm

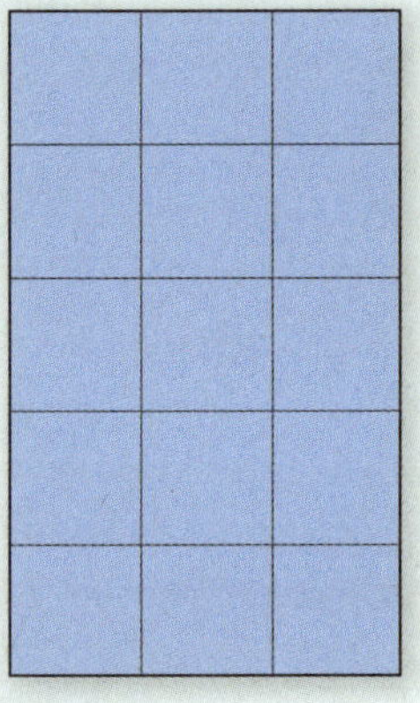

Perimeter: ☐ cm

☐ sq. cm

B

☐ sq. cm

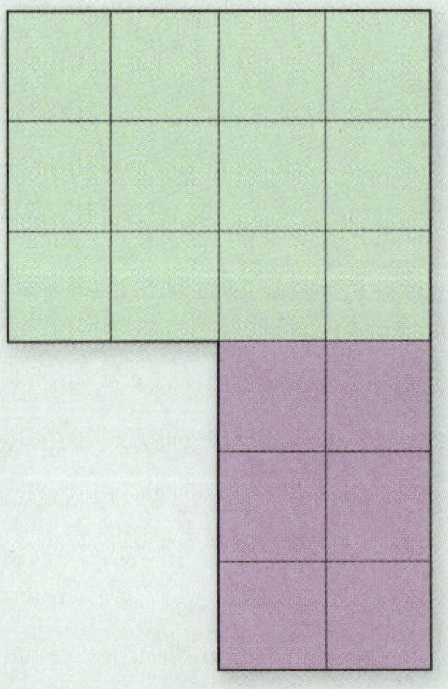

☐ sq. cm

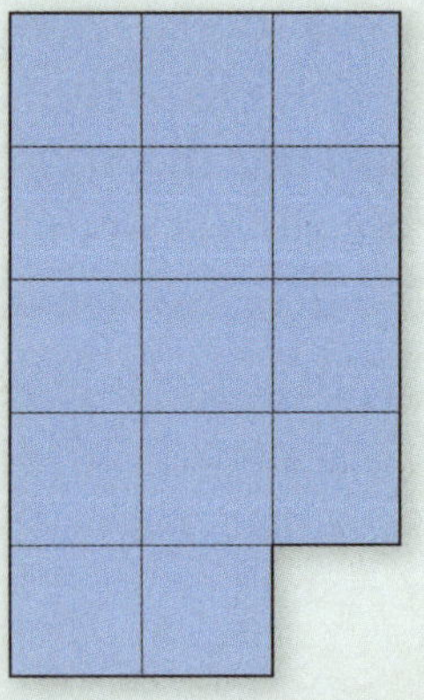

☐ sq. cm

Practice

Find the area of each shape.

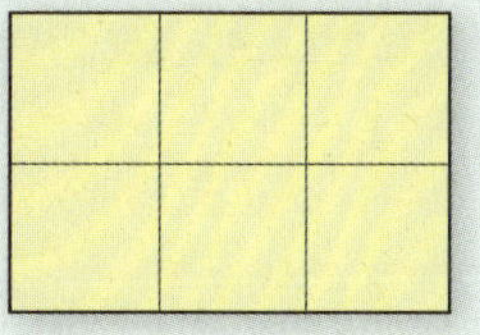

☐ sq. cm

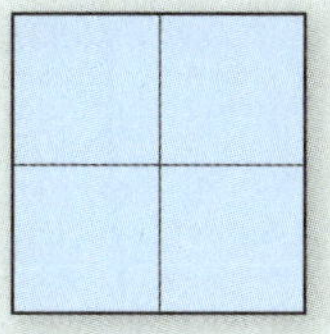

☐ sq. cm

☐ sq. cm

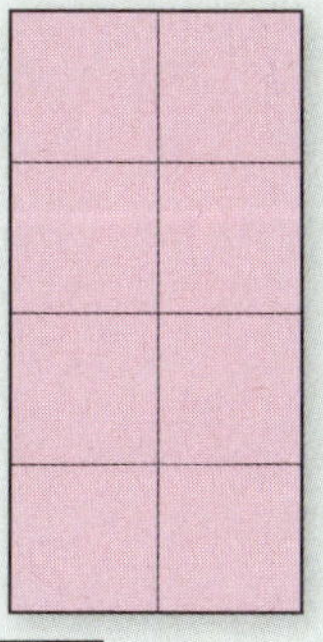

☐ sq. cm

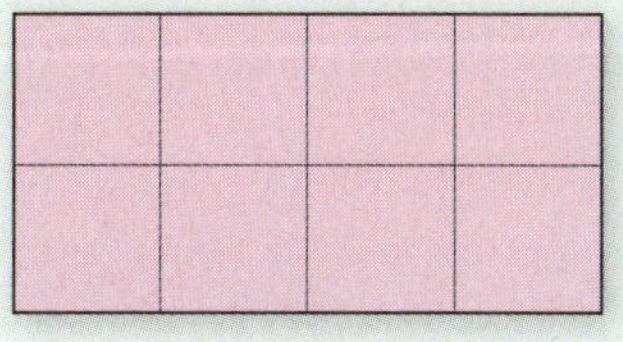

☐ sq. cm

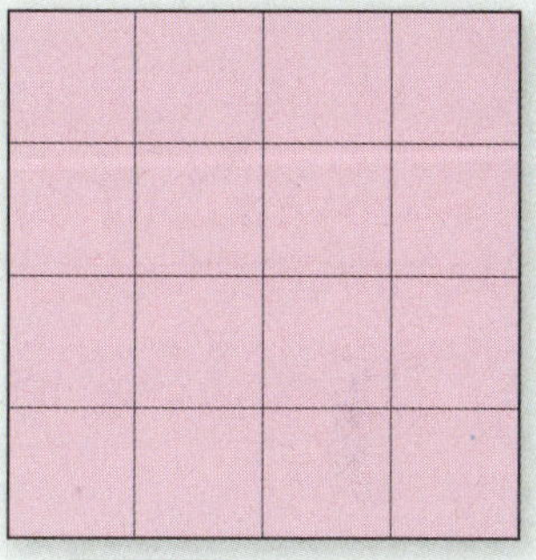

☐ sq. cm

☐ sq. cm

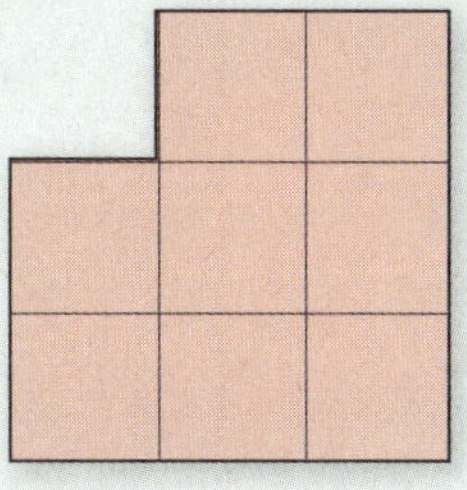

☐ sq. cm

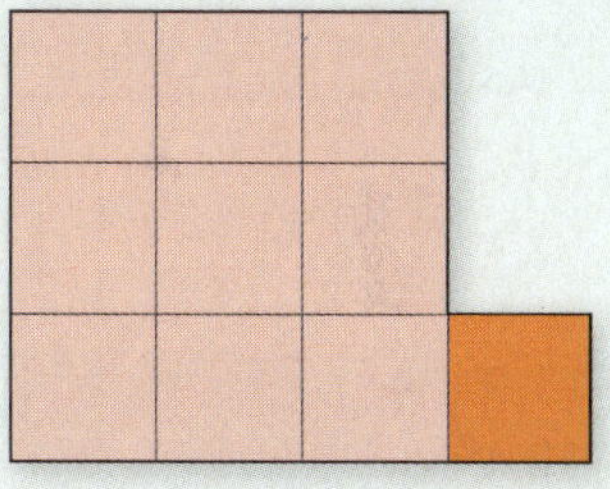

☐ sq. cm

☐ sq. cm

☐ sq. cm

☐ sq. cm

Review

Use the pictograph to answer the questions.
Write a multiplication equation to match each question.

How many minutes did Ryan practice on Tuesday?

How many minutes did Ryan practice on Thursday?

How many minutes did Ryan practice on Saturday?

Complete.

$$\begin{array}{r} 646 \\ -\ 209 \\ \hline \end{array}$$

$$\begin{array}{r} 431 \\ +\ 569 \\ \hline \end{array}$$

Complete.

$$\begin{array}{r} 7 \\ \times\ 9 \\ \hline \end{array} \qquad \begin{array}{r} 6 \\ \times\ 6 \\ \hline \end{array} \qquad \begin{array}{r} 4 \\ \times\ 8 \\ \hline \end{array}$$

$$\begin{array}{r} 9 \\ \times\ 6 \\ \hline \end{array} \qquad \begin{array}{r} 5 \\ \times\ 9 \\ \hline \end{array} \qquad \begin{array}{r} 8 \\ \times\ 7 \\ \hline \end{array}$$

Solve. Write the equations you use.

Aaron has $37.
He buys 4 books.
Each book costs $8.
How much money does he have left?

Lesson Activities

A

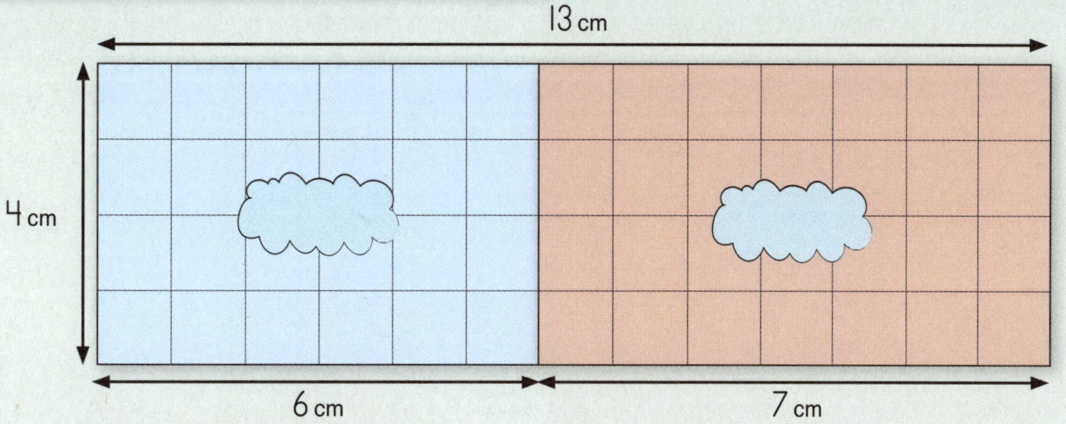

☐ sq. cm

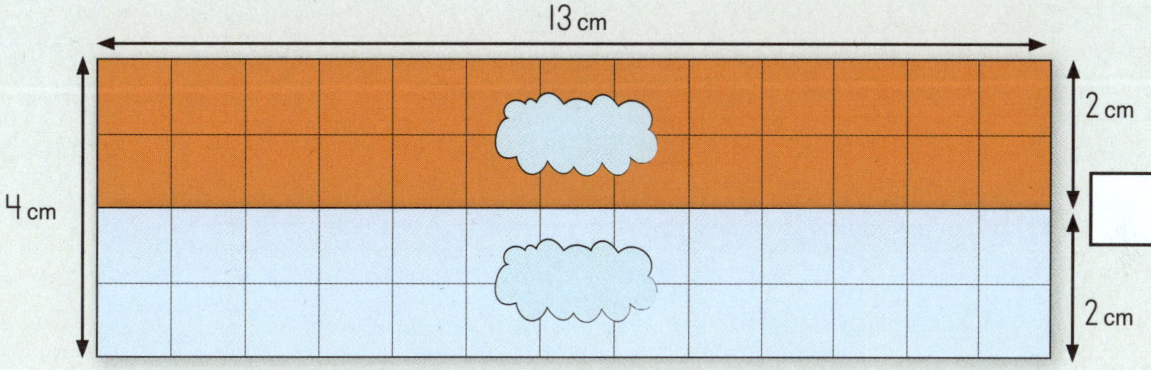

☐ sq. cm

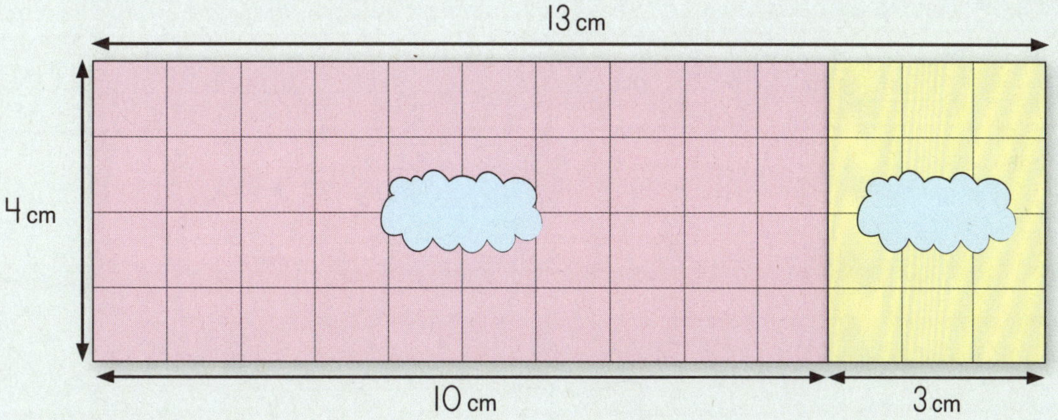

☐ sq. cm

B

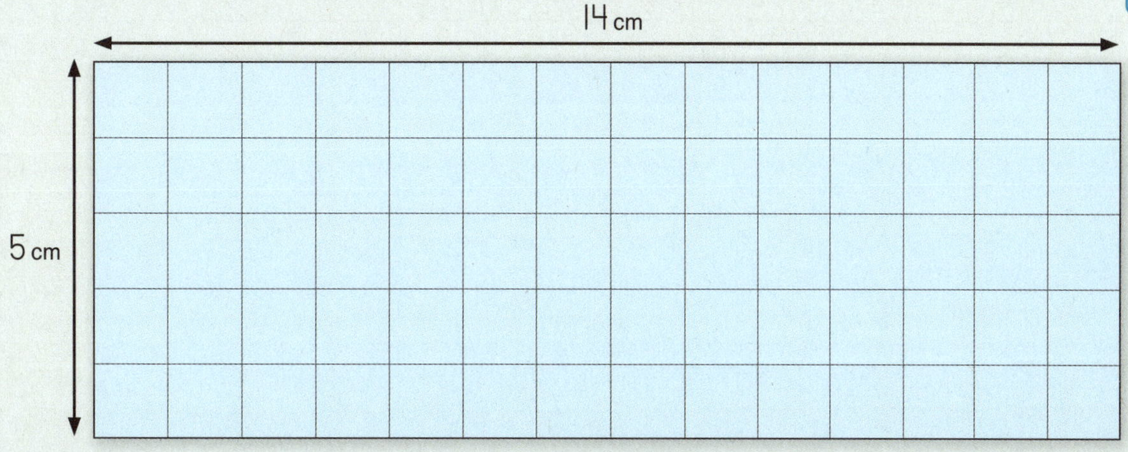

☐ sq. cm

Practice

Split each rectangle into smaller rectangles. Then, find the area of the whole rectangle. The first rectangle has already been split for you.

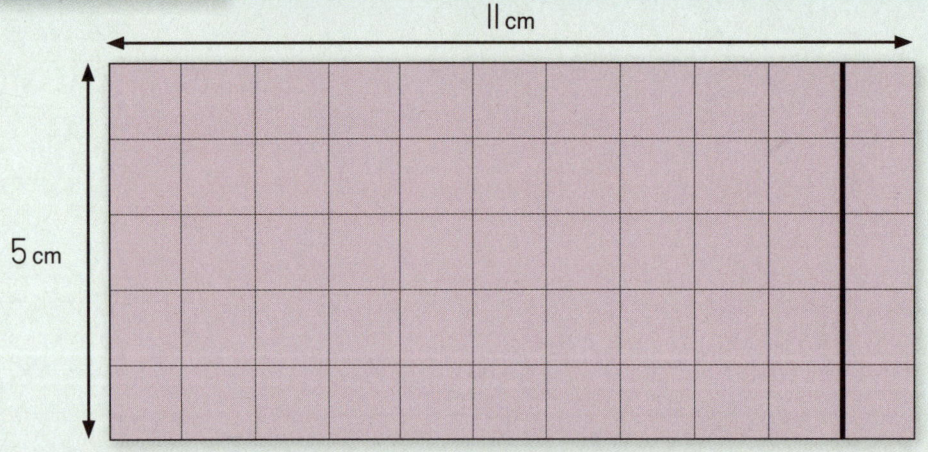

☐ sq. cm

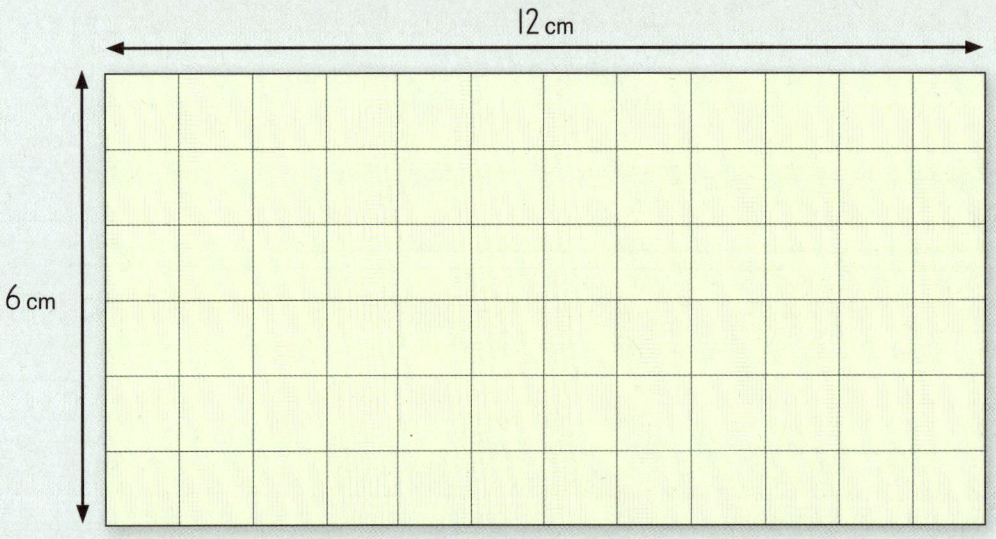

☐ sq. cm

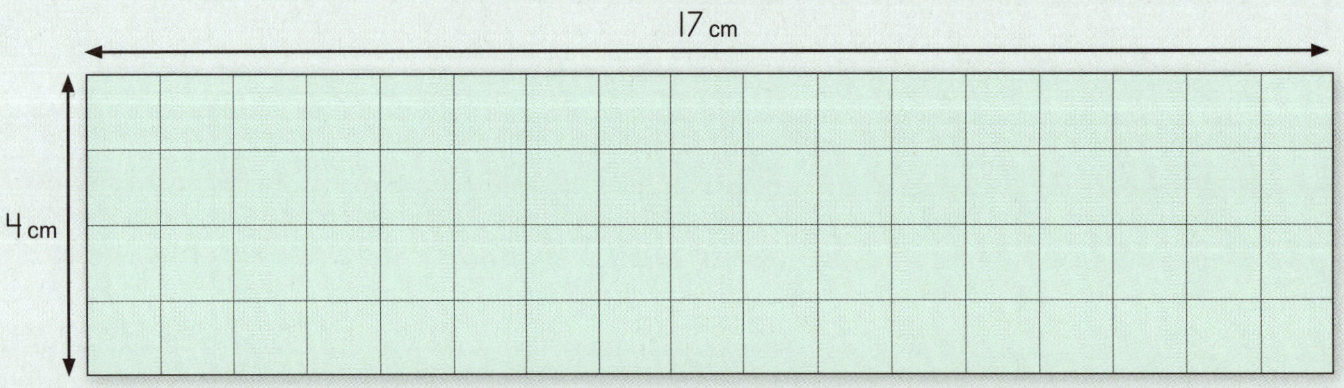

☐ sq. cm

Review

Choose the more sensible unit for each item.

Height of a mug

4 feet	4 inches

Height of a door

8 feet	8 inches

Height of a tree

20 yards	20 miles

Complete.

$7 \times 6 + 1 = \square$

$8 \times 8 + 2 = \square$

$9 \times 7 + 7 = \square$

$6 \times 8 + 2 = \square$

$7 \times 8 + 5 = \square$

Complete.

$47 + \square = 52$

$\square + 6 = 77$

$100 - \square = 55$

$\square - 12 = 48$

$40 - \square = 2$

Solve. Write the equations you use.

★ The dinosaur costs \$1.35 less than the yo-yo. The deck of cards costs \$0.79 more than the dinosaur. How much does the deck of cards cost?

Lesson Activities

A

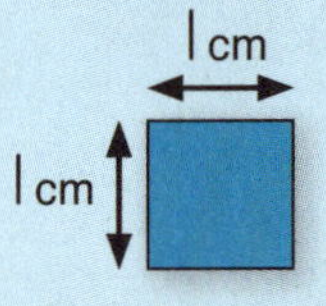

1 square centimeter
(sq. cm)

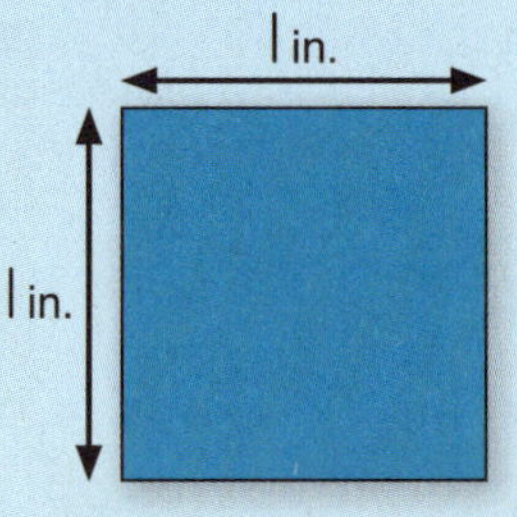

1 square inch
(sq. in.)

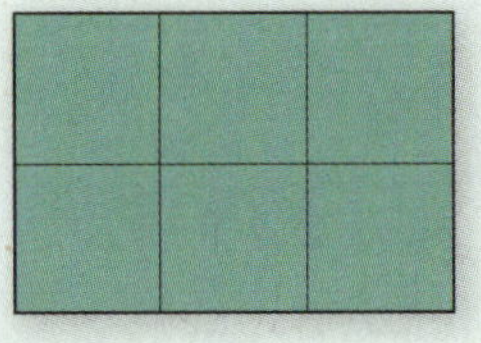

B

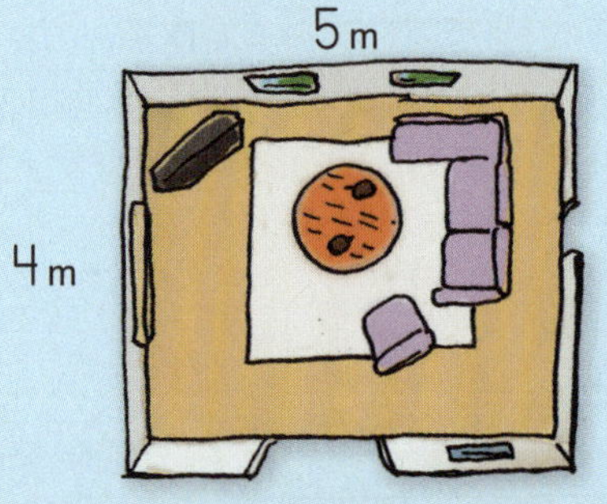

What is the area of the room?

Practice

Use the grid lines to find the area of each shape. Circle the correct units.

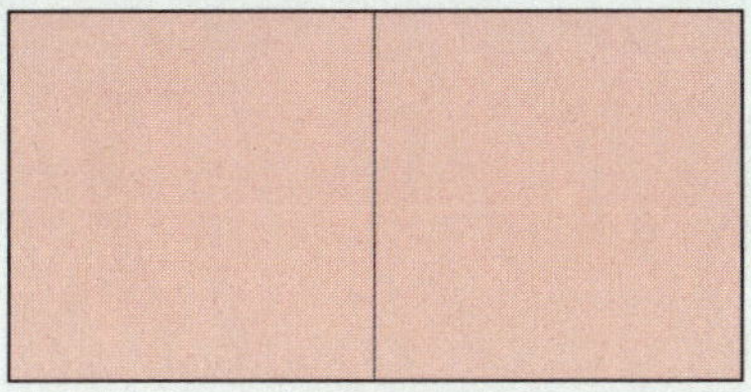

☐ sq. in. / sq. cm

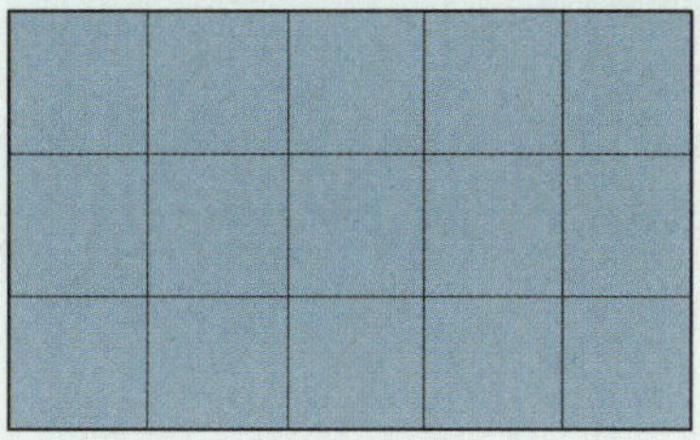

☐ sq. in. / sq. cm

Find the area of each item.

5 m

5 m

☐

12 ft.

10 ft.

☐

10 in.

13 in.

☐

10 cm

15 cm

☐

Review

Circle the more sensible measurement for each item.

Height of a mug

10 centimeters | 10 meters

Height of a door

2 centimeters | 2 meters

Height of a tree

20 meters | 20 kilometers

Complete.

$3 \times 4 = \square$	$7 \times 8 = \square$	$2 \times 9 = \square$
$6 \times 9 = \square$	$8 \times 4 = \square$	$8 \times 3 = \square$
$4 \times 5 = \square$	$8 \times 8 = \square$	$9 \times 4 = \square$
$0 \times 7 = \square$	$7 \times 3 = \square$	$9 \times 9 = \square$
$9 \times 3 = \square$	$7 \times 9 = \square$	$6 \times 4 = \square$

Solve. Write the equations you use.

Mark's book is 319 pages long. Vera's book is 278 pages long. How many pages longer is Mark's book than Vera's?

Mark's book is 319 pages long. Vera's book is 278 pages long. How many pages are in both books?

Lesson Activities

A

Serafina made a poster 10 inches long and 6 inches wide. What is the area of the poster?

Jeffrey helped his dad plant sod in a square part of the yard. Each side of the square was 8 feet long. How many square feet did they cover?

B

The shorter side of the rug is 6 feet long. The other side is 4 feet longer. What is the area of the rug?

The longer side of the pool is 5 meters long. The other side is 1 meter shorter. What is the area of the pool?

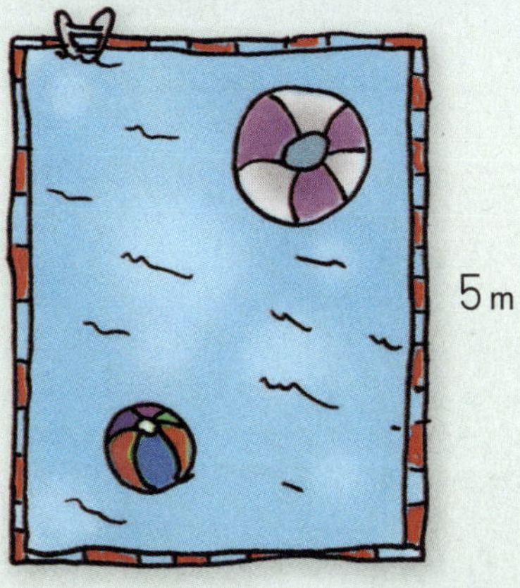

Practice

Solve. Write the equations you use.

Caroline's bedroom is shaped like a rectangle. It is 12 feet long and 10 feet wide. What is the area of her bedroom?

Zayne used 4 craft sticks to make a square. Each craft stick is 5 inches long. What is the area of the square?

The shorter side of the pool is 4 yards long. The other side is 3 yards longer. What is the area of the pool?

★ The perimeter of this garden bed is 14 feet. What is its area?

Review

Use the numbers to complete the blanks. You will use each number once.

1	2	3	4	5	6	7	8	9

$\square \times 8 = 16$	$3 \times \square = 12$	$10 \times \square = 90$
$\square \times 4 = 20$	$6 \times \square = 18$	$3 \times \square = 24$
$\square \times 5 = 35$	$10 \times \square = 60$	$17 \times \square = 17$

Complete.

	× 7
7	
9	
6	
8	

	× 8
6	
8	
9	
7	

	× 9
9	
7	
8	
6	

Copy the shapes.

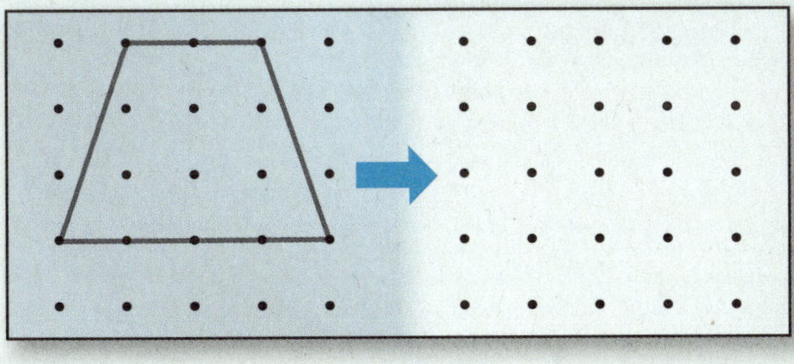

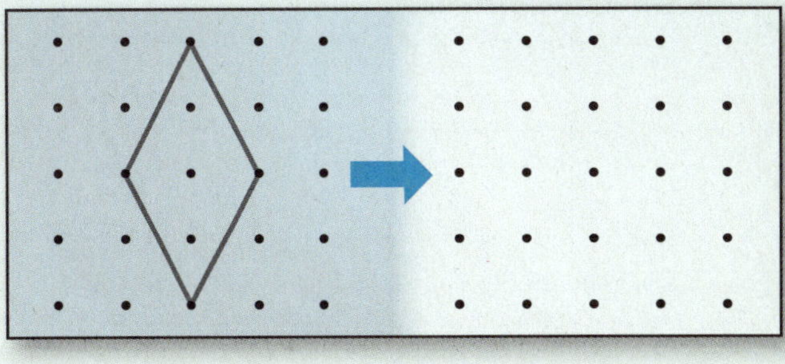

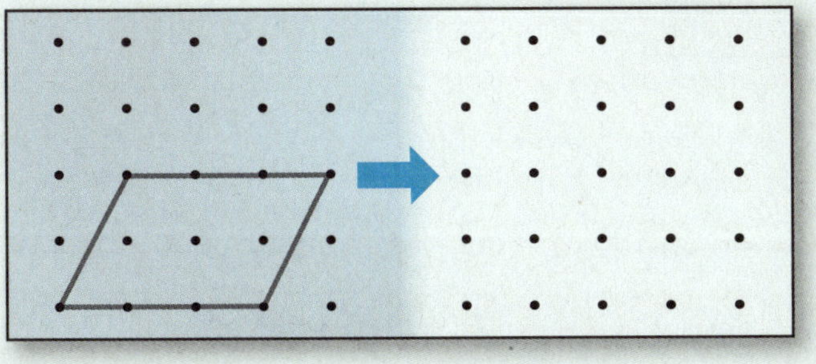

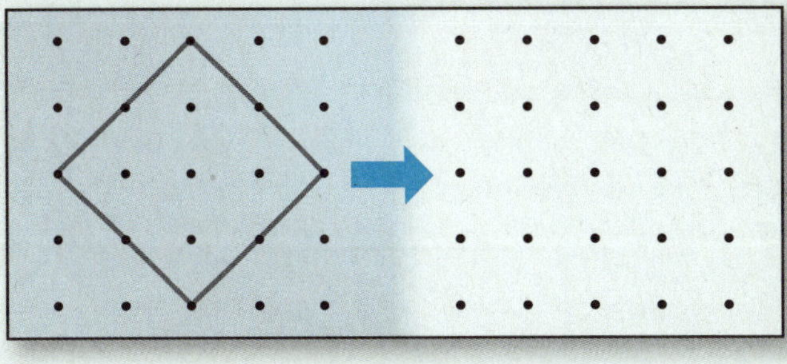

9.12

Unit Wrap-Up

Use a ruler to measure the sticks to the nearest quarter-inch.

Circle the more sensible unit for each item.

Area of a rug

40 sq. ft.	40 sq. in.

Area of a sticky note

25 sq. cm	25 sq. m

Area of a parking lot

300 sq. m	300 sq. km

Find the perimeter. Include the correct unit.

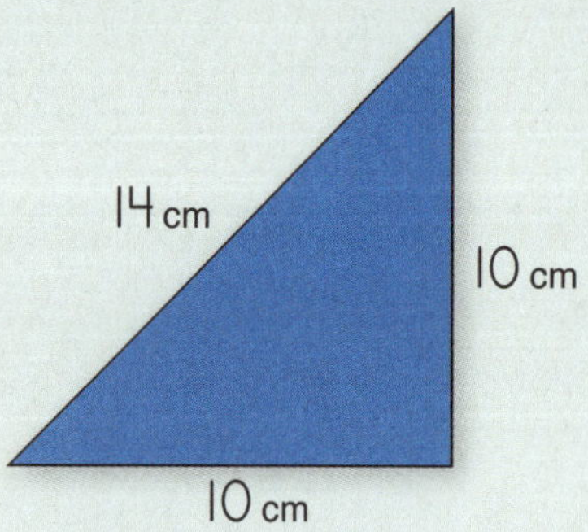

Perimeter: ______

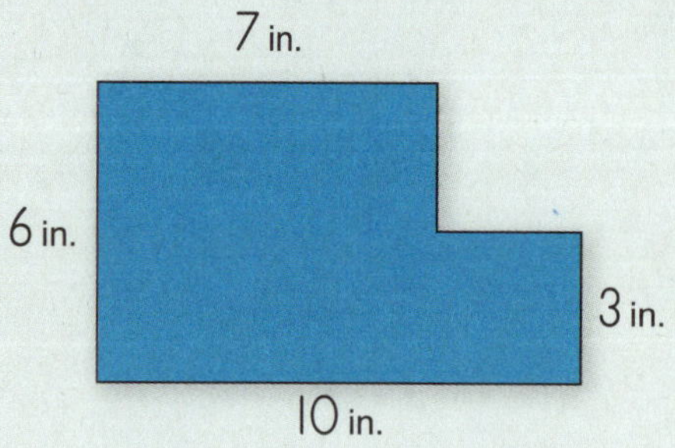

Perimeter: ______

All sides are 6 m.

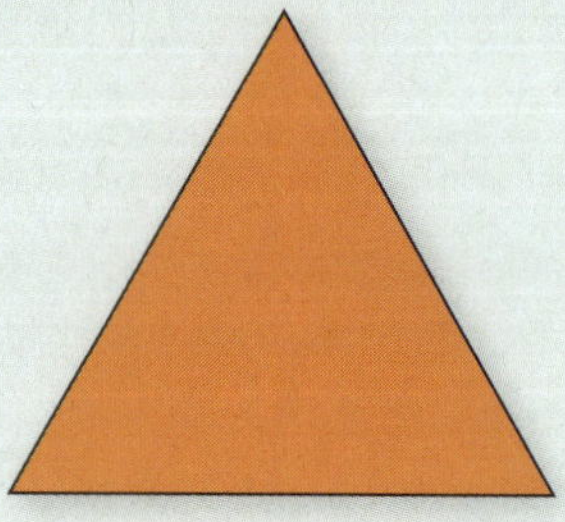

Perimeter: ______

Unit Wrap-Up

Find the area. Include the correct unit.

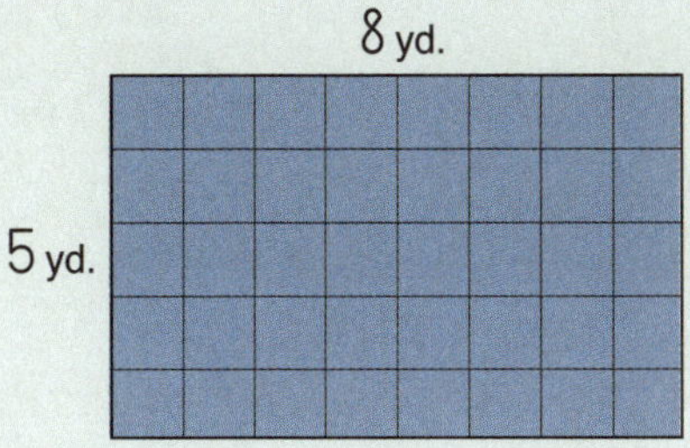

Area: ______

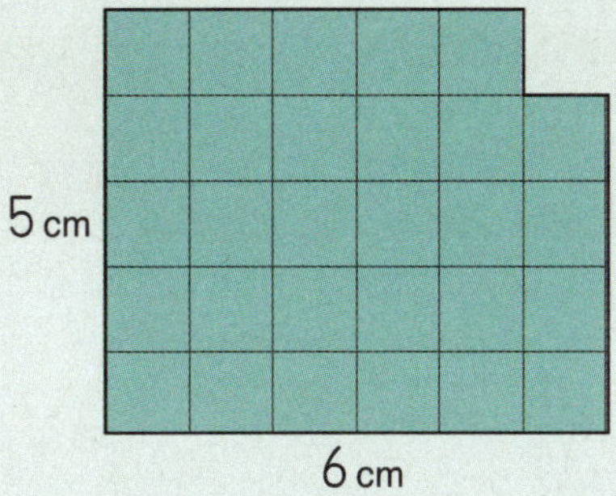

Area: ______

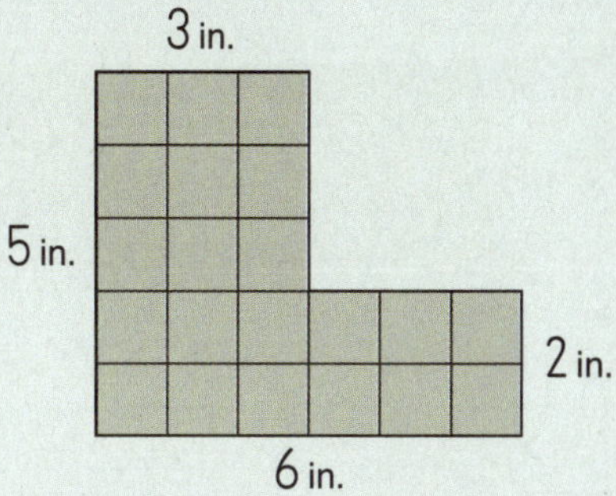

Area: ______

Split the rectangle into smaller rectangles. Then, find the area of the whole rectangle.

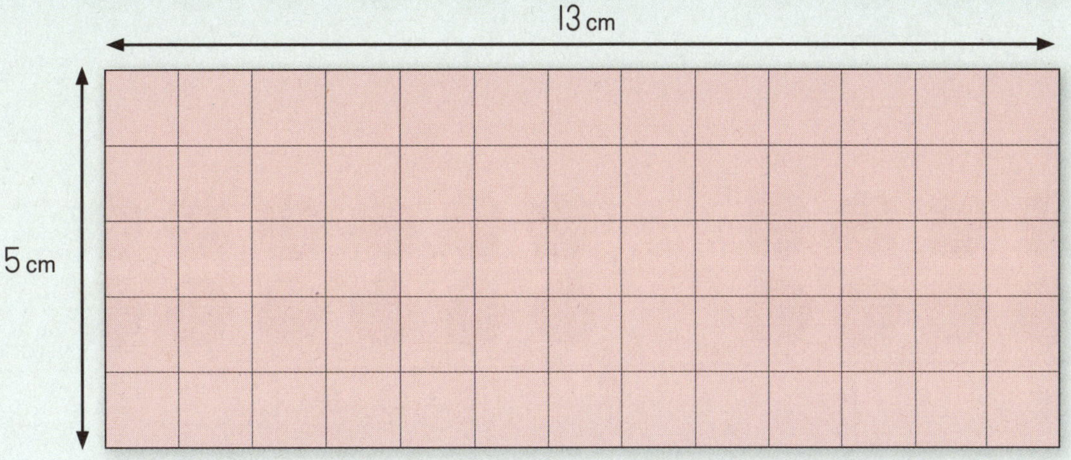

☐ sq. cm

Solve. Write the equations you use.

Hannah's kitchen is 20 ft. long and 18 ft. wide. What is the perimeter of the kitchen?

The shorter side of the sandbox is 8 ft. long. The other side is 2 ft. longer. What is the perimeter of the sandbox?

Lesson Activities

A

Multiplication

$3 \times 4 = 12$

number of groups — size of each group — total

Division

$12 \div 3 = 4$

total — number of groups — size of each group

$12 \div 6 = \square$

$12 \div 2 = \square$

$12 \div 4 = \square$

$12 \div 12 = \square$

B

Total Number of Cookies	Number of People	Division Equation
6	3	
10	2	
10	5	
0	4	
15	15	

Practice

Complete. Draw rings around the crackers to show how you divided them.

Split 16 into 2 equal groups.
How many are in each group?

$16 \div 2 =$ ☐

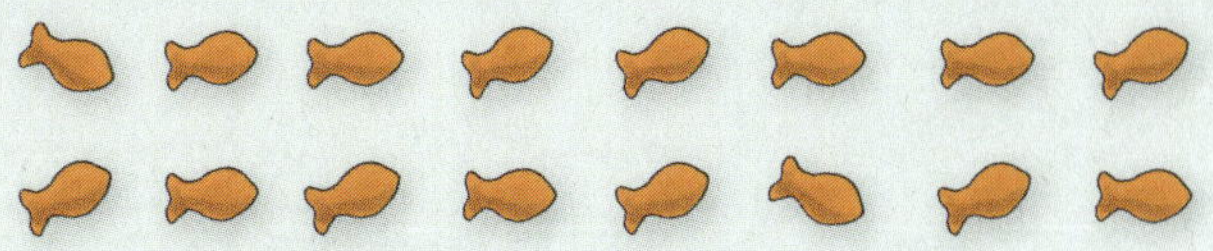

Split 16 into 8 equal groups.
How many are in each group?

$16 \div 8 =$ ☐

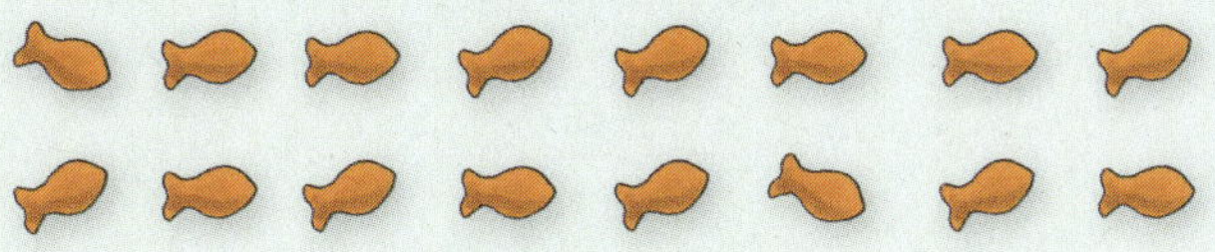

$16 \div 4 =$ ☐

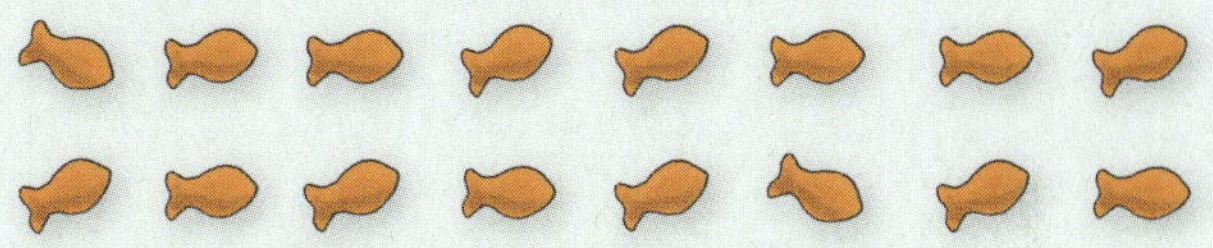

$16 \div 16 =$ ☐

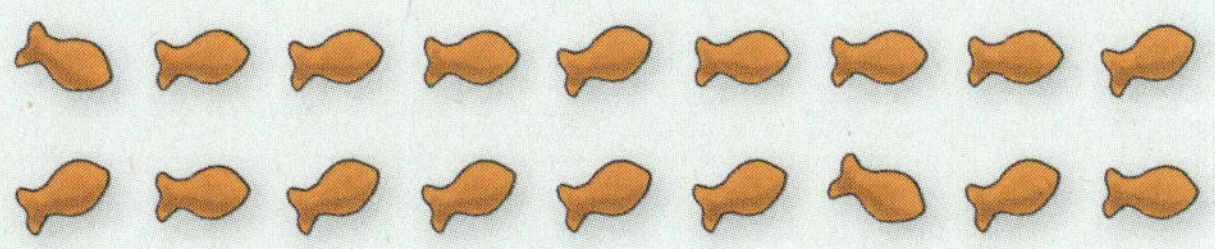

$18 \div 3 =$ ☐

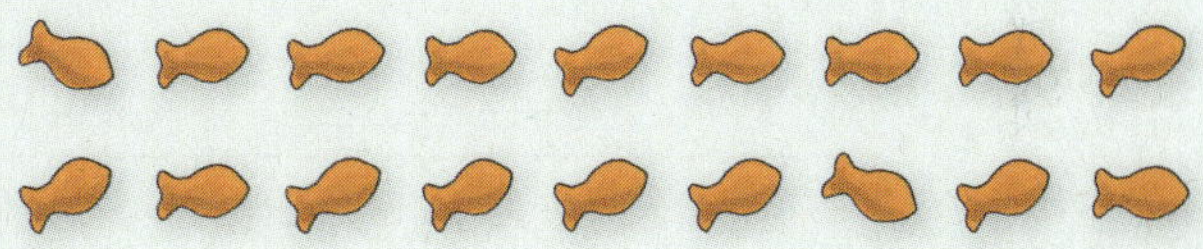

$18 \div 6 =$ ☐

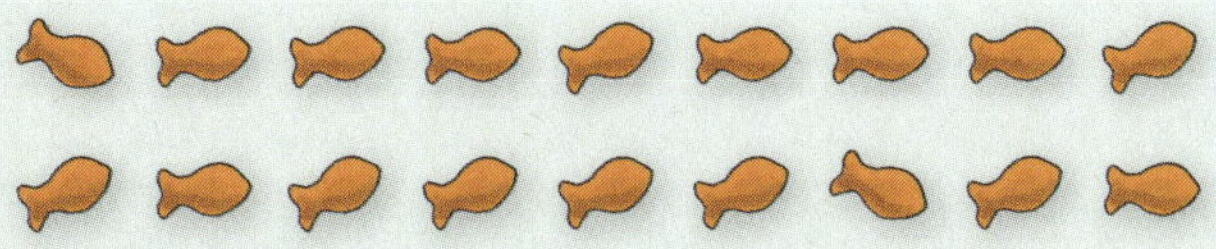

$18 \div 9 =$ ☐

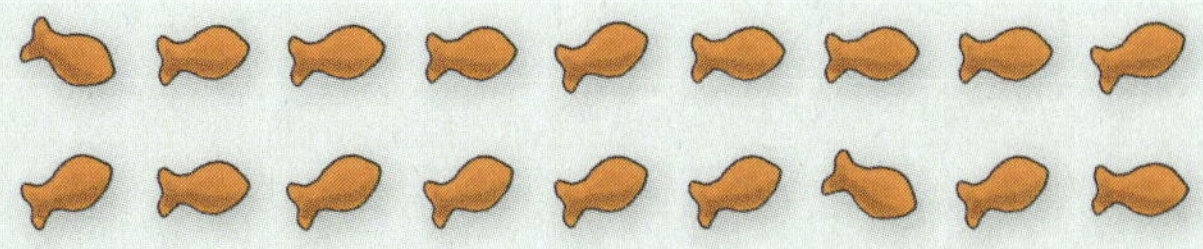

$18 \div 2 =$ ☐

Review

Complete the sequences.

Count by 50s							950	1,000

Count by 25s							975	1,000

Count by 20s							980	1,000

Find the perimeter and area of each rectangle.

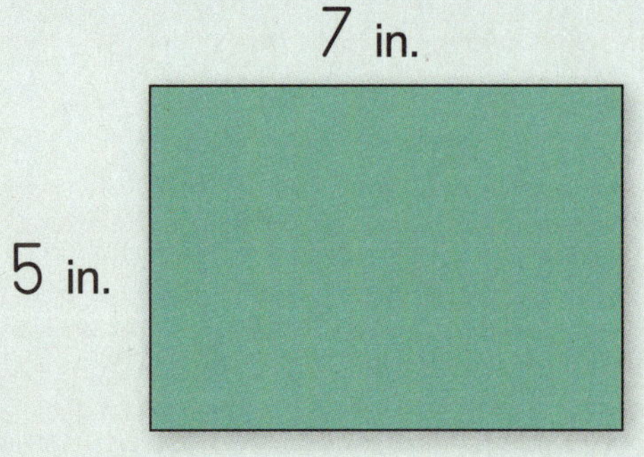

Perimeter: ______

______

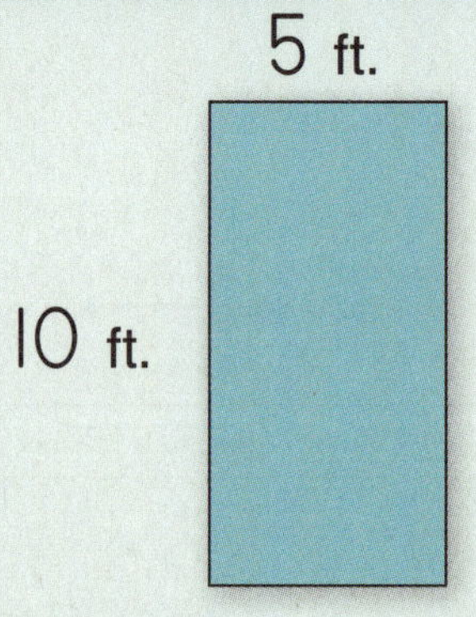

Perimeter: ______

______

Complete.

	Half
20	
10	
18	
14	
16	

Complete.

$8 \times 7 =$ ☐ $\quad 9 \times 6 =$ ☐

$5 \times 9 =$ ☐ $\quad 8 \times 4 =$ ☐

$6 \times 6 =$ ☐ $\quad 7 \times 7 =$ ☐

$8 \times 9 =$ ☐ $\quad 8 \times 8 =$ ☐

Lesson Activities

A

You have 14 cookies.
You split them equally with your brother.
How many do each of you get?

$14 \div 2 = \square$

Half of 14 is $\square$.

$16 \div 2 = \square$	$20 \div 2 = \square$	$8 \div 2 = \square$
$10 \div 2 = \square$	$6 \div 2 = \square$	$4 \div 2 = \square$
$2 \div 2 = \square$	$18 \div 2 = \square$	$12 \div 2 = \square$

B

Division Race (÷2)

Practice

Complete.

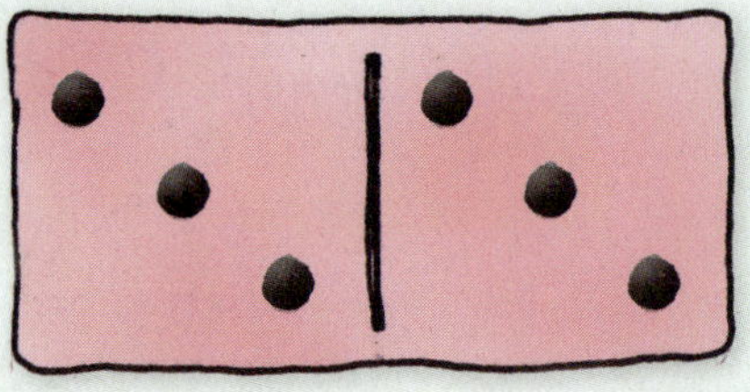

$6 \div 2 = \square$

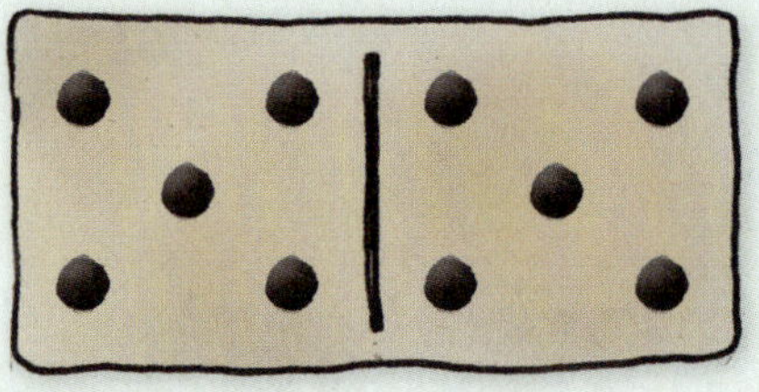

$10 \div 2 = \square$

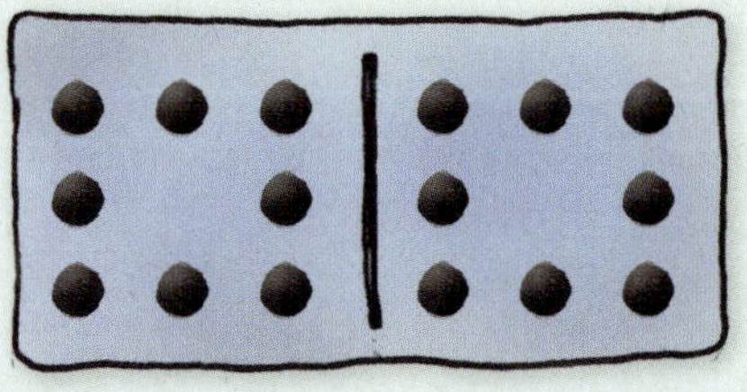

$16 \div 2 = \square$

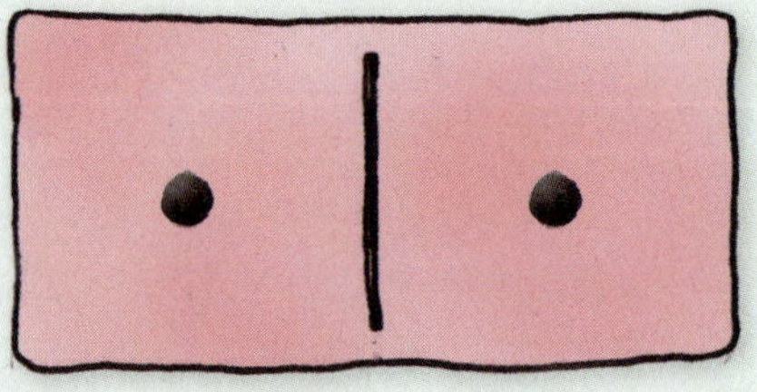

$2 \div 2 = \square$

$14 \div 2 = \square$

$12 \div 2 = \square$

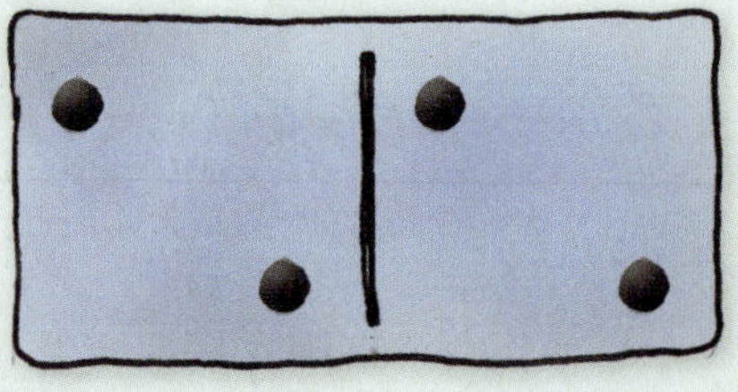

$4 \div 2 = \square$

$18 \div 2 = \square$

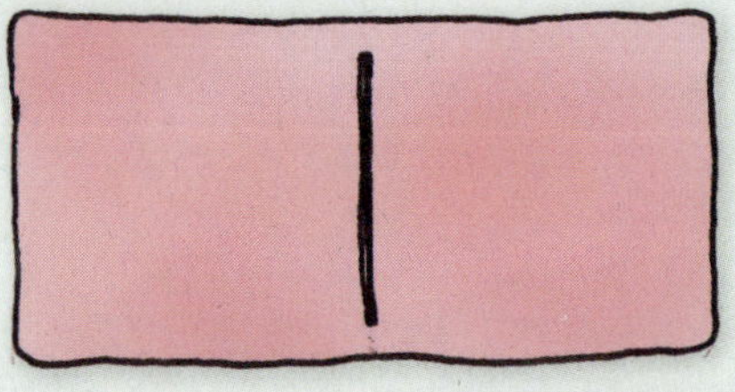

$0 \div 2 = \square$

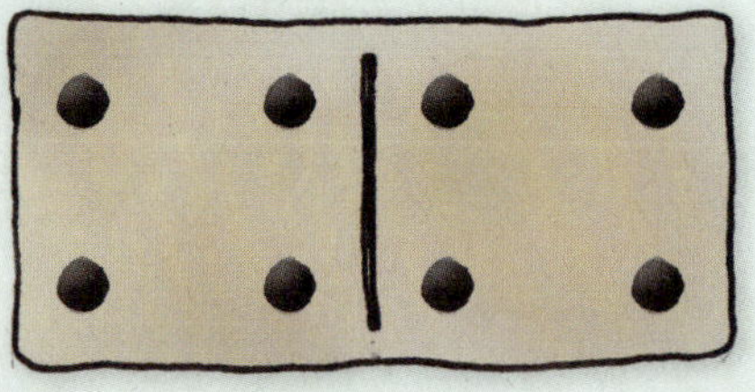

$8 \div 2 = \square$

Review

Find the area of each shape.

☐ sq. cm

☐ sq. cm

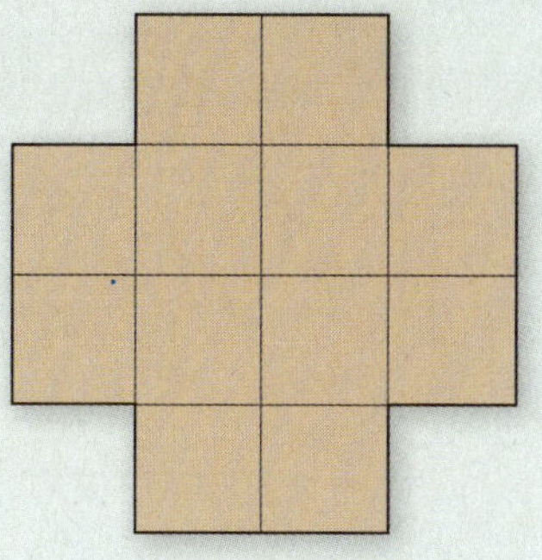

☐ sq. cm

Complete the fact family.

7 + 9 = 16

☐ + ☐ = ☐

☐ - ☐ = ☐

☐ - ☐ = ☐

Complete.

	3	5	7
+	2	4	6

	3	1	2
-	1	7	5

Solve. Write the equations you use.

Sarah has $23.
She buys 2 craft kits.
Each craft kit costs $10.
How much money does she have left?

Liam buys yarn for $5.39 and a crochet hook for $2.74. How much does he spend?

Lesson Activities

A

☐ × ☐ = ☐

☐ × ☐ = ☐

☐ ÷ ☐ = ☐

☐ ÷ ☐ = ☐

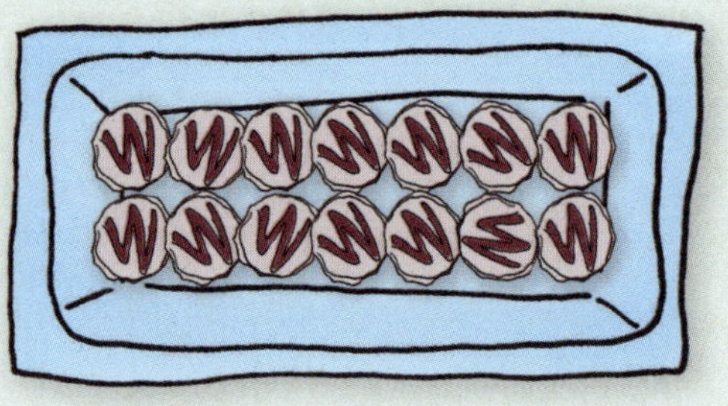

☐ × ☐ = ☐

☐ × ☐ = ☐

☐ ÷ ☐ = ☐

☐ ÷ ☐ = ☐

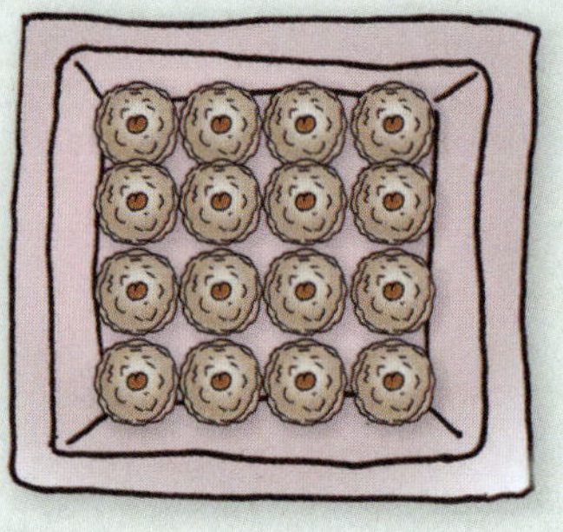

☐ × ☐ = ☐

☐ ÷ ☐ = ☐

B

18 ÷ 3 = ☐

3 × ☐ = 18

20 ÷ 5 = ☐

5 × ☐ = 20

30 ÷ 3 = ☐

3 × ☐ = 30

12 ÷ 4 = ☐

4 × ☐ = 12

21 ÷ 3 = ☐

3 × ☐ = 21

Practice

Complete the fact families to match the arrays.

2 × 9 = 18

□ × □ = □

□ ÷ □ = □

□ ÷ □ = □

□ × □ = □

□ × □ = □

□ ÷ □ = □

□ ÷ □ = □

Complete the equations to match the arrays.

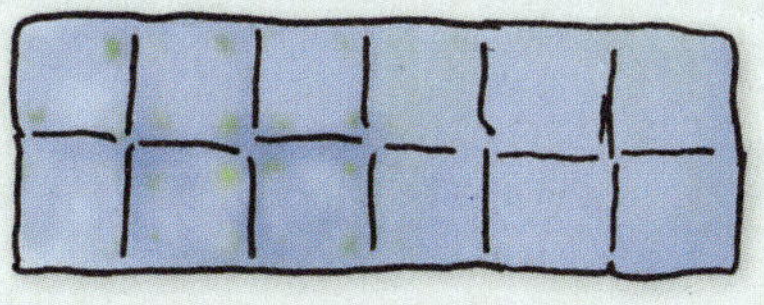

2 × □ = 12

12 ÷ 2 = □

3 × □ = 9

9 ÷ 3 = □

5 × □ = 25

25 ÷ 5 = □

4 × □ = 24

24 ÷ 4 = □

10.3

Review

Use the grid lines to find the area of each shape. Circle the correct units.

☐ sq. in. / sq. cm

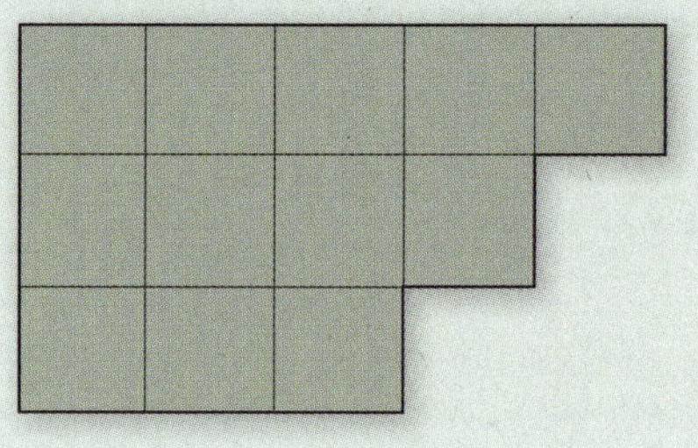

☐ sq. in. / sq. cm

Write the multiples in order.

Multiples of 8	8	16	24							80
Multiples of 9	9	18								90

Round to the nearest hundred.

373	692	817	436	501	760

Complete.

593 +10 → ☐ +10 → ☐ +10 → ☐ +10 → 633

477 +20 → ☐ +20 → ☐ +20 → ☐ +20 → 557

645 +50 → ☐ +50 → ☐ +50 → ☐ +50 → 845

Lesson Activities

A

12 children split into groups of 2.
How many groups do they make?

12 ÷ 2 = ☐

total — size of each group — number of groups

12 ÷ 4 = ☐

12 ÷ 6 = ☐

12 ÷ 3 = ☐

12 ÷ 12 = ☐

B

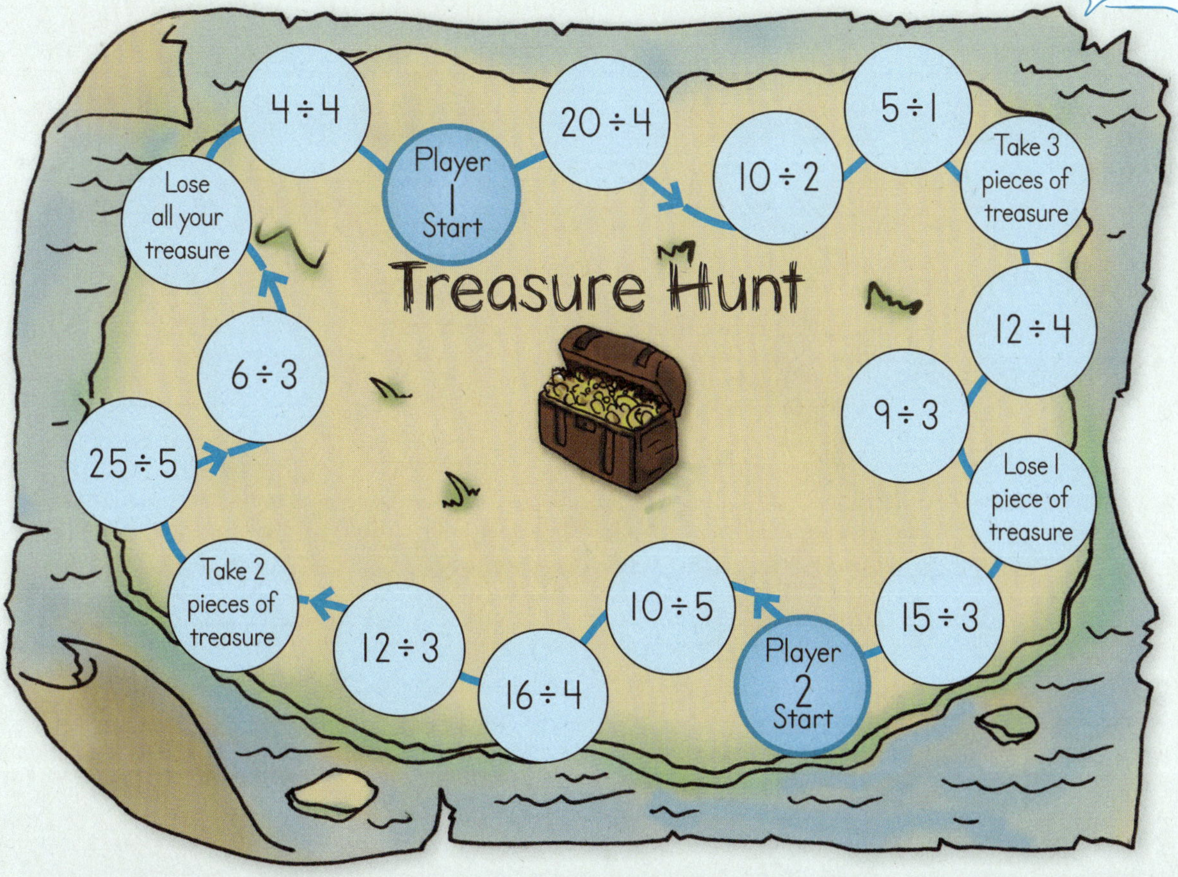

Practice

Complete. Draw rings around the candies to show how you divided them.

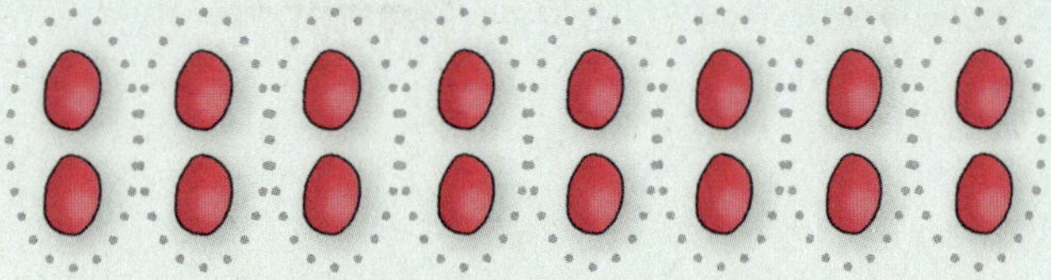

How many groups of 2 equal 16?

$16 \div 2 = $ 8

How many groups of 8 equal 16?

$16 \div 8 = $ ☐

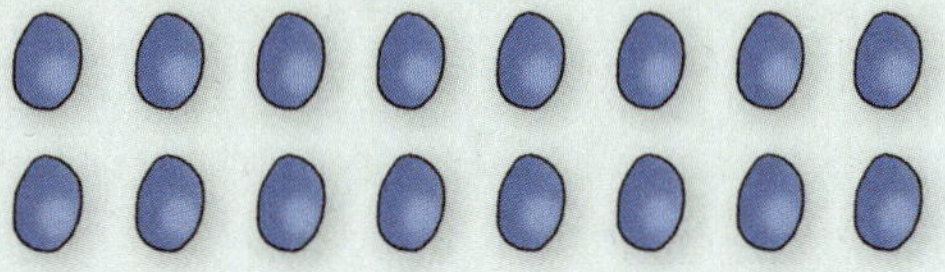

How many groups of 4 equal 16?

$16 \div 4 = $ ☐

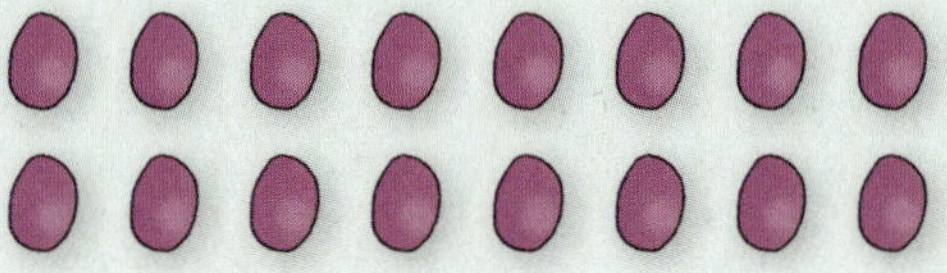

How many groups of 16 equal 16?

$16 \div 16 = $ ☐

How many groups of 3 equal 18?

$18 \div 3 = $ ☐

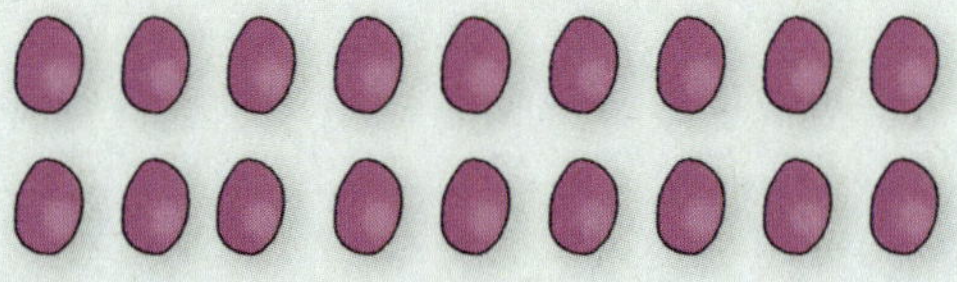

How many groups of 6 equal 18?

$18 \div 6 = $ ☐

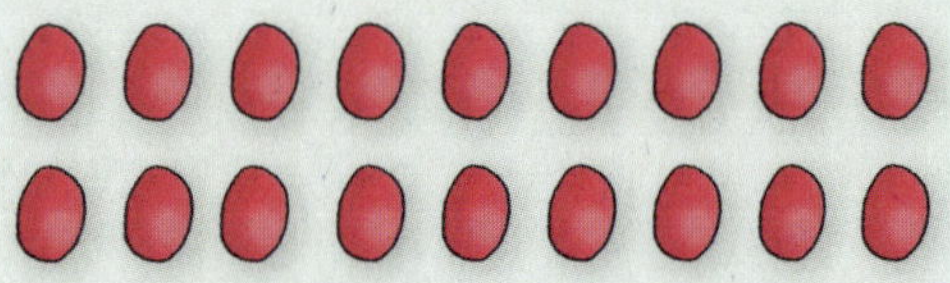

How many groups of 9 equal 18?

$18 \div 9 = $ ☐

How many groups of 2 equal 18?

$18 \div 2 = $ ☐

Review

Choose the more sensible unit for each item.

Area of a bulletin board

6 sq. ft.	6 sq. in.

Area of a zoo

1 sq. mi.	1 sq. yd.

Area of a book's cover

54 sq. ft.	54 sq. in.

Match.

\$2.50 + \$3.25	\$5.75	\$6.00 - \$2.50
\$1.50 + \$2.50	\$3.50	\$6.00 - \$1.75
\$2.75 + \$0.75	\$4.00	\$6.00 - \$0.25
\$1.75 + \$2.50	\$4.25	\$6.00 - \$2.00

Complete.

1 minute = ☐ seconds

1 hour = ☐ minutes

1 day = ☐ hours

1 week = ☐ days

Complete.

$7 \times 9 =$ ☐

$9 \times 9 =$ ☐

$10 \times 10 =$ ☐

$7 \times 8 =$ ☐

$7 \times 5 =$ ☐

$6 \times 7 =$ ☐

Lesson Activities

A

70 ÷ 10 = ☐

☐ × 10 = 70

90 ÷ 10 = ☐	40 ÷ 10 = ☐	60 ÷ 10 = ☐
30 ÷ 10 = ☐	10 ÷ 10 = ☐	100 ÷ 10 = ☐
50 ÷ 10 = ☐	20 ÷ 10 = ☐	80 ÷ 10 = ☐

B

Four in a Row

4	9	7	20 ÷ 10	70 ÷ 10	5
50 ÷ 10	8	100 ÷ 10	6	5	18 ÷ 2
9	30 ÷ 10	2	10 ÷ 2	12 ÷ 2	60 ÷ 10
20 ÷ 2	14 ÷ 2	10	90 ÷ 10	7	8
10	80 ÷ 10	6	16 ÷ 2	40 ÷ 10	3

Practice

Match.

40 ÷ 10	3	10 ÷ 2
30 ÷ 10	4	8 ÷ 2
60 ÷ 10	5	12 ÷ 2
80 ÷ 10	6	6 ÷ 2
90 ÷ 10	7	18 ÷ 2
50 ÷ 10	8	20 ÷ 2
100 ÷ 10	9	14 ÷ 2
70 ÷ 10	10	16 ÷ 2

Solve. Write a division equation to match.

There are 14 children.
They split into 2 equal teams.
How many children are on each team?

☐ ÷ ☐ = ☐

You have 30 flowers.
You put 10 flowers in each vase. How many vases do you fill?

☐ ÷ ☐ = ☐

Review

Find the perimeter and area.

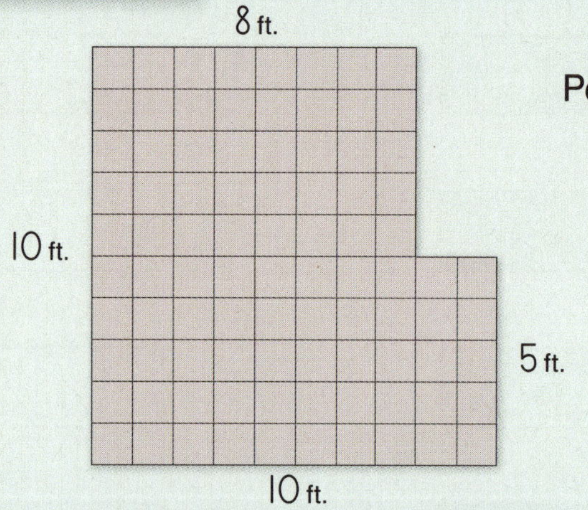

Perimeter: ____

____

Complete the sequences.

Complete.

2 weeks, 4 days = ____ days

4 weeks, 1 day = ____ days

8 weeks, 2 days = ____ days

7 weeks, 3 days = ____ days

★ 11 weeks = ____ days

Copy the shapes.

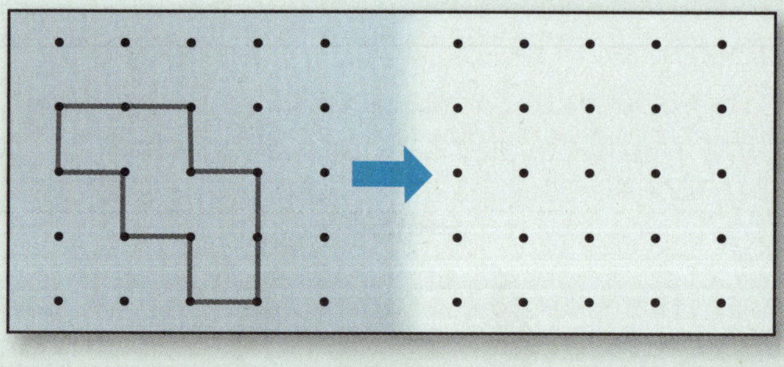

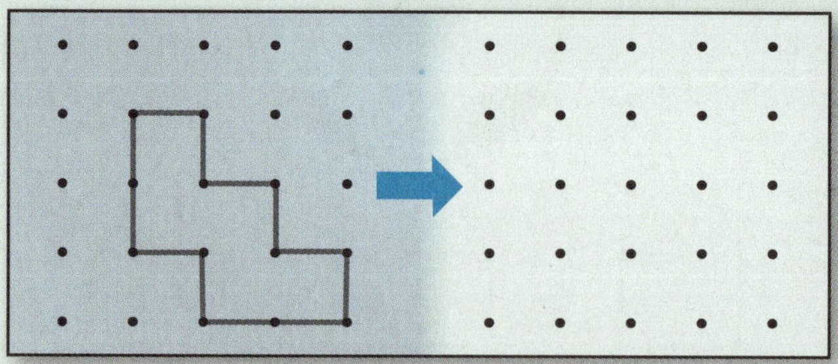

Lesson Activities

A

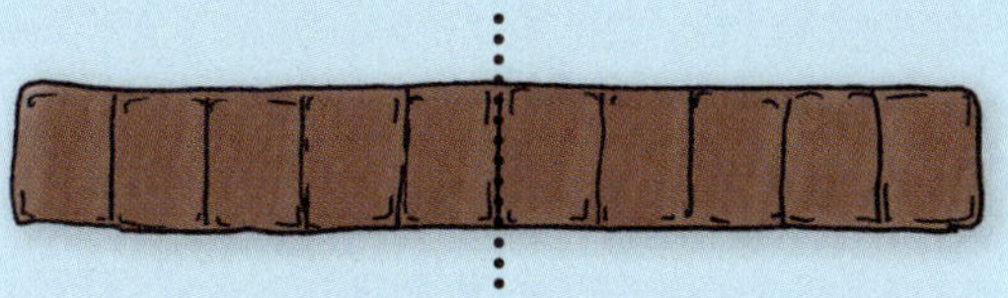

10 ÷ 5 = ☐

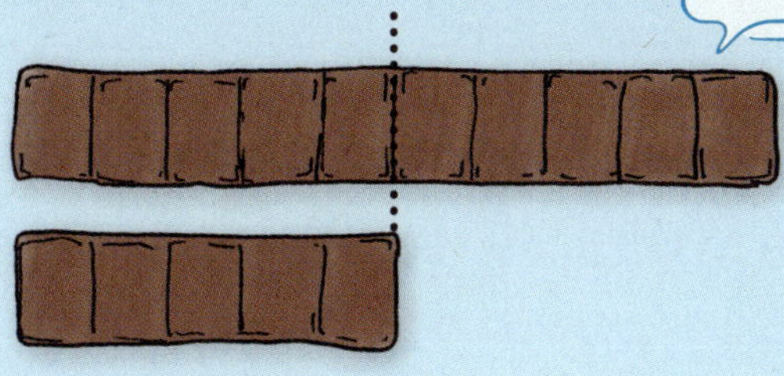

15 ÷ 5 = ☐

20 ÷ 5 = ☐

25 ÷ 5 = ☐

30 ÷ 5 = ☐

35 ÷ 5 = ☐

40 ÷ 5 = ☐

45 ÷ 5 = ☐

B

Player 1

1 2 3 4 5 6 7 8 9 10

Player 2

1 2 3 4 5 6 7 8 9 10

Practice

Complete.

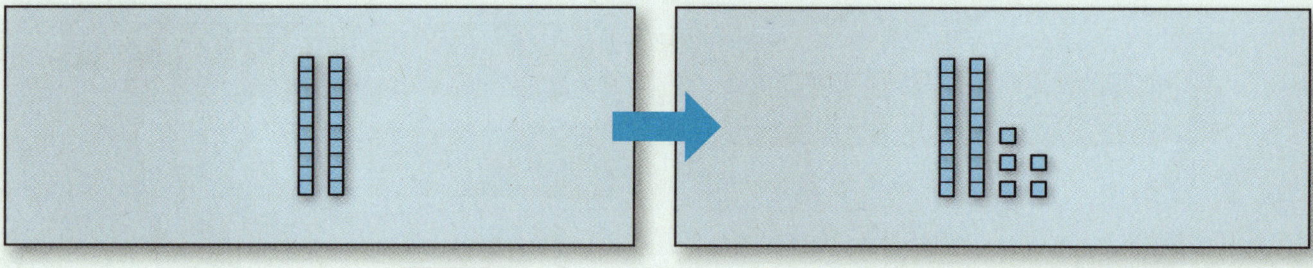

$20 \div 5 =$ ☐ $25 \div 5 =$ ☐

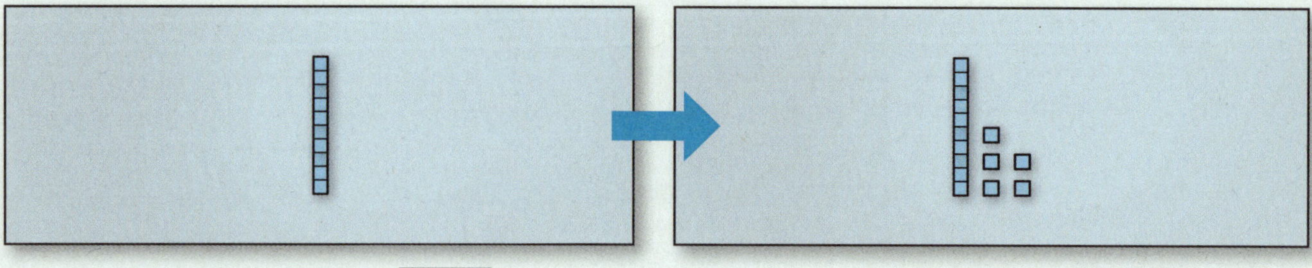

$10 \div 5 =$ ☐ $15 \div 5 =$ ☐

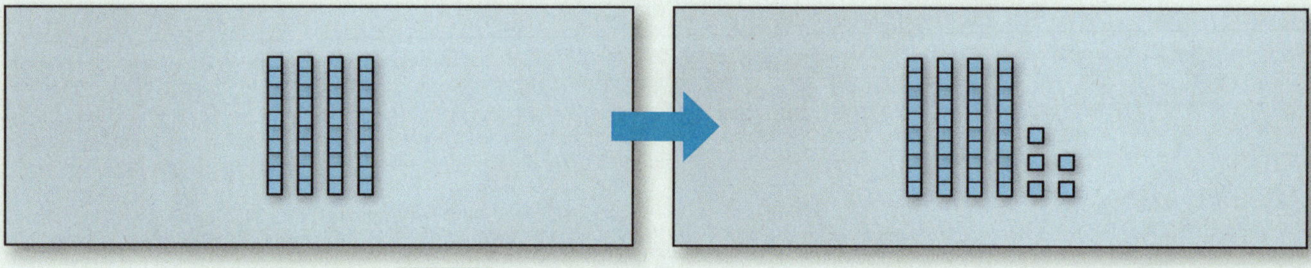

$40 \div 5 =$ ☐ $45 \div 5 =$ ☐

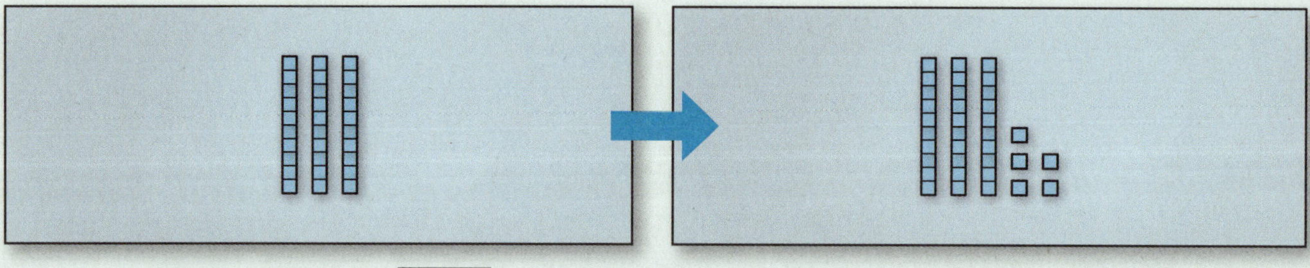

$30 \div 5 =$ ☐ $35 \div 5 =$ ☐

★ $100 \div 5 =$ ☐ → ★ $105 \div 5 =$ ☐

Review

Circle the more sensible unit for each item.

Area of a cellphone screen

100 sq. m	100 sq. cm

Area of a rug

3 sq. m	3 sq. km

Area of a zoo

2 sq. m	2 sq. km

Complete.

$ ______

$ ______

Complete.

$6 \times 8 =$ ☐

$4 \times 7 =$ ☐

$8 \times 7 =$ ☐

$9 \times 4 =$ ☐

$7 \times 7 =$ ☐

Solve. Write the equations you use.

Noah made a square quilt. Each side is 3 feet long. What is the perimeter of the quilt?

Noah made a square quilt. Each side is 3 feet long. What is the area of the quilt?

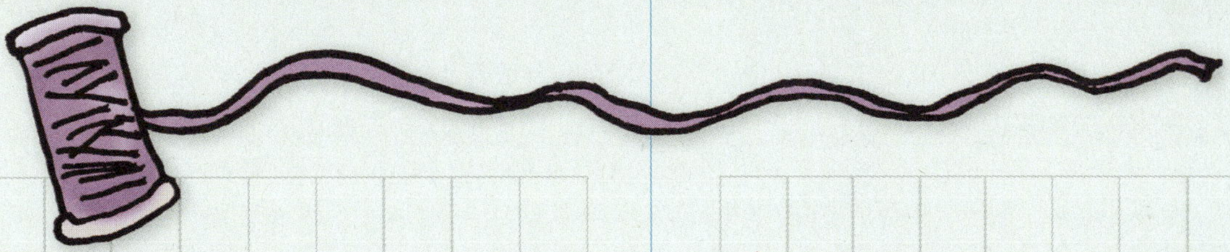

Lesson Activities

A

Division Crash (÷5)

15 ÷ 5	25 ÷ 5	40 ÷ 5	10 ÷ 5	35 ÷ 5
45 ÷ 5	20 ÷ 5	5 ÷ 5	30 ÷ 5	50 ÷ 5

B

$8 \div 2 = 4$

dividend divisor quotient

C

5 friends equally share 20 lollipops.
How many lollipops does each friend get?

You have 20 lollipops.
You put 5 lollipops in each goodie bag.
How many goodie bags do you make?

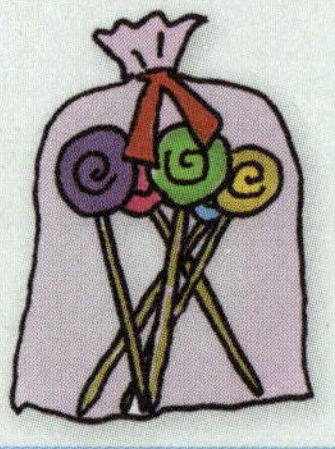

You need 80 markers.
How many packs should you buy?

You have 16 feet of rope.
You cut it into 2 equal pieces.
How long is each piece?

Practice

Complete.

☐ × 5 = 20	20 ÷ 5 = ☐
☐ × 5 = 40	40 ÷ 5 = ☐
☐ × 5 = 25	25 ÷ 5 = ☐
☐ × 5 = 35	35 ÷ 5 = ☐
☐ × 5 = 45	45 ÷ 5 = ☐
☐ × 5 = 30	30 ÷ 5 = ☐
☐ × 5 = 50	50 ÷ 5 = ☐

Solve. Write a division problem to match.

There are 10 doughnuts in each box.
You need 50 doughnuts.
How many boxes should you buy?

☐ ÷ ☐ = ☐

You have 20 inches of ribbon. You need 5 inches of ribbon for each bookmark.
How many bookmarks can you make?

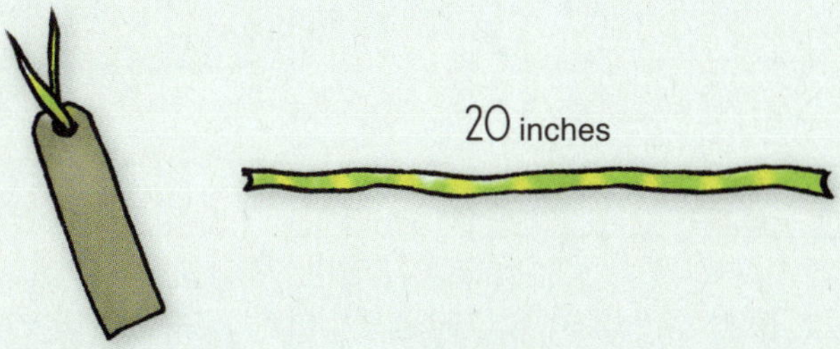

☐ ÷ ☐ = ☐

Review

Split the rectangle into smaller rectangles. Then, find the area of the whole rectangle.

☐ sq. cm

Complete the fact family.

3	×	7	=	21
7	×	☐	=	☐
21	÷	☐	=	☐
21	÷	☐	=	☐

Complete.

$10 \times 4 + 6 =$ ☐

$9 \times 5 + 3 =$ ☐

$2 \times 9 + 1 =$ ☐

$6 \times 5 + 3 =$ ☐

Use a ruler to measure each line to the nearest quarter-inch.

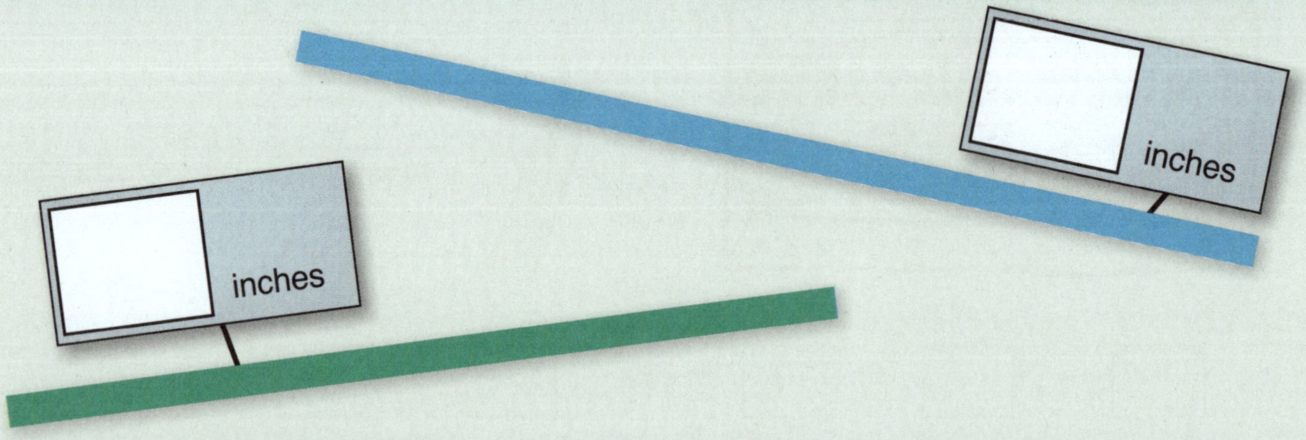

Lesson Activities

A

$13 \div 4 =$ ☐

$11 \div 2 =$ ☐

$10 \div 3 =$ ☐

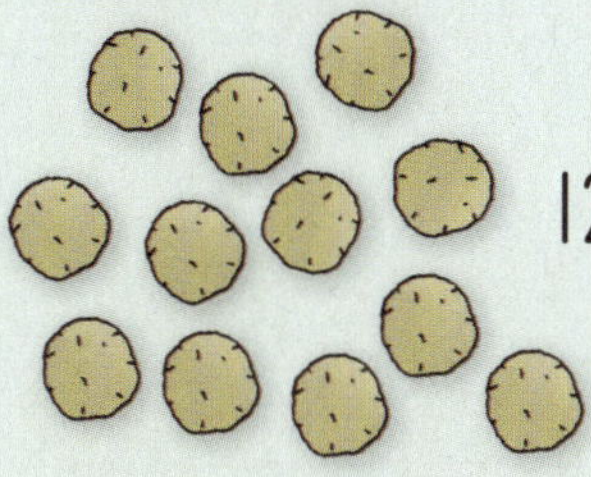

$12 \div 5 =$ ☐

$15 \div 4 =$ ☐

B

Roll and Divide

Player 1	Player 2
14 ÷ ☐ = ☐	14 ÷ ☐ = ☐
8 ÷ ☐ = ☐	8 ÷ ☐ = ☐
9 ÷ ☐ = ☐	9 ÷ ☐ = ☐
16 ÷ ☐ = ☐	16 ÷ ☐ = ☐
21 ÷ ☐ = ☐	21 ÷ ☐ = ☐
Sum of remainders ☐	Sum of remainders ☐

10.8

Practice

Complete.

$16 \div 5 =$ ☐

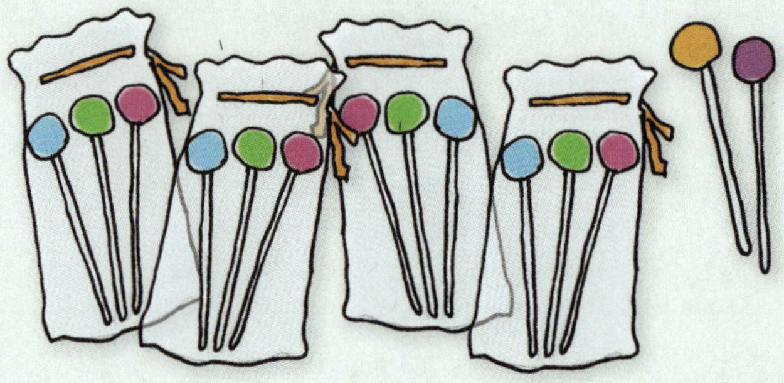

$14 \div 3 =$ ☐

$23 \div 4 =$ ☐

$23 \div 6 =$ ☐

$34 \div 10 =$ ☐

$34 \div 5 =$ ☐

Review

Complete.

Start

172 - 5 = ☐	299 + 14 = ☐
172 - 3 = ☐	299 + 4 = ☐
172 - 2 = ☐	299 + 1 = ☐

2 × 39 = ☐	21 × 10 = ☐
2 × 36 = ☐	20 × 10 = ☐
2 × 35 = ☐	19 × 10 = ☐

Complete.

	Half
60	
64	
70	
72	
76	

Complete.

4 × 4 = ☐	6 × 7 = ☐
9 × 5 = ☐	5 × 6 = ☐
8 × 1 = ☐	8 × 8 = ☐
9 × 7 = ☐	6 × 4 = ☐

Color the odd numbers red. Color the even numbers pink.

898 98 9 988 899 8 89 989 809

10.9

Unit Wrap-Up

Complete.

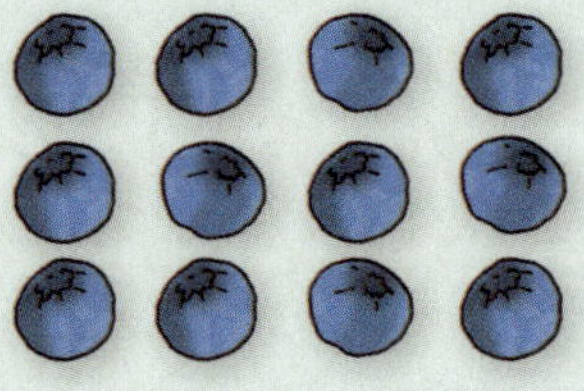

$12 \div 3 =$ ____

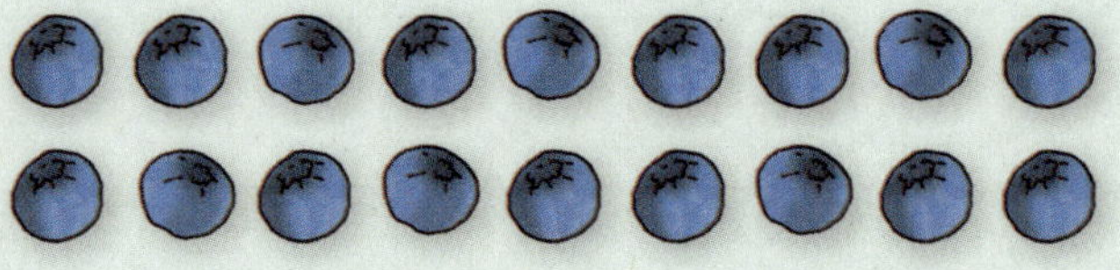

$18 \div 2 =$ ____

$7 \div 7 =$ ____

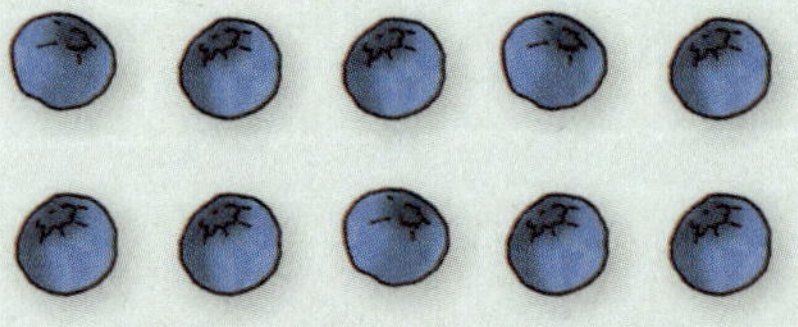

$10 \div 5 =$ ____

Complete the fact family to match the array.

____ × ____ = ____

____ × ____ = ____

____ ÷ ____ = ____

____ ÷ ____ = ____

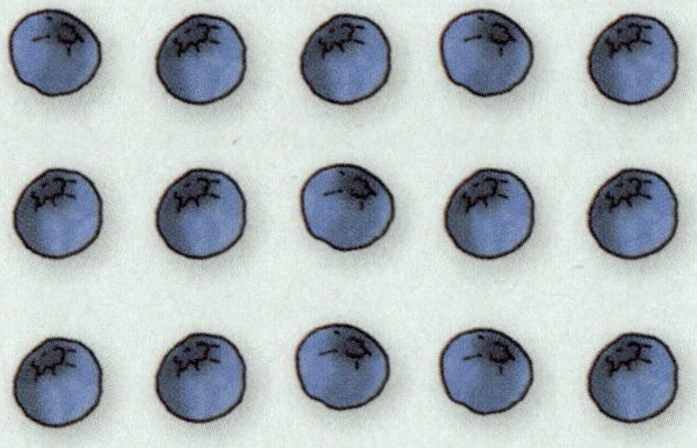

Use the words in the word bank to complete the sentences.

$24 \div 4 = 6$

24 is the ________________________.

4 is the ________________________.

6 is the ________________________.

Word bank
divisor
quotient
dividend

Unit Wrap-Up

Complete.

$20 \div 5 =$ □ $90 \div 10 =$ □ $16 \div 2 =$ □

$30 \div 10 =$ □ $25 \div 5 =$ □ $15 \div 5 =$ □

$10 \div 1 =$ □ $20 \div 2 =$ □ $50 \div 5 =$ □

$45 \div 5 =$ □ $40 \div 10 =$ □ $14 \div 2 =$ □

$18 \div 2 =$ □ $35 \div 5 =$ □ $70 \div 10 =$ □

Complete.

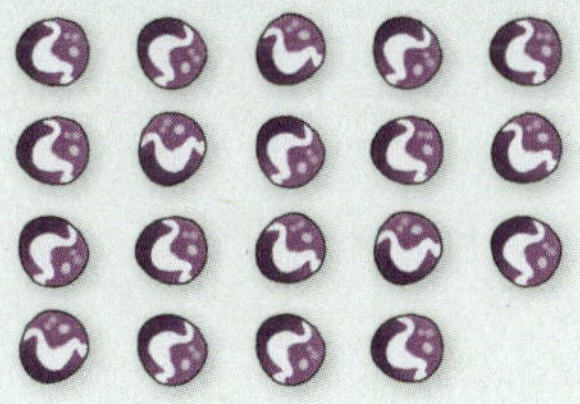

$19 \div 5 =$ □

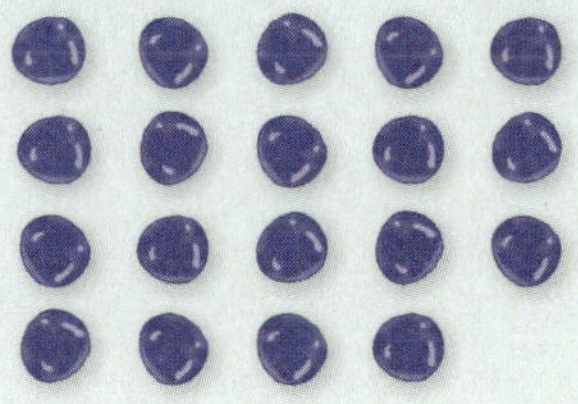

$19 \div 2 =$ □

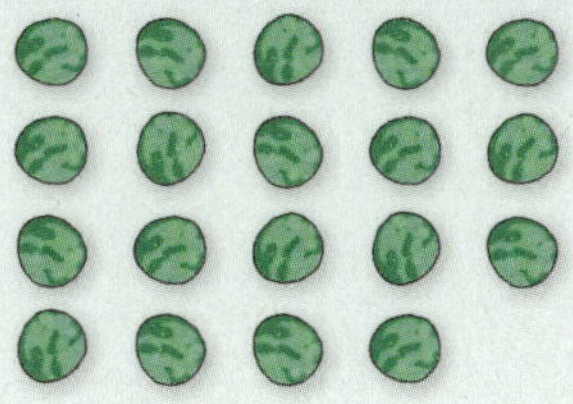

$19 \div 10 =$ □

Solve. Write the equations you use.

30 children are at swim lessons. They divide into groups with 10 children in each group. How many groups do they make?

□ $\div$ □ $=$ □

Maya sets up 15 chairs. She arranges them in rows of 5. How many rows does she make?

□ $\div$ □ $=$ □

Lesson Activities

A

Base-ten Blocks

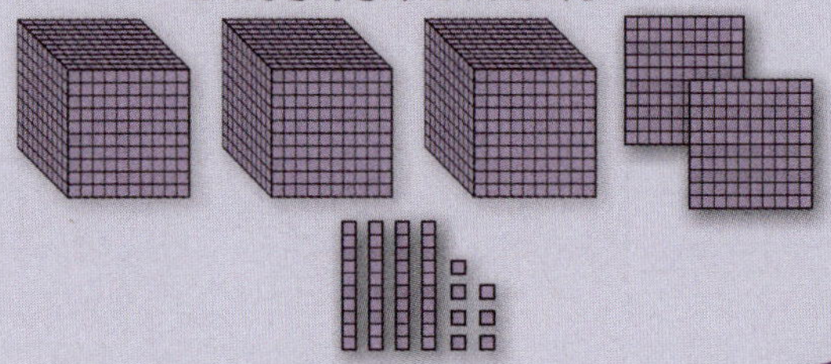

Money

3,247

Expanded Form

3,000 + 200 + 40 + 7

Number Line

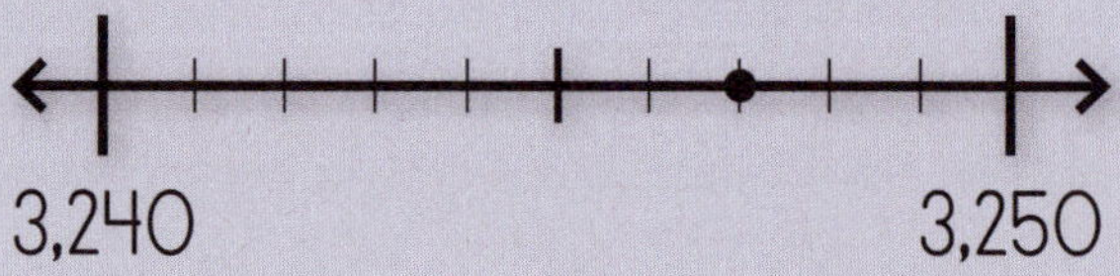

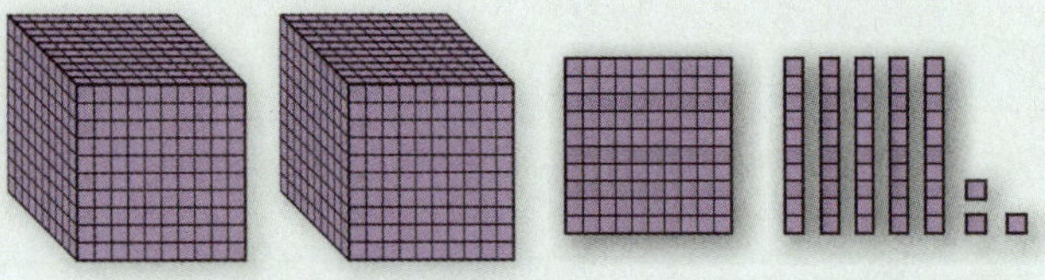

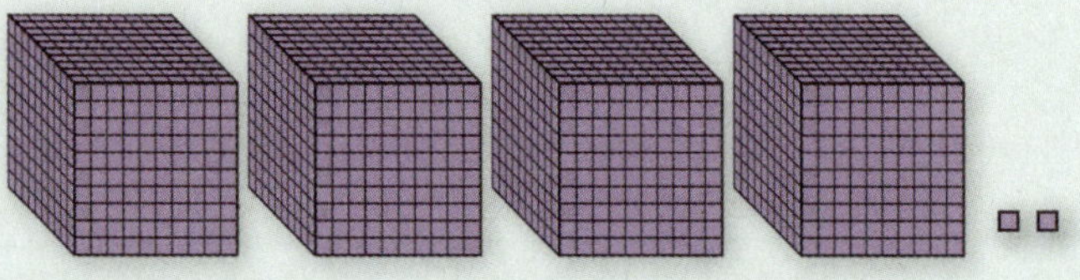

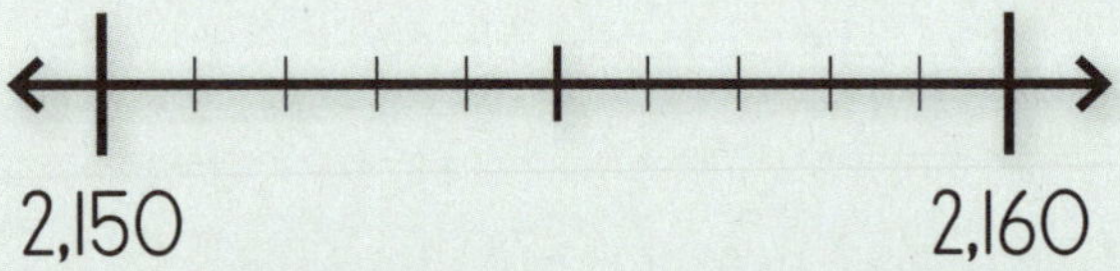

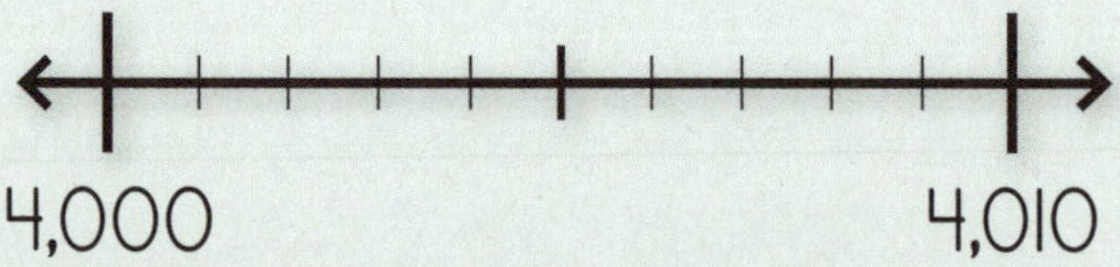

B

Number Riddles

2,247 4,247 4,052 2,053 2,253 3,227 4,012 2,152 3,267 4,000 2,154 3,999

Practice

Complete.

Expanded Form	Number
5,000 + 900 + 60 + 2	5,962
3,000 + 400 + 50 + 7	
	6,831
	7,999
8,000 + 8	
4,000 + 40	

Complete.

$ ______

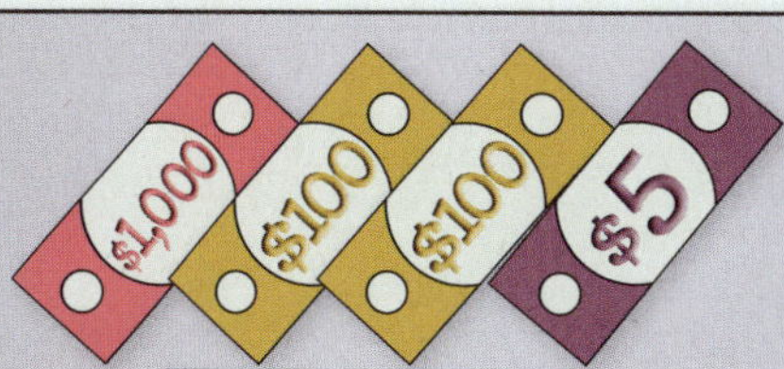

$ ______

Connect each number to its place on the number line.

2,993 | 2,999 | 3,004 | 3,006

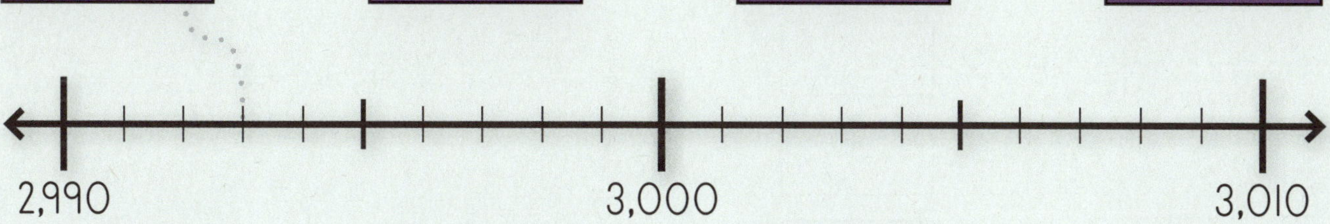

2,991 | 2,995 | 3,001 | 3,008

Match.

4,264 + 1	4,364
4,264 + 100	4,274
4,264 + 10	5,264
4,264 + 1,000	4,265

4,264 - 1	4,254
4,264 - 10	4,164
4,264 - 100	4,263
4,264 - 1,000	3,264

Review

Match.

90 ÷ 10	5	30 ÷ 5
50 ÷ 10	6	40 ÷ 5
70 ÷ 10	7	45 ÷ 5
80 ÷ 10	8	25 ÷ 5
60 ÷ 10	9	35 ÷ 5

Complete.

$70 \times 3 =$ ☐

$40 \times 8 =$ ☐

$50 \times 5 =$ ☐

$90 \times 7 =$ ☐

$60 \times 8 =$ ☐

Complete with <, >, or =.

$\frac{4}{8} \bigcirc \frac{1}{8}$

$\frac{1}{6} \bigcirc \frac{1}{3}$

$\frac{3}{6} \bigcirc \frac{1}{2}$

Circle pairs that make 1,000.

450	550	125	875
650	250	850	225
350	750	150	775

Lesson Activities

A

3,678 | 5,070 | 4,000 | 6,999

B

1,899 ◯ 2,015

4,600 ◯ 4,700

9,265 ◯ 9,256

8,791 ◯ 891

3,100 ◯ 3,040

C

Greatest Possible Number

Least Possible Number

11.2

Practice

Complete the circles with <, >, or =.

4,629 ◯ 5,000	3,890 ◯ 3,265	1,698 ◯ 698
7,001 ◯ 7,010	5,000 ◯ 4,000	6,245 ◯ 6,145
6,000 ◯ 5,999	4,309 ◯ 4,390	8,972 ◯ 8,972

Circle the greatest number in each group.

7,258	3,115	4,400
5,287	3,151	4,404
8,785	3,515	4,440
2,875	3,551	4,040
8,572	3,155	4,004

Write a number in the blank that makes the statement true.

5,000 > ☐	5,000 < ☐	5,000 = ☐
☐ < 3,946	☐ > 3,946	☐ = 3,946

Review

Color the problems that match the number in the star.

280
- 190 + 90
- 300 - 20
- 80 × 4

300
- 150 + 150
- 340 - 50
- 60 × 5

350
- 325 + 25
- 420 - 60
- 70 × 5

420
- 350 + 80
- 490 - 70
- 60 × 7

540
- 380 + 60
- 600 - 60
- 90 × 6

560
- 490 + 80
- 600 - 40
- 80 × 7

Round to the nearest hundred.

919	990	999	909	991	911

Solve. Write the equations you use.

Sofia earns $5 each time she shovels snow. How many times must she shovel snow to earn $30?

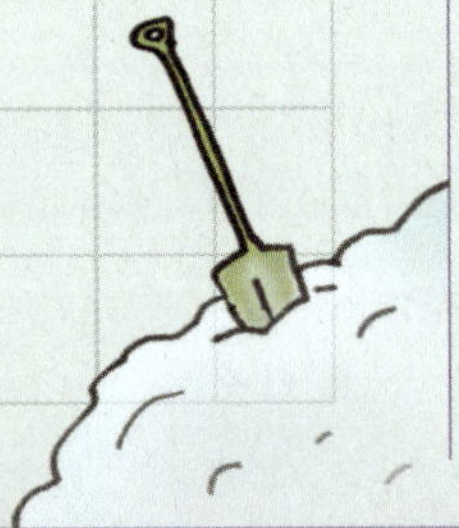

James earns $8 per hour for babysitting. If he babysits for 4 hours, how much does he earn?

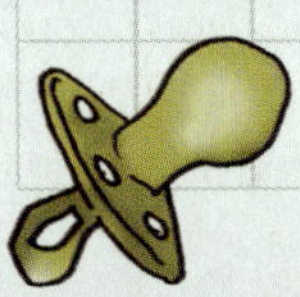

Lesson Activities

A

Multiplication Undercover (×7)

Player										
Player 1	7	14	21	28	35	42	49	56	63	70
Player 2	7	14	21	28	35	42	49	56	63	70

B

Distance Between Cities

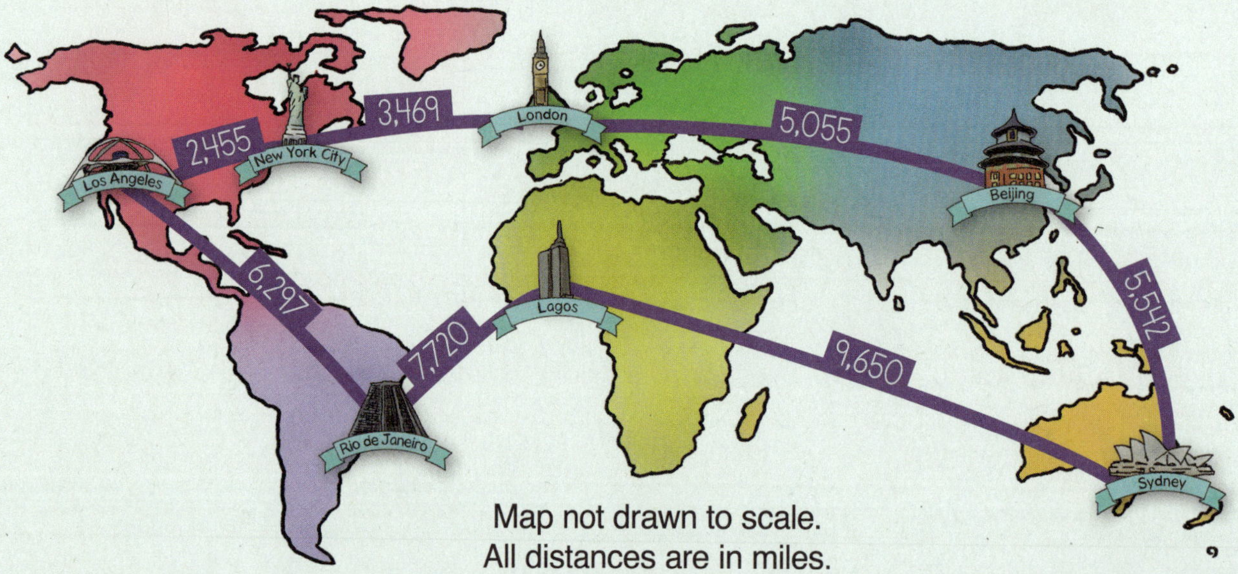

Map not drawn to scale.
All distances are in miles.

C

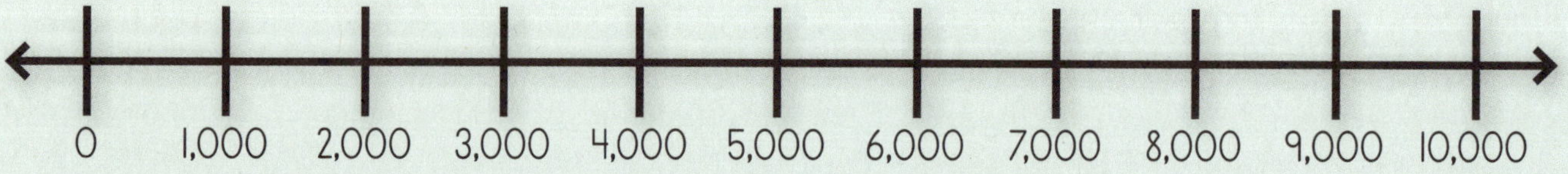

2,455	3,469	5,055	5,542	9,650	7,720	6,297

Practice

Connect each number to its dot on the number line.

7,274 | 7,450 | 7,972

7,193 | 7,625 | 7,816

Round each number to the nearest thousand. Use the number line to help.

7,816	7,450	7,193	7,625	7,972	7,274

Round each number to the nearest thousand.

About ☐ pages

About ☐ dollars

About ☐ kilometers

Review

Complete.

Start

$3{,}000 + 4{,}000 = \square$

$300 + 400 = \square$

$30 + 40 = \square$

$4{,}000 - 3{,}000 = \square$

$400 - 300 = \square$

$40 - 30 = \square$

★ $5{,}120 + 1{,}650 = \square$

$5{,}120 + 1{,}600 = \square$

$5{,}120 + 1{,}000 = \square$

★ $3{,}750 - 1{,}520 = \square$

$3{,}750 - 1{,}500 = \square$

$3{,}750 - 1{,}000 = \square$

Complete.

$18 \div 2 = \square$	$40 \div 5 = \square$	$16 \div 2 = \square$
$25 \div 5 = \square$	$12 \div 2 = \square$	$20 \div 2 = \square$
$45 \div 5 = \square$	$14 \div 2 = \square$	$30 \div 5 = \square$

Solve. Write the equations you use.

Jo has \$4.38. She earns \$3.75.
Then, she spends \$2.49.
How much money does she have now?

Lesson Activities

A

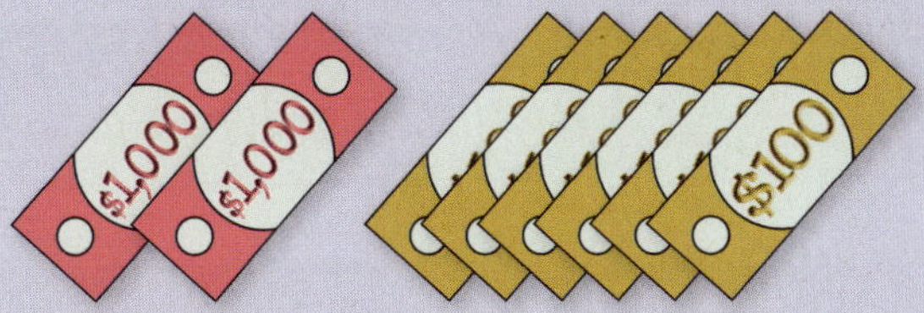

2,600 + ☐ = 3,000

8,900 + ☐ = 9,000	6,500 + ☐ = 7,000
4,300 + ☐ = 5,000	1,200 + ☐ = 2,000

B

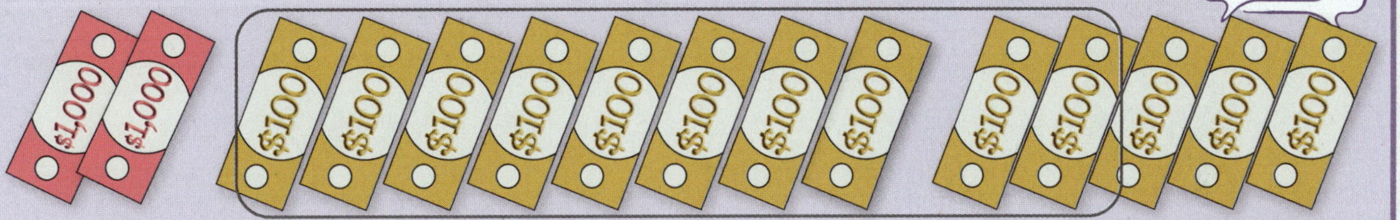

2,800 + 500 = ☐

8,900 + 400 = ☐	6,500 + 700 = ☐
4,300 + 900 = ☐	1,200 + 900 = ☐

C

Race to 10,000 Scoring Guide

= 100

= 200

= 300

= 400

= 500

= 600

1 or 2 of a Kind = 0

4 of a Kind = 900

5 of a Kind = 2,000

6 of a Kind = 3,000

Practice

Circle pairs that equal 5,000.

4,500	400	4,300	700
500	4,600	100	4,700
4,800	200	4,900	300

Complete.

Start

3,700 + 300 = ☐
3,700 + 400 = ☐
3,700 + 500 = ☐

8,900 + 100 = ☐
8,900 + 400 = ☐
8,900 + 700 = ☐

6,500 + 500 = ☐
6,500 + 800 = ☐
6,500 + 900 = ☐

★ 7,750 + 250 = ☐
★ 7,750 + 450 = ☐
★ 7,750 + 950 = ☐

Solve. Write the equations you use.

Tim's mom tries to walk 8,000 steps per day. One day, she walks 7,400 steps. How many more steps does she need to walk to meet her goal?

Madison's family drives 800 miles to visit her grandparents. Then, they drive 800 miles home. How far do they drive in all?

Review

Match.

20 ÷ 2	6	40 ÷ 5
14 ÷ 2	7	30 ÷ 5
18 ÷ 2	8	50 ÷ 5
16 ÷ 2	9	45 ÷ 5
12 ÷ 2	10	35 ÷ 5

Write the multiples in order.

Multiples of 7	7	14	21							70
Multiples of 8	8	16								80

Complete.

$$\begin{array}{r} 457 \\ +\ 359 \\ \hline \end{array}$$

$$\begin{array}{r} 608 \\ -\ 275 \\ \hline \end{array}$$

Solve. Write the equations you use.

Josh organized his model cars. He has 4 shelves, and he put 6 cars on each shelf. He had 5 cars left, so he put them on his desk. How many model cars does Josh have?

Lesson Activities

A

3,000 - 200 = ☐

4,000 - 600 = ☐

2,000 - 100 = ☐

5,000 - 400 = ☐

6,000 - 500 = ☐

8,000 - 900 = ☐

B

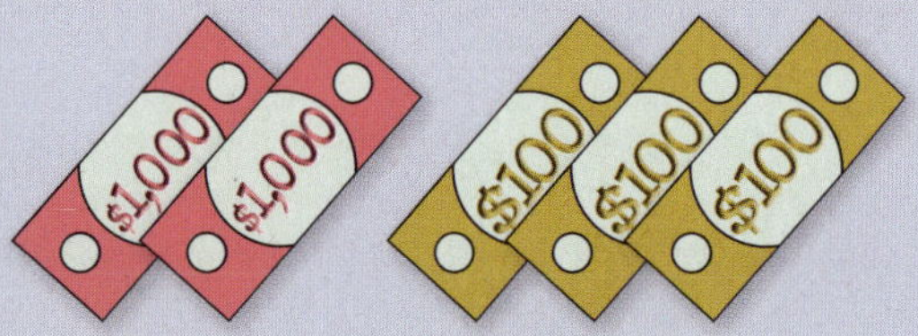

2,300 - 400 = ☐

3,100 - 200 = ☐

5,200 - 500 = ☐

2,600 - 800 = ☐

4,500 - 700 = ☐

C

Race to 0 Scoring Guide

= 100

= 200

= 300

= 400

= 500

= 600

1 or 2 of a Kind = 0

4 of a Kind = 900

5 of a Kind = 2,000

6 of a Kind = 3,000

Practice

Match.

5,000 - 500	4,400	5,100 - 400
5,000 - 400	4,500	5,100 - 700
5,000 - 600	4,600	5,300 - 400
5,000 - 100	4,700	5,300 - 800
5,000 - 300	4,800	5,200 - 600
5,000 - 200	4,900	5,700 - 900

Complete.

7,000 → -500 → ☐ → -600 → ☐ → -400 → 5,500

8,000 → -900 → ☐ → -700 → ☐ → -400 → 6,000

9,000 → -800 → ☐ → -500 → ☐ → -700 → 7,000

★ 6,350 → -500 → ☐ → -900 → ☐ → -350 → 4,600

11.5

Review

Write the multiples in order.

Multiples of 6	6	12	18							60
Multiples of 9	9	18								90

Find the perimeter and area.

6 ft.

5 ft.

Perimeter: ____________

____

Write the time.

___ : ___

___ : ___

___ : ___

___ : ___

Solve. Write the equations you use.

Ava's family drove 274 miles in the morning and 189 miles in the afternoon. How far did they drive in all?

Ava's family drove 274 miles in the morning and 189 miles in the afternoon. How much farther did they drive in the morning than the afternoon?

Lesson Activities

A

	3,	9	8	4
+	2,	6	3	2

Estimate

\+ ______

	4,	1	9	6
-	2,	8	7	9

Estimate

\- ______

B

Distance Between Cities

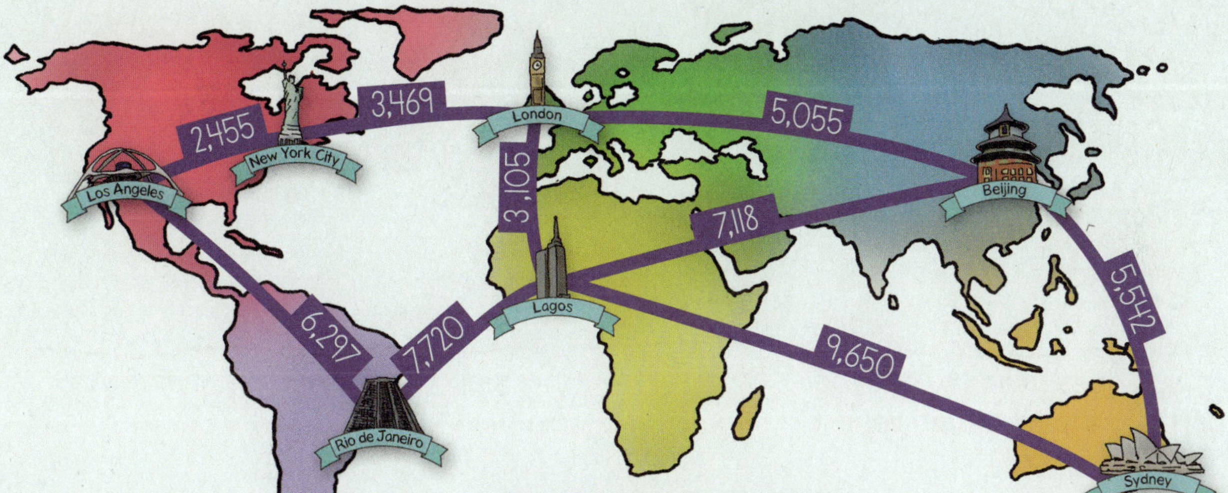

Map not drawn to scale.
All distances are in miles.

Itinerary	Total Distance Traveled	Difference in Flight Lengths
______ ✈ ______ ✈ ______		
______ ✈ ______ ✈ ______		

Practice

Complete.

	6,	9	2	7
+	1,	4	6	2

	4,	1	5	8
-	2,	6	4	1

	5,	0	6	5
-	3,	2	4	8

Use the ad to solve. Write the equations you use.

How much does it cost to buy the golf cart and the all-terrain vehicle?

How much more does the motorcycle cost than the golf cart?

You have $4,500. You buy the golf cart. How much money do you have left?

How much does it cost to buy the motorcycle and the golf cart?

Review

Use the chart to complete the pictograph.

Favorite Season	Number of People
Winter	6
Spring	10
Summer	14
Fall	8

Complete.

$\frac{2}{4} + \frac{1}{4} = \frac{\square}{\square}$ $\frac{1}{3} + \frac{2}{3} = \frac{\square}{\square}$ $\frac{3}{6} + \frac{2}{6} = \frac{\square}{\square}$

$\frac{3}{4} - \frac{1}{4} = \frac{\square}{\square}$ $\frac{3}{3} - \frac{1}{3} = \frac{\square}{\square}$ $\frac{5}{6} - \frac{2}{6} = \frac{\square}{\square}$

Complete.

$23 \div 5 = \square$

$23 \div 4 = \square$

$23 \div 10 = \square$

Lesson Activities

A

1,500

4,200

1,900

B

Inventions Timeline

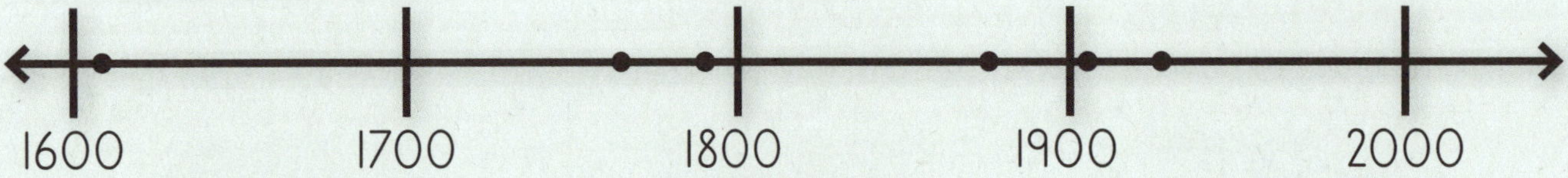

C

Practice

Match.

two thousand four hundred	1,600	forty-five hundred
three thousand seven hundred	2,400	sixteen hundred
four thousand five hundred	3,700	twenty-four hundred
one thousand six hundred	4,500	thirty-seven hundred

Write the current year in the chart. Then, use the chart to answer the questions.

Current year	
First person walks on the moon	1969
Pluto discovered	1930
Saturn's rings discovered	1610

How many years ago were Saturn's rings discovered?

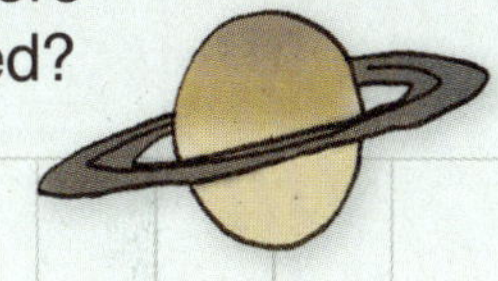

How many years ago was Pluto discovered?

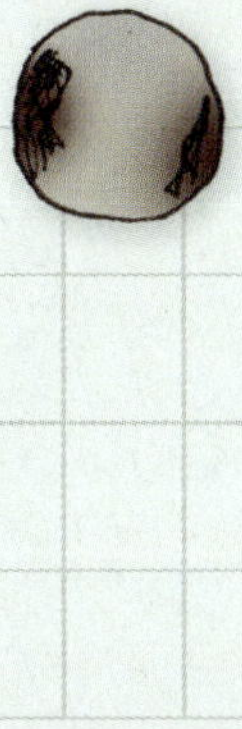

How many years ago did the first person walk on the moon?

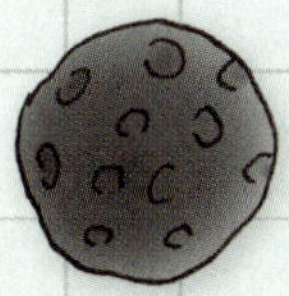

Review

Use the numbers to complete the blanks.
You will use each number once.

1	2	3	4	5	6	7	8	9

☐ × 3 = 6	3 × ☐ = 21	3 × ☐ = 9
☐ × 3 = 24	3 × ☐ = 3	3 × ☐ = 27
☐ × 3 = 12	3 × ☐ = 18	3 × ☐ = 15

Find the area and perimeter of each shape.

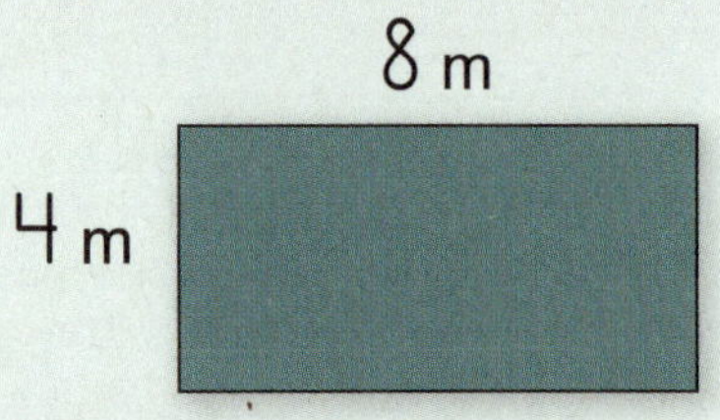

Perimeter: ☐

☐

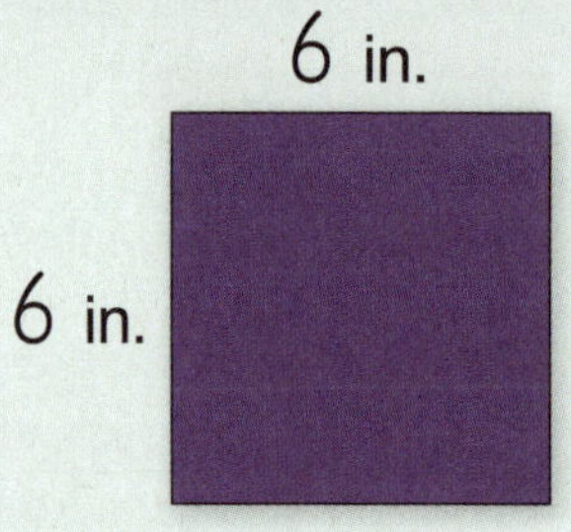

Perimeter: ☐

☐

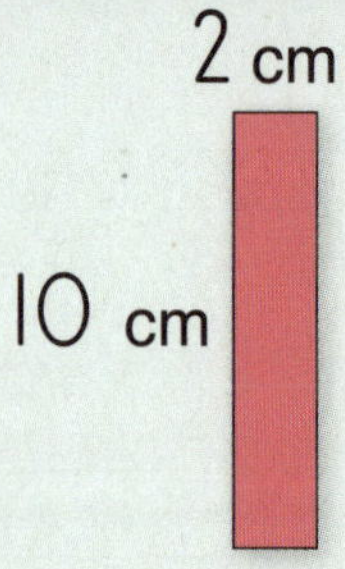

Perimeter: ☐

☐

Complete.

5 weeks, 2 days = ☐ days

4 weeks, 6 days = ☐ days

8 weeks, 3 days = ☐ days

★ 3 weeks, ☐ days = 24 days

Copy the shapes.

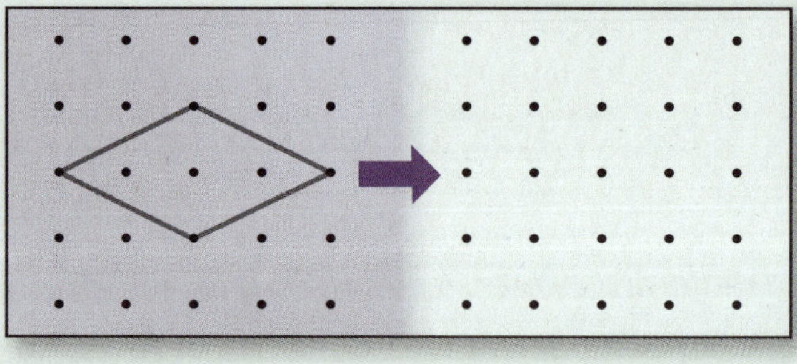

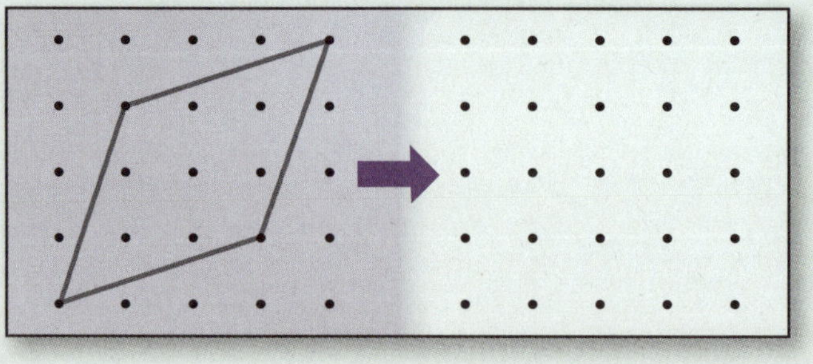

Unit Wrap-Up

Write the value of each set of base-ten blocks.

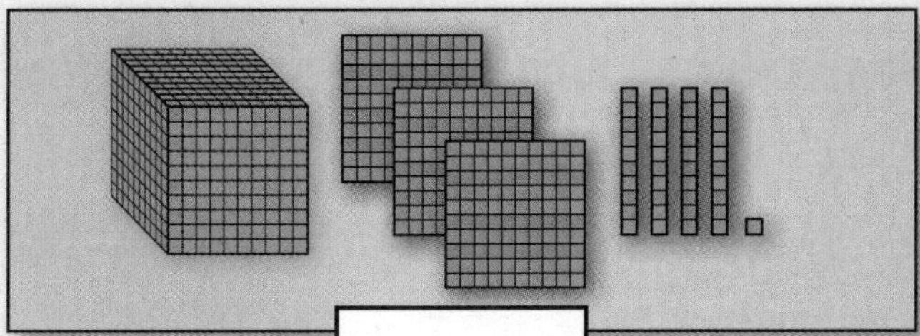

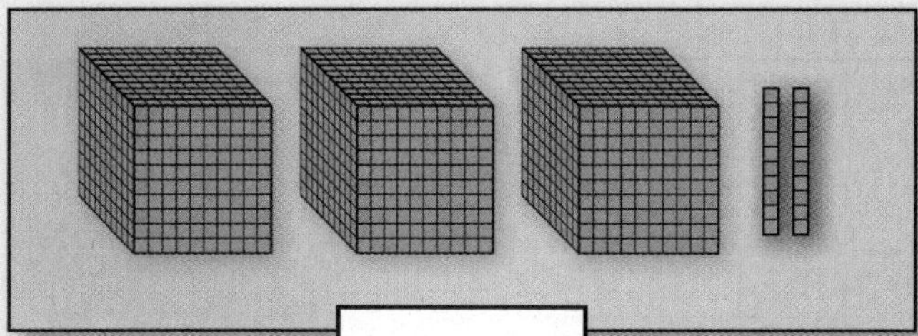

Connect each number to its place on the number line.

7,997 | 7,992 | 8,005 | 8,001

Round to the nearest thousand.

6,704	8,962	7,135	4,500

Complete.

Expanded Form	Number
5,000 + 400 + 20	
	6,125
9,000 + 9	
	4,078

Complete with <, >, or =.

3,768 ◯ 3,786

9,645 ◯ 9,642

4,000 ◯ 3,979

11.8

Unit Wrap-Up

Match.

2,900 + 200	3,000
2,700 + 500	3,100
2,800 + 700	3,200
2,600 + 400	3,500

4,100 - 200	3,900
4,000 - 500	3,800
4,200 - 600	3,600
4,300 - 500	3,500

Complete the sequences.

Count by						
1s	7,307					7,312
10s	6,780					6,830
100s	4,700					5,200

Complete.

	3,	5	9	2
+	4,	4	4	6

	8,	3	5	0
-	3,	6	2	8

Lesson Activities

A

12 ÷ 3 = ☐

☐ × 3 = 12

6 ÷ 3 = ☐	9 ÷ 3 = ☐	3 ÷ 3 = ☐
15 ÷ 3 = ☐	18 ÷ 3 = ☐	30 ÷ 3 = ☐
21 ÷ 3 = ☐	27 ÷ 3 = ☐	24 ÷ 3 = ☐

B

Climb and Slide

Practice

Complete.

$\square \times 3 = 12$

$12 \div 3 = \square$

$\square \times 3 = 6$

$6 \div 3 = \square$

$\square \times 3 = 15$

$15 \div 3 = \square$

$\square \times 3 = 24$

$24 \div 3 = \square$

$\square \times 3 = 3$

$3 \div 3 = \square$

$\square \times 3 = 30$

$30 \div 3 = \square$

$\square \times 3 = 27$

$27 \div 3 = \square$

$\square \times 3 = 9$

$9 \div 3 = \square$

$\square \times 3 = 21$

$21 \div 3 = \square$

$\square \times 3 = 18$

$18 \div 3 = \square$

Review

Draw a shape to match.

Triangle | Rectangle | Square

Isabella made a bar graph to show how many people came to the skating rink each day. Use the bar graph to complete the chart and answer the questions.

People at the Skating Rink

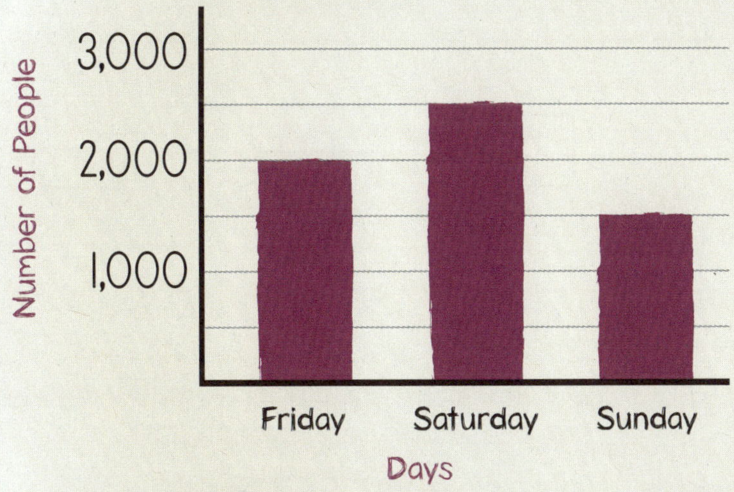

Day	Number of People
Friday	
Saturday	
Sunday	

How many more people came on Saturday than Friday?

How many fewer people came on Sunday than Saturday?

How many people came in all on Saturday and Sunday?

How many people came in all 3 days?

12.2

Lesson Activities

A

9 ÷ 2 = 4 R1

B

There is 1 brownie. 3 friends want to share it equally. How many brownies does each person get?

1 ÷ 3 = ☐

There are 3 brownies. 1 friend wants to eat them all by himself! How many brownies does he get?

3 ÷ 1 = ☐

2 ÷ 1 = ☐

4 ÷ 1 = ☐

100 ÷ 1 = ☐

C

There are 0 brownies. 3 friends want to share them equally. How many brownies does each person get?

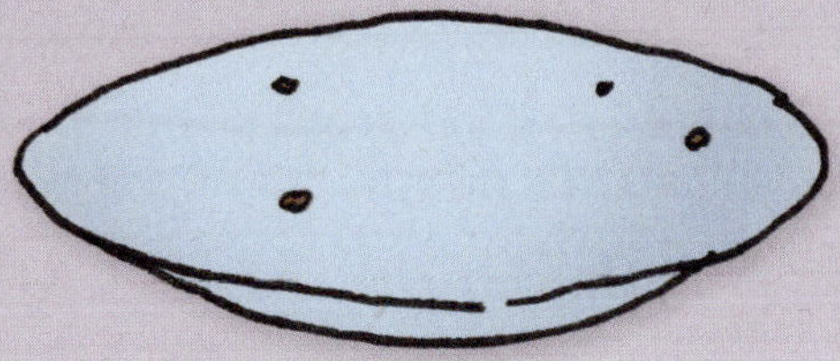

0 ÷ 3 = ☐

There are 3 brownies. 0 friends want to share them equally. How many brownies does each person get?

3 ÷ 0 = ☐

0 ÷ 5 = ☐

5 ÷ 0 = ☐

7 ÷ 0 = ☐

0 ÷ 7 = ☐

0 ÷ 100 = ☐

100 ÷ 0 = ☐

Practice

Complete the problems that can be solved.
Cross out the problems that cannot be solved.

$0 \div 3 =$ 0	$6 \div 0 =$ ☐	$8 \div 1 =$ ☐
~~$3 \div 0 =$ ☐~~	$0 \div 6 =$ ☐	$0 \div 8 =$ ☐
$0 \div 9 =$ ☐	$1 \div 0 =$ ☐	$0 \div 50 =$ ☐
$9 \div 0 =$ ☐	$10 \div 1 =$ ☐	$50 \div 0 =$ ☐

Complete.

$12 \div 3 =$ ☐	$30 \div 3 =$ ☐	$27 \div 3 =$ ☐
$9 \div 3 =$ ☐	$21 \div 3 =$ ☐	$18 \div 3 =$ ☐
$24 \div 3 =$ ☐	$15 \div 3 =$ ☐	$6 \div 3 =$ ☐

Solve. Write a division equation to match.

Amir buys 3 movie tickets. He pays $27.
How much does each movie ticket cost?

☐ ÷ ☐ = ☐

Brooklyn has 25 feet of ribbon.
She cuts it into pieces that are 5 feet long.
How many pieces does she get?

☐ ÷ ☐ = ☐

Review

Use the numbers to complete the blanks.
You will use each number once.

1	2	3	4	5	6	7	8	9

☐ × 4 = 12	4 × ☐ = 20	4 × ☐ = 16
☐ × 4 = 32	4 × ☐ = 4	4 × ☐ = 36
☐ × 4 = 8	4 × ☐ = 28	4 × ☐ = 24

Complete with <, >, or =.

6 × 7 ◯ 40

7 × 7 ◯ 50

8 × 6 ◯ 50

9 × 6 ◯ 50

9 × 9 ◯ 80

Round to the nearest thousand.

6,742	
8,499	
3,500	
2,077	
4,601	

Complete the sequences.

Count by 5s

6,000					6,025

Count by 10s

5,480					5,530

Lesson Activities

A

16 ÷ 4 = ☐

☐ × 4 = 16

12 ÷ 4 = ☐	20 ÷ 4 = ☐	32 ÷ 4 = ☐
24 ÷ 4 = ☐	8 ÷ 4 = ☐	4 ÷ 4 = ☐
28 ÷ 4 = ☐	40 ÷ 4 = ☐	36 ÷ 4 = ☐

B

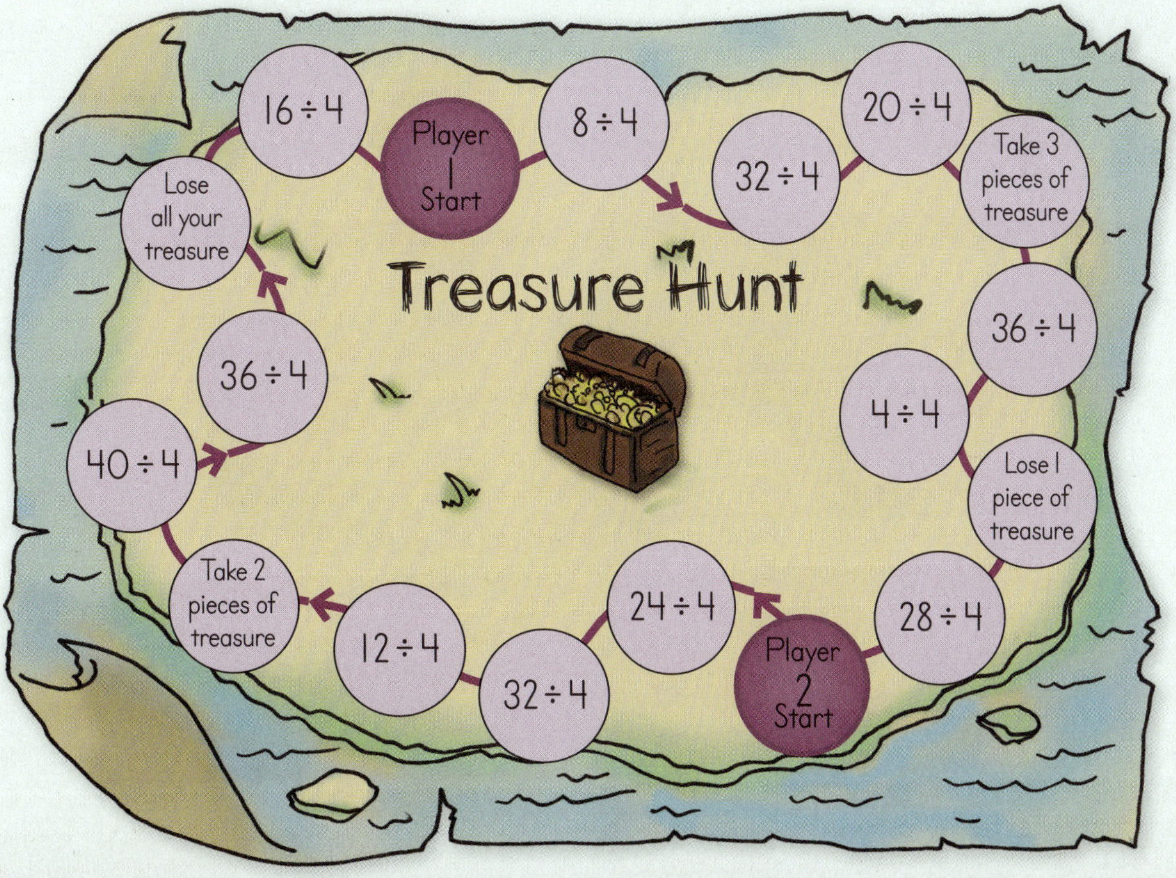

Practice

Complete.

$\square \times 4 = 8$

$8 \div 4 = \square$

$\square \times 4 = 20$

$20 \div 4 = \square$

$\square \times 4 = 40$

$40 \div 4 = \square$

$\square \times 4 = 12$

$12 \div 4 = \square$

$\square \times 4 = 4$

$4 \div 4 = \square$

$\square \times 4 = 24$

$24 \div 4 = \square$

$\square \times 4 = 28$

$28 \div 4 = \square$

$\square \times 4 = 16$

$16 \div 4 = \square$

$\square \times 4 = 36$

$36 \div 4 = \square$

$\square \times 4 = 32$

$32 \div 4 = \square$

Review

Circle the more sensible unit for each item.

Area of a sticky note

4 sq. ft.	4 sq. in.

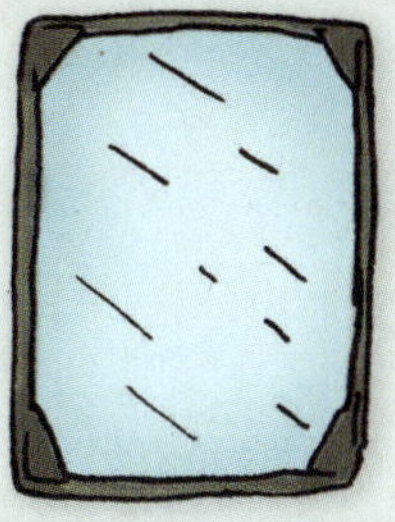

Area of a mirror

3 sq. ft.	3 sq. in.

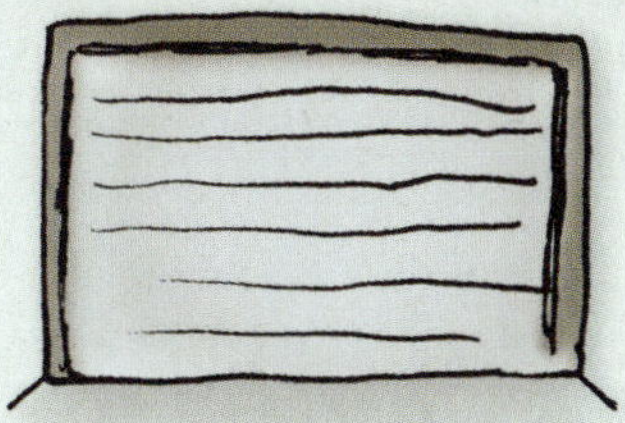

Area of a garage door

15 sq. yd.	15 sq. ft.

Color the multiples in order from Start to End.

Multiples of 8

16	24	32	40	44
8	20	36	48	54
14	28	40	56	64
18	36	44	63	72
12	21	35	70	80

Start: 8 — END: 80

Complete.

3,500 + 500 = ____

4,900 + 400 = ____

6,000 - 200 = ____

7,100 - 300 = ____

Solve. Write the equations you use.

A sandwich costs $6.39.
A drink costs $4.48 less than a sandwich.
How much does it cost to buy a sandwich and a drink?

Lesson Activities

A

12 children split into 2 groups.
How many children are in each group?

$12 \div 2 = \square$

total — number of groups — size of each group

12 children split into groups of 2.
How many groups do they make?

$12 \div 2 = \square$

total — size of each group — number of groups

B

There are 30 children at gymnastics lessons. The coaches divide the children into 5 equal groups. How many children are in each group?

20 children carpool together to the museum. 4 children fit in each car. How many cars do they need?

Eden arranges 24 chairs for the piano recital. She makes 3 rows. How many chairs are in each row?

Simon has 12 inches of yarn.
He cuts the yarn into 4 equal pieces.
How long is each piece?

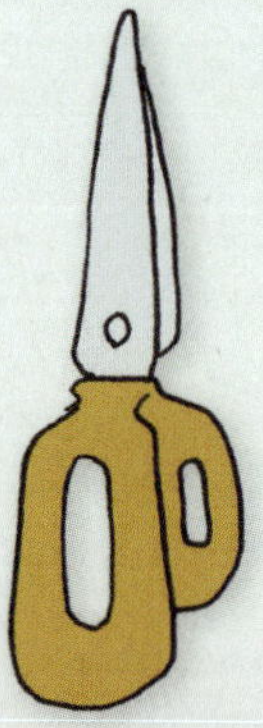

Practice

Complete.

$40 \div 4 = \square$	$24 \div 4 = \square$	$16 \div 4 = \square$
$8 \div 4 = \square$	$20 \div 4 = \square$	$32 \div 4 = \square$
$28 \div 4 = \square$	$36 \div 4 = \square$	$12 \div 4 = \square$
$27 \div 3 = \square$	$21 \div 3 = \square$	$24 \div 3 = \square$
$6 \div 1 = \square$	$12 \div 1 = \square$	$20 \div 1 = \square$

Solve. Write the equations you use.

4 donuts fit in a box.
If you have 24 donuts, how many boxes can you fill completely?

There are 15 children on the soccer team. They split into 5 equal groups at practice. How many children are in each group?

Sara has 28 feet of rope. She cuts the rope into pieces that are 4 feet long. How many pieces does she get?

4 friends earn $20 at a lemonade stand. They share the money equally.
How much money does each person get?

Review

Use the numbers to complete the blanks. You will use each number once.

1	2	3	4	5	6	7	8	9

☐ × 6 = 24	6 × ☐ = 36	6 × ☐ = 18
☐ × 6 = 30	6 × ☐ = 12	6 × ☐ = 48
☐ × 6 = 54	6 × ☐ = 6	6 × ☐ = 42

Complete with <, >, or =.

6 × 6 ◯ 35

6 × 7 ◯ 40

8 × 7 ◯ 60

8 × 8 ◯ 60

8 × 9 ◯ 70

Complete.

65 - 63 = ☐

71 - 65 = ☐

127 - 125 = ☐

153 - 148 = ☐

Complete the sequences.

Count by 2s	5,100					5,110
Count by 20s	5,100					5,200

Lesson Activities

A

42 ÷ 6 = ☐

☐ × 6 = 42

60 ÷ 6 = ☐	12 ÷ 6 = ☐	24 ÷ 6 = ☐
30 ÷ 6 = ☐	6 ÷ 6 = ☐	36 ÷ 6 = ☐
54 ÷ 6 = ☐	48 ÷ 6 = ☐	18 ÷ 6 = ☐

B

Dice Tic-Tac-Toe

18 ÷ 6	36 ÷ 6	60 ÷ 6	54 ÷ 6	30 ÷ 6
54 ÷ 6	48 ÷ 6	12 ÷ 6	24 ÷ 6	54 ÷ 6
24 ÷ 6	6 ÷ 6	30 ÷ 6	48 ÷ 6	42 ÷ 6
60 ÷ 6	42 ÷ 6	36 ÷ 6	42 ÷ 6	6 ÷ 6
12 ÷ 6	36 ÷ 6	18 ÷ 6	30 ÷ 6	48 ÷ 6

Practice

Complete.

☐ × 6 = 18

18 ÷ 6 = ☐

☐ × 6 = 54

54 ÷ 6 = ☐

☐ × 6 = 24

24 ÷ 6 = ☐

☐ × 6 = 60

60 ÷ 6 = ☐

☐ × 6 = 48

48 ÷ 6 = ☐

☐ × 6 = 30

30 ÷ 6 = ☐

☐ × 6 = 12

12 ÷ 6 = ☐

☐ × 6 = 6

6 ÷ 6 = ☐

☐ × 6 = 42

42 ÷ 6 = ☐

☐ × 6 = 36

36 ÷ 6 = ☐

Review

Complete the equivalent fractions.

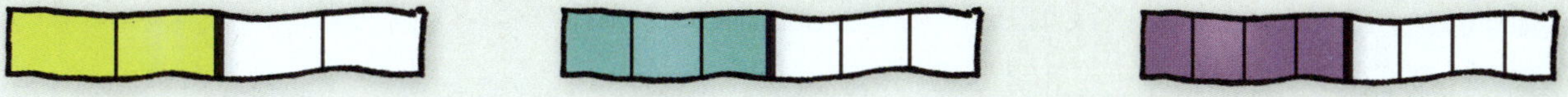

$\frac{1}{2} = \frac{\square}{4}$ $\frac{1}{2} = \frac{\square}{6}$ $\frac{1}{2} = \frac{\square}{8}$

Color the multiples in order from Start to End.

Multiples of 7

Start →

7	14	21	28	35
12	16	54	49	42
24	48	64	56	60
45	36	40	63	70
35	30	32	72	80

END

Complete.

	3,	5	0	8
+	2,	7	6	4

Solve.

You pay the clerk $10.00.
How much change do you get?

Change
$

Copy the lines.

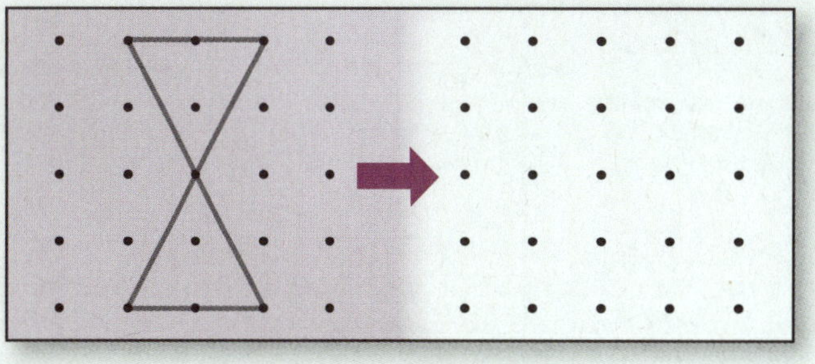

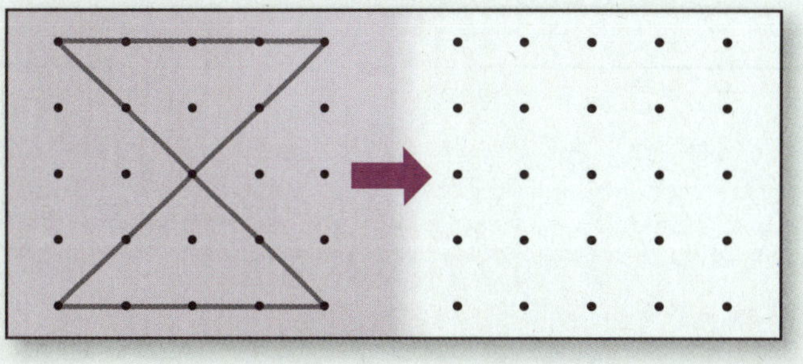

Lesson Activities

A

20 Striped Chocolates
(4 in each box)

$20 \div 4 =$ ☐

$4\overline{)20}$

15 Caramel Chocolates
(5 in each box)

14 Cherry Chocolates
(7 in each box)

24 Dark Chocolates
(6 in each box)

B

Dice Tic-Tac-Toe

$3\overline{)27}$	$6\overline{)60}$	$5\overline{)40}$	$5\overline{)25}$	$6\overline{)24}$
$4\overline{)32}$	$6\overline{)12}$	$3\overline{)21}$	$6\overline{)48}$	$4\overline{)28}$
$6\overline{)30}$	$3\overline{)24}$	$6\overline{)42}$	$6\overline{)54}$	$4\overline{)36}$
$3\overline{)30}$	$5\overline{)35}$	$6\overline{)18}$	$4\overline{)40}$	$5\overline{)45}$
$5\overline{)30}$	$6\overline{)36}$	$4\overline{)24}$	$3\overline{)18}$	$6\overline{)6}$

Practice

Complete.

$3\overline{)15}$	$4\overline{)24}$	$5\overline{)35}$	$4\overline{)40}$	$2\overline{)16}$
$2\overline{)10}$	$3\overline{)27}$	$4\overline{)36}$	$5\overline{)40}$	$4\overline{)32}$
$6\overline{)12}$	$6\overline{)60}$	$6\overline{)24}$	$6\overline{)18}$	$6\overline{)36}$
$6\overline{)\ \ 6}$	$6\overline{)30}$	$6\overline{)48}$	$6\overline{)42}$	$6\overline{)54}$

Solve. Write each problem with a division bracket.

You need 35 pencils.
How many packs should you buy?

You need 10 staplers.
How many packs should you buy?

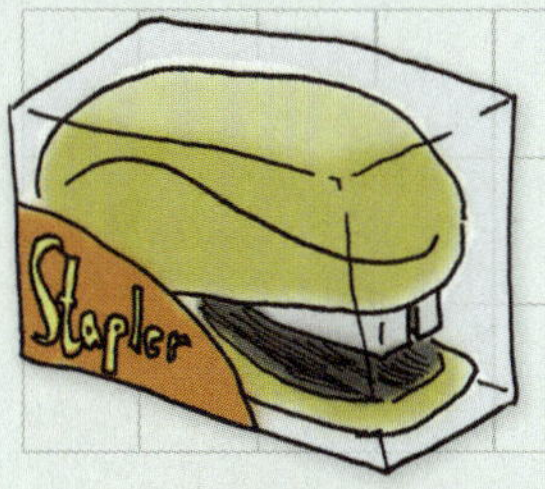

You need 90 markers.
How many packs should you buy?

You need 18 scissors.
How many packs should you buy?

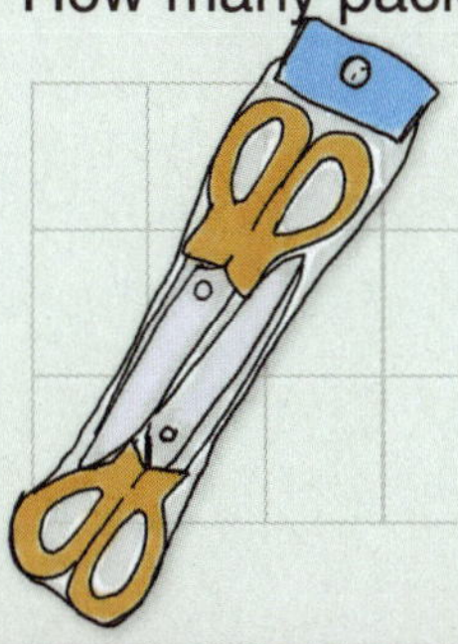

Review

Complete.

$$\begin{array}{r} 9{,}768 \\ -\ 4{,}285 \\ \hline \square \end{array} \qquad \begin{array}{r} 3{,}097 \\ -\ 1{,}644 \\ \hline \square \end{array} \qquad \begin{array}{r} 6{,}000 \\ -\ 3{,}850 \\ \hline \square \end{array}$$

Complete the equivalent fractions.

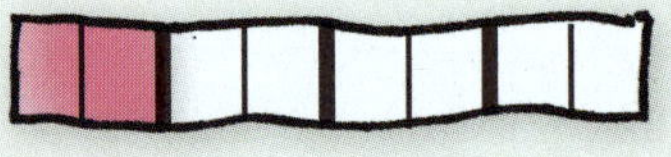

$\frac{1}{4} = \frac{\square}{8}$

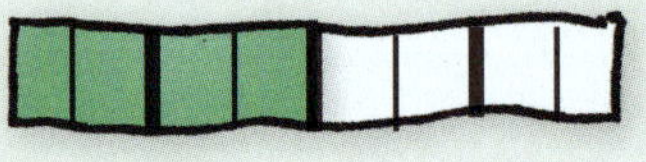

$\frac{2}{4} = \frac{\square}{8}$

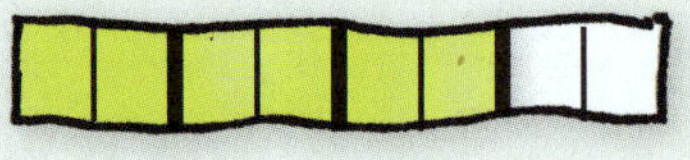

$\frac{3}{4} = \frac{\square}{8}$

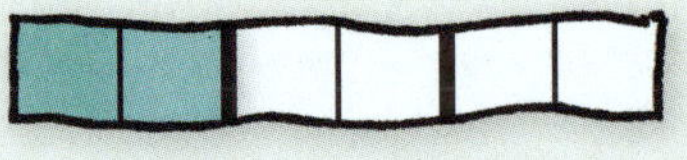

$\frac{1}{3} = \frac{\square}{6}$

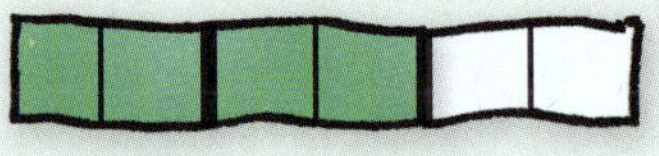

$\frac{2}{3} = \frac{\square}{6}$

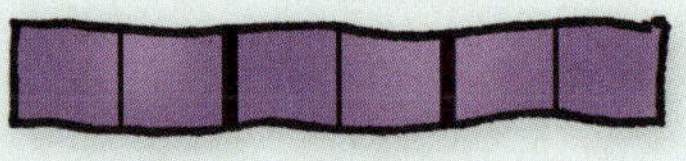

$\frac{3}{3} = \frac{\square}{6}$

Use the grid lines to find the area of each shape. Circle the correct units.

☐ sq. in.
sq. cm

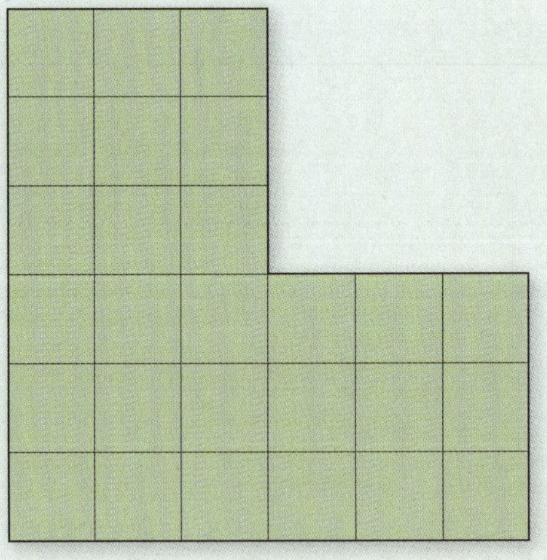

☐ sq. in.
sq. cm

Lesson Activities

A

Hit the Target

B

Striped Chocolates

			full boxes
4	2	3	
			chocolates in the full boxes
			chocolates left

Caramel Chocolates

			full boxes
5	1	6	
			chocolates in the full boxes
			chocolates left

Cherry Chocolates

			full boxes
3	2	0	
			chocolates in the full boxes
			chocolates left

Dark Chocolates

			full boxes
2	1	9	
			chocolates in the full boxes
			chocolates left

Milk Chocolates

				full boxes
1	0	4	3	
				chocolates in the full boxes
				chocolates left

Practice

Color the problems that match the number in the star.

5
- 15 ÷ 3
- 24 ÷ 4
- 30 ÷ 6

8
- 24 ÷ 3
- 32 ÷ 4
- 42 ÷ 6

4
- 18 ÷ 3
- 16 ÷ 4
- 24 ÷ 6

6
- 18 ÷ 3
- 24 ÷ 4
- 48 ÷ 6

9
- 30 ÷ 3
- 36 ÷ 4
- 54 ÷ 6

7
- 21 ÷ 3
- 32 ÷ 4
- 42 ÷ 6

Review

Write the time.

:

:

:

:

Color the multiples in order from Start to End.

Multiples of 9

	24	30	32	35	80
	18	27	36	40	90	END
Start →	9	12	45	48	81
	15	20	54	63	72
	21	25	56	70	64

Complete.

$60 \times 4 =$ ☐

$70 \times 9 =$ ☐

$70 \times 6 =$ ☐

$40 \times 5 =$ ☐

$80 \times 8 =$ ☐

Complete.

Expanded Form	Number
2,000 + 900 + 80 + 4	
	6,245
3,000 + 8	
	9,040
	3,107

Solve.

Aaron finds $\frac{7}{8}$ of a leftover pizza in the fridge.

He eats $\frac{1}{8}$ of the pizza.

What fraction of the whole pizza is left?

Lesson Activities

A

Long Division

1. Divide — How many groups can I make?
2. Multiply — How many are in the groups?
3. Subtract — How many are left?

3 ⟌ 2 2

1. Divide
2. Multiply
3. Subtract

2 ⟌ 1 7 5 ⟌ 2 7 3 ⟌ 2 0 4 ⟌ 3 1

B

Roll and Divide

Player 1	⟌ 1 9	⟌ 2 3	⟌ 2 8	Sum of remainders
Player 2	⟌ 1 9	⟌ 2 3	⟌ 2 8	Sum of remainders

Practice

Complete. Follow the steps.

1. Divide
2. Multiply
3. Subtract

$2\overline{)11}$ $5\overline{)24}$ $3\overline{)17}$ $4\overline{)13}$

Complete.

Start

$30 \div 3 =$ ___
$27 \div 3 =$ ___
$24 \div 3 =$ ___

$20 \div 4 =$ ___
$24 \div 4 =$ ___
$28 \div 4 =$ ___

$30 \div 6 =$ ___
$36 \div 6 =$ ___
$42 \div 6 =$ ___

$15 \div 3 =$ ___
$18 \div 3 =$ ___
$21 \div 3 =$ ___

$40 \div 4 =$ ___
$36 \div 4 =$ ___
$32 \div 4 =$ ___

$60 \div 6 =$ ___
$54 \div 6 =$ ___
$48 \div 6 =$ ___

Review

Find the perimeter and area of each rectangle.

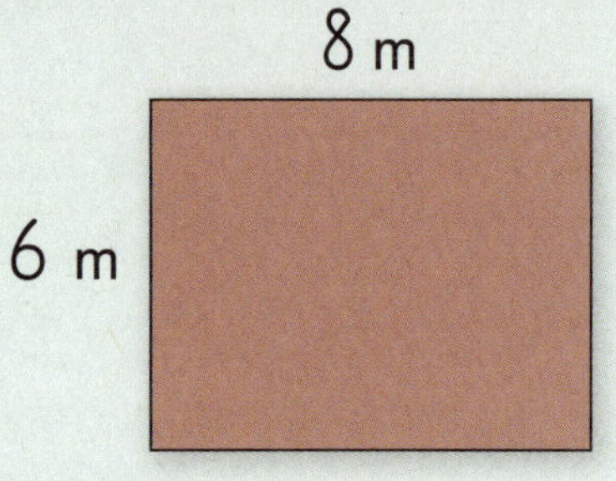

Perimeter: ______

______

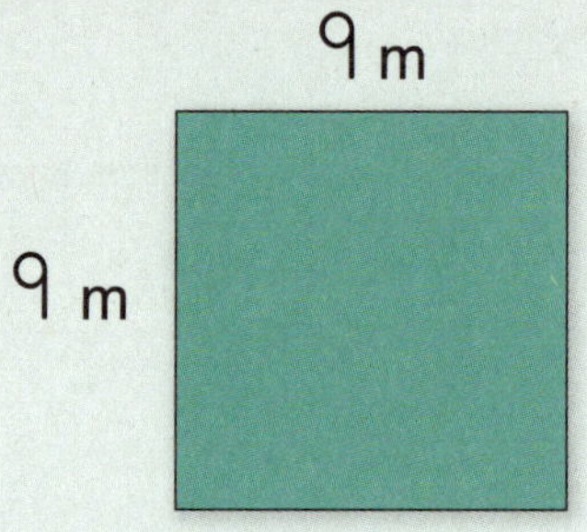

Perimeter: ______

______

Label the numbers on the number line.

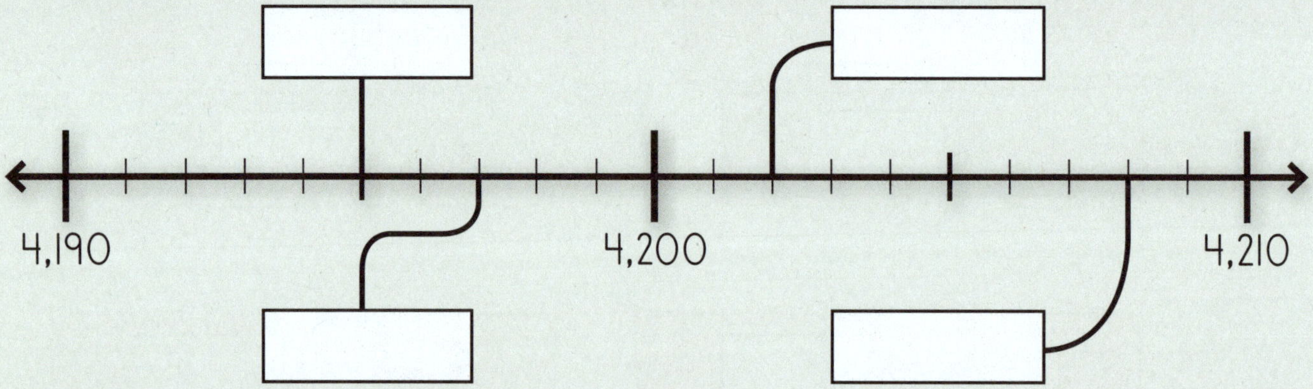

Complete with <, >, or =.

$\frac{5}{8}$ ◯ $\frac{3}{8}$

$\frac{1}{4}$ ◯ $\frac{1}{2}$

2 ◯ $\frac{1}{2}$

★ $3\frac{1}{4}$ ◯ $2\frac{3}{4}$

★ $\frac{7}{3}$ ◯ $\frac{8}{3}$

Match.

9 × 8	56
8 × 8	63
9 × 7	64
9 × 9	72
8 × 7	81

Lesson Activities

A

1. Divide
2. Multiply
3. Subtract

$4\overline{)23}$ $5\overline{)32}$ $3\overline{)25}$ $6\overline{)20}$

B

There are 32 children at gymnastics lessons.
The teachers divide the children into 5 groups.
They make the groups as even as possible.
How many children are in each group?

23 children carpool together to the museum.
4 children fit in each car.
How many cars do they need?

Eden arranges 25 chairs for the piano recital.
She makes 3 rows.
Then, she puts away any extra chairs.
How many chairs are in each row?

Simon has 20 inches of yarn.
He cuts the yarn into as many 6-inch-long pieces as he can.
How much yarn is left over?

Practice

Complete. Follow the steps.

1. Divide
2. Multiply
3. Subtract

$4\overline{)25}$ $5\overline{)17}$ $4\overline{)31}$ $4\overline{)21}$

Solve. Use the completed problems above to help find the answers. You do not need to write equations for the problems.

4 donuts fit in a box.
If you have 25 donuts, how many boxes can you fill completely?

There are 17 children on the soccer team.
They split into 5 groups.
They make the groups as equal as possible.
How many children are in each group?

Sara has 31 feet of rope. She cuts the rope into pieces that are 4 feet long.
How much rope is left over?

★ 4 friends earn $21 at a lemonade stand. They share the money equally.
How much money does each person get?

Review

Split the rectangle into smaller rectangles. Then, find the area of the whole rectangle.

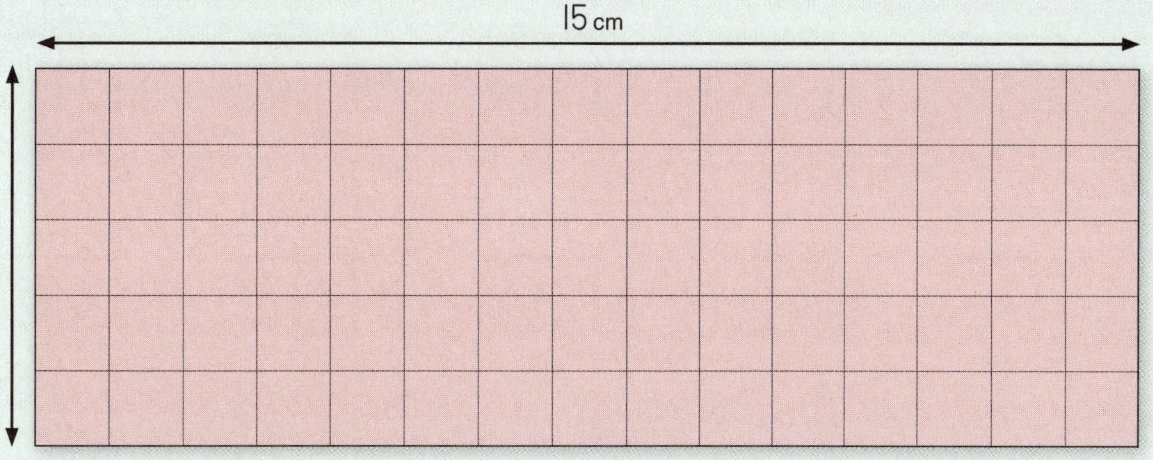

☐ sq. cm

Complete.

$\frac{5}{8} + \frac{2}{8} = \frac{\square}{\square}$

$\frac{1}{6} + \frac{4}{6} = \frac{\square}{\square}$

$\frac{3}{3} - \frac{1}{3} = \frac{\square}{\square}$

★ $\frac{5}{3} - \frac{1}{3} = \frac{\square}{\square}$

Circle the least number in each row.

3,294	3,094	3,904
5,065	5,056	5,650
8,011	8,101	8,010

Solve.

40 ÷ 10 = ☐	20 ÷ 4 = ☐	24 ÷ 6 = ☐
40 ÷ 5 = ☐	20 ÷ 2 = ☐	24 ÷ 3 = ☐
28 ÷ 4 = ☐	36 ÷ 6 = ☐	70 ÷ 10 = ☐
28 ÷ 2 = ☐	★ 36 ÷ 3 = ☐	★ 70 ÷ 5 = ☐

Unit Wrap-Up

Complete.

$3\overline{)15}$ $4\overline{)24}$ $6\overline{)60}$ $3\overline{)12}$ $6\overline{)30}$

$4\overline{)16}$ $3\overline{)21}$ $6\overline{)36}$ $4\overline{)36}$ $3\overline{)24}$

$6\overline{)54}$ $4\overline{)40}$ $3\overline{)27}$ $4\overline{)28}$ $6\overline{)42}$

$4\overline{)20}$ $6\overline{)24}$ $6\overline{)48}$ $3\overline{)18}$ $4\overline{)32}$

Complete. Cross out any problems that cannot be solved.

$0 \div 4 =$ ☐	$6 \div 0 =$ ☐	$0 \div 127 =$ ☐
$4 \div 0 =$ ☐	$0 \div 6 =$ ☐	$127 \div 0 =$ ☐

Match each number in the equation to the correct word.

16 ÷ 5 = 3 R1

divisor | remainder | dividend | quotient

Unit Wrap-Up

Complete. Follow the steps.

1. Divide
2. Multiply
3. Subtract

$5\overline{)24}$ $3\overline{)25}$ $6\overline{)19}$ $4\overline{)39}$

Solve. Write the equations you use.

Darius has 26 googly eyes. He puts 4 googly eyes on each monster puppet. He makes as many puppets as he can. How many googly eyes does he have left over?

There are 27 children at swim lessons. They split into 3 groups and make the groups as equal as possible. How many children are in each group?

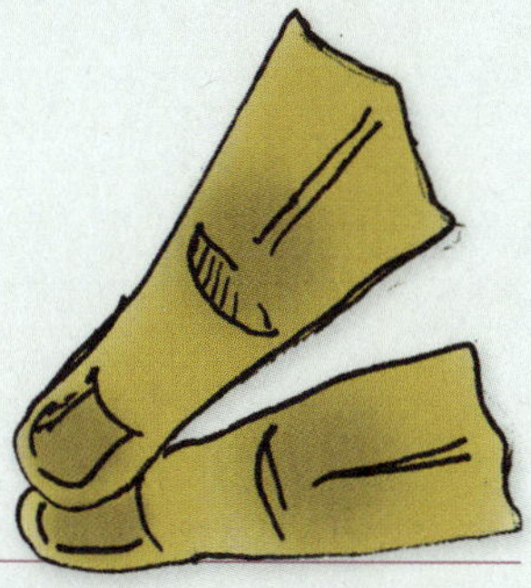

Mariana helps her grandpa plant peas. They have 24 seeds. They plant 6 seeds in each row. How many rows do they plant?

Brayden helps his mom decorate for a party. They blow up 50 balloons and tie them in 6 bunches. They make the bunches as equal as possible. How many balloons are in each bunch?

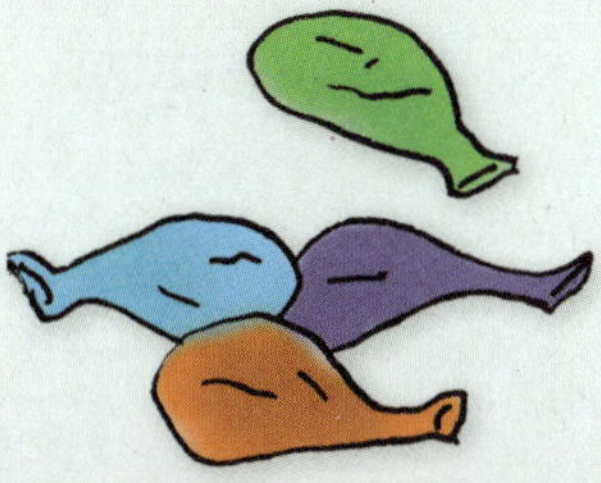

Lesson Activities

A

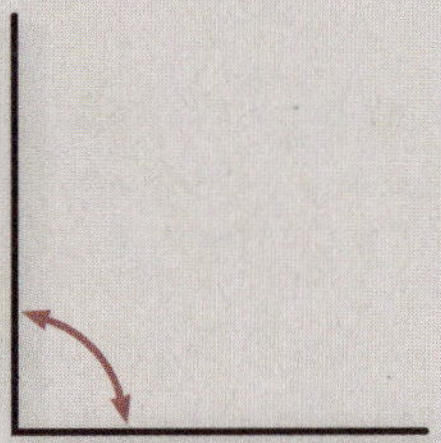

Right angle

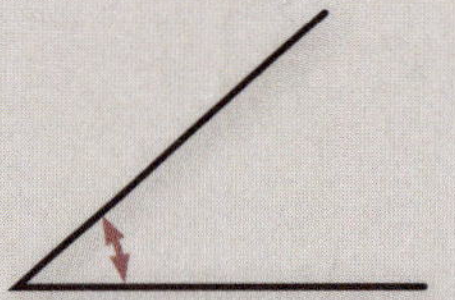

Smaller than a right angle

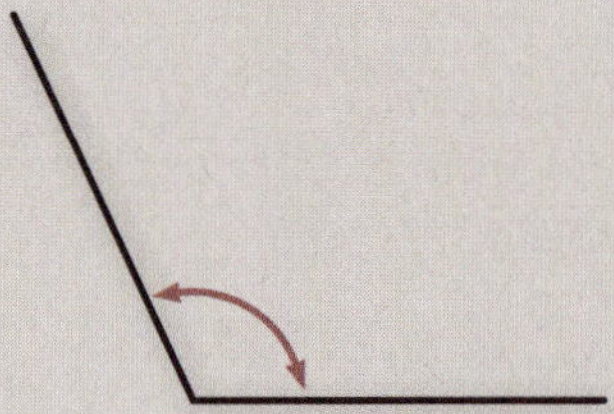

Larger than a right angle

B

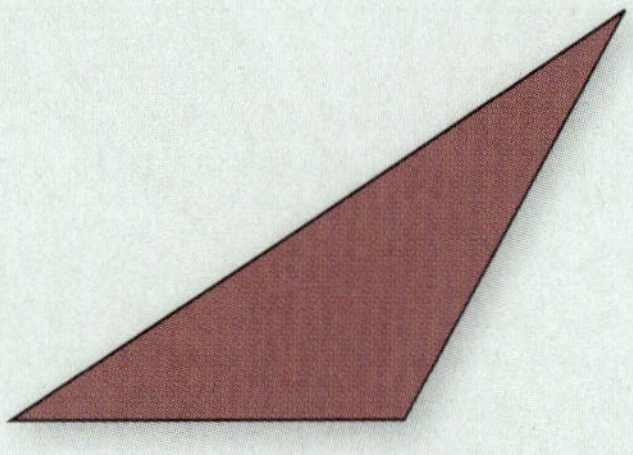

☐ right angles

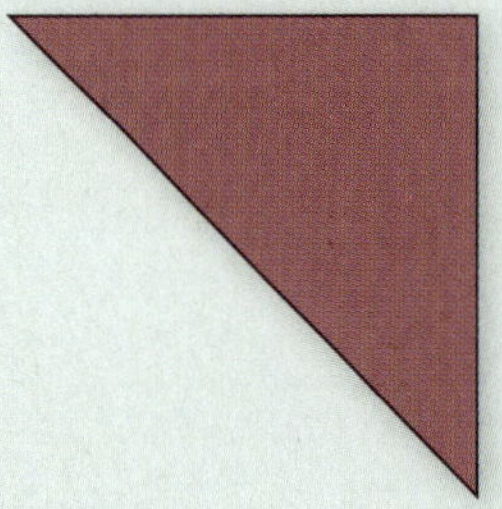

☐ right angles

☐ right angles

☐ right angles

☐ right angles

☐ right angles

Practice

Circle the description that matches the highlighted angle.

Right angle
Smaller than a right angle
Larger than a right angle

Right angle
Smaller than a right angle
Larger than a right angle

Right angle
Smaller than a right angle
Larger than a right angle

Right angle
Smaller than a right angle
Larger than a right angle

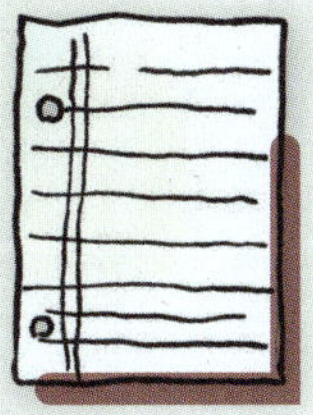

Right angle
Smaller than a right angle
Larger than a right angle

Right angle
Smaller than a right angle
Larger than a right angle

Tell how many right angles each shape has.

☐ right angles

☐ right angles

☐ right angles

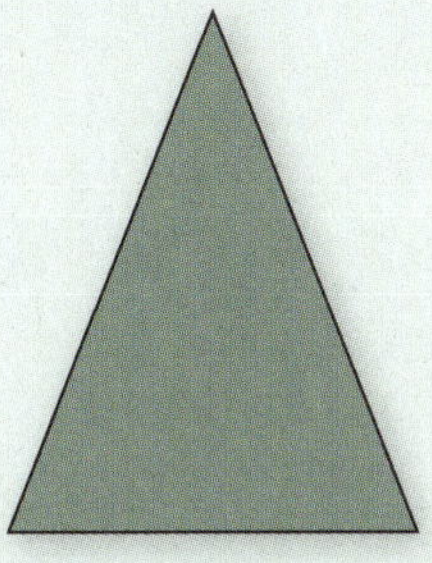

☐ right angles

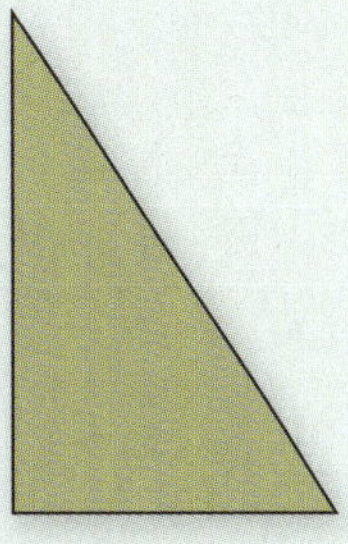

☐ right angles

☐ right angles

Review

Complete. Follow the steps.

1. Divide
2. Multiply
3. Subtract

$2\overline{)17}$ $5\overline{)42}$ $4\overline{)37}$ $3\overline{)28}$

Write the numbers that come before and after each number.

Before		After
3,464	3,465	3,466
	8,949	
	6,100	
	7,000	
	4,003	

Complete.

1 year = ☐ months

1 week = ☐ days

1 day = ☐ hours

1 hour = ☐ minutes

1 minute = ☐ seconds

Complete.

36 ÷ 4 = ☐	24 ÷ 4 = ☐	40 ÷ 4 = ☐
42 ÷ 6 = ☐	40 ÷ 5 = ☐	24 ÷ 3 = ☐
60 ÷ 6 = ☐	36 ÷ 6 = ☐	18 ÷ 2 = ☐
18 ÷ 3 = ☐	32 ÷ 4 = ☐	30 ÷ 3 = ☐

Lesson Activities

A

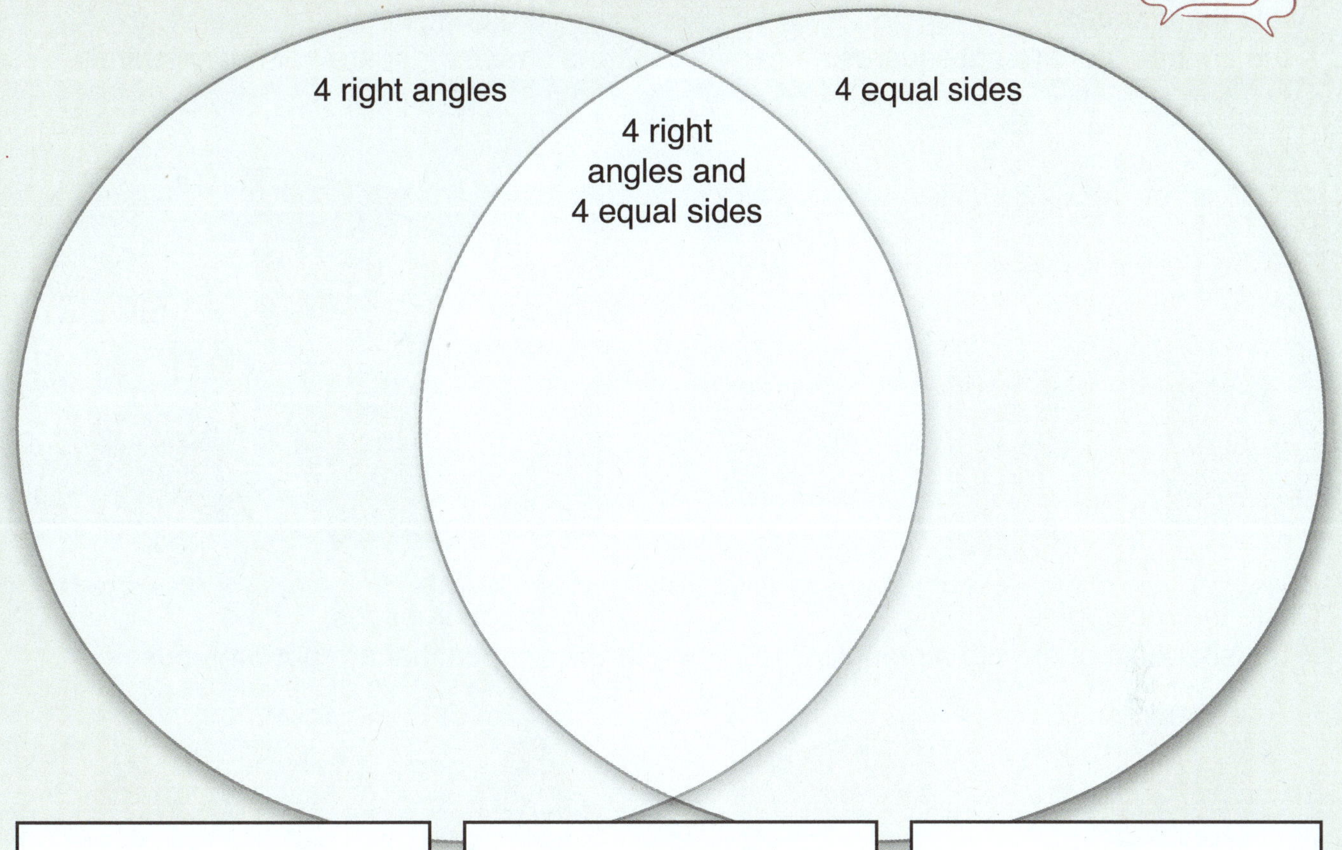

B

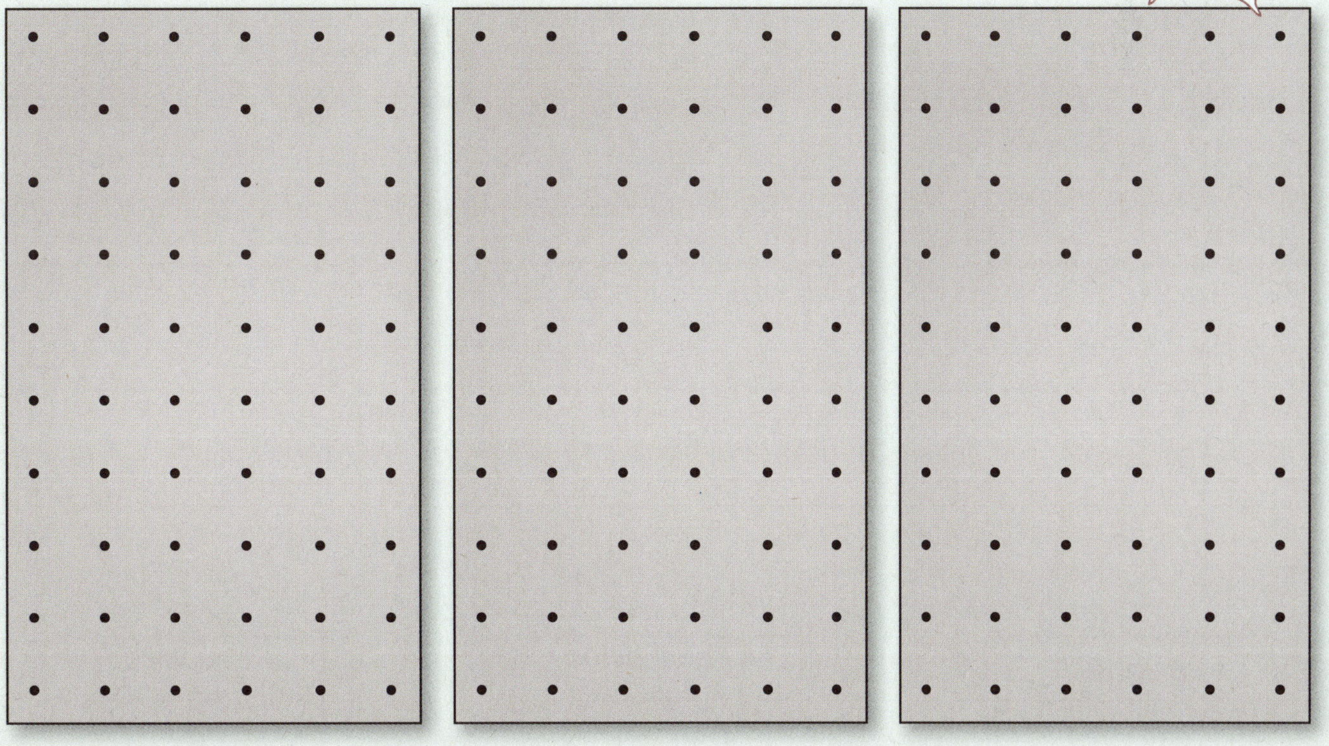

Practice

Follow the directions for each group of shapes.

Circle the squares.
X the shapes that are not squares.

Circle the quadrilaterals.
X the shapes that are not quadrilaterals.

Circle the rectangles.
X the shapes that are not rectangles.

Circle the rhombuses.
X the shapes that are not rhombuses.

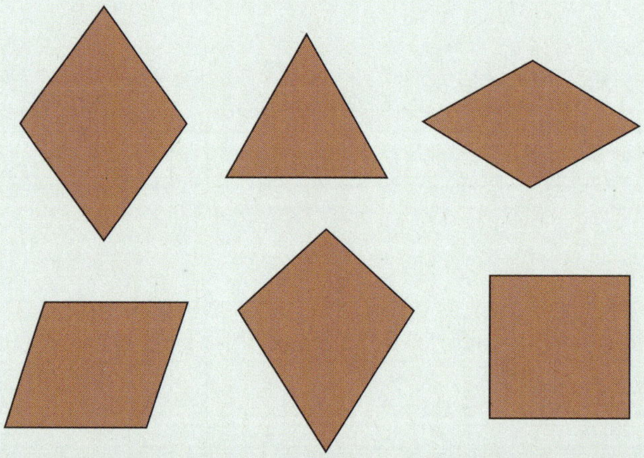

Draw a quadrilateral that matches each description.

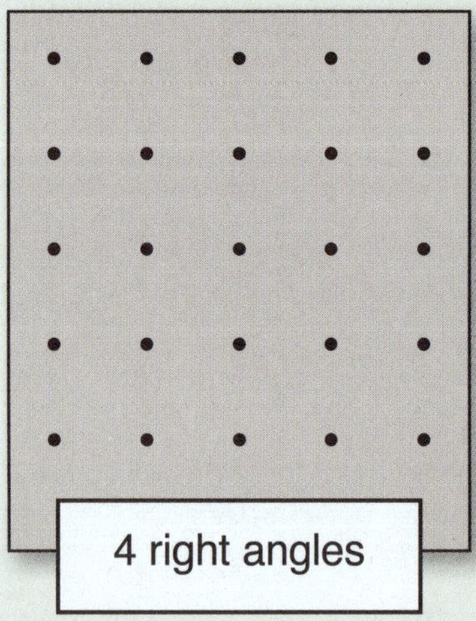

4 right angles

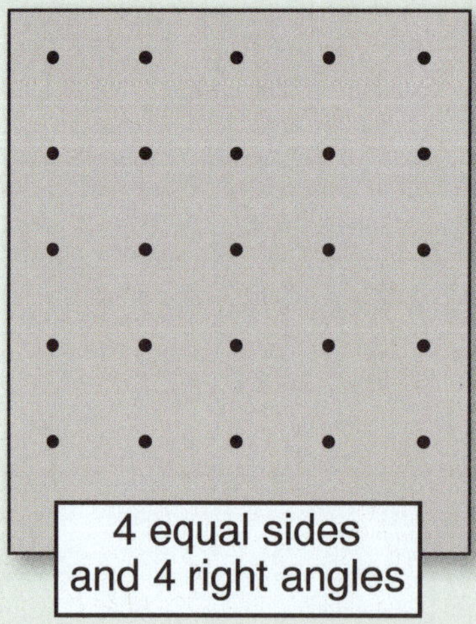

4 equal sides
and 4 right angles

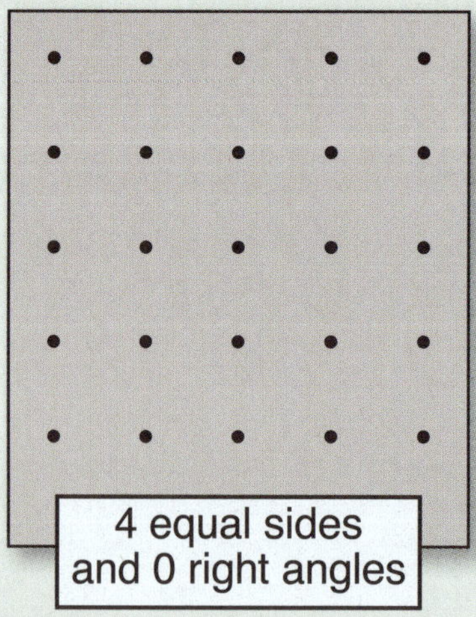

4 equal sides
and 0 right angles

Review

Write the time.

__ : __

__ : __

__ : __

__ : __

Complete.

	5,	0	9	7
+	2,	4	6	8

	5,	0	9	7
-	2,	4	6	8

Complete.

$6\overline{)30}$ $3\overline{)30}$ $4\overline{)36}$

$6\overline{)42}$ $6\overline{)54}$ $3\overline{)27}$

$4\overline{)28}$ $5\overline{)45}$ $6\overline{)48}$

Solve. Write the equations you use to solve the problems.

There are 36 children at baseball practice.
They divide into 4 groups.
How many children are in each group?

There are 39 children at baseball practice.
They divide into 4 groups.
How many children are in each group?

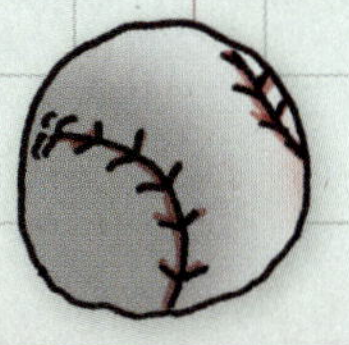

Lesson Activities

A

Pentomino Rules

- Every pentomino has 5 squares.
- Each square must touch at least one other square.
- Squares may only touch along their edges. They must touch from corner to corner.

Pentominoes

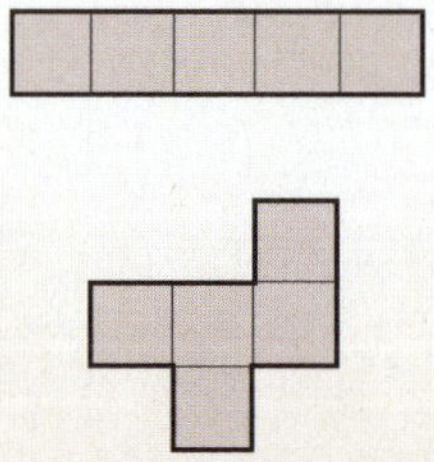

Not Pentominoes

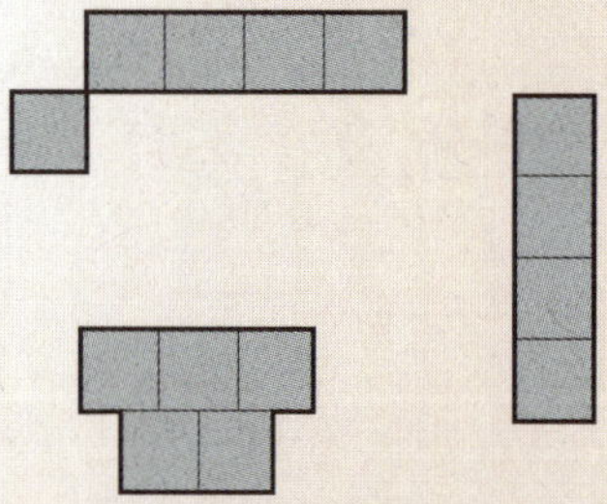

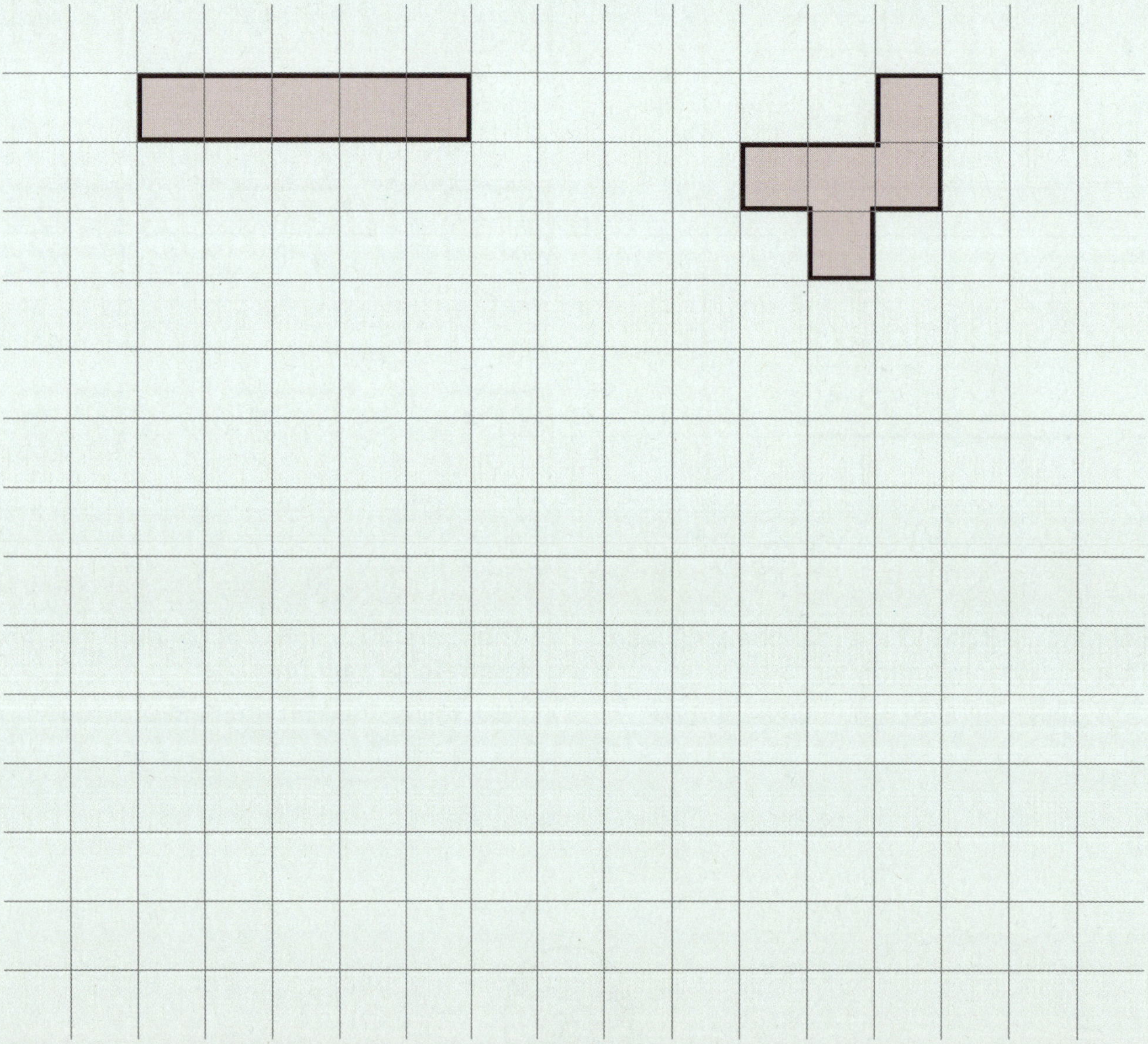

Practice

Find two different ways to cover each shape with pentominoes. Draw lines to show where you put each piece.

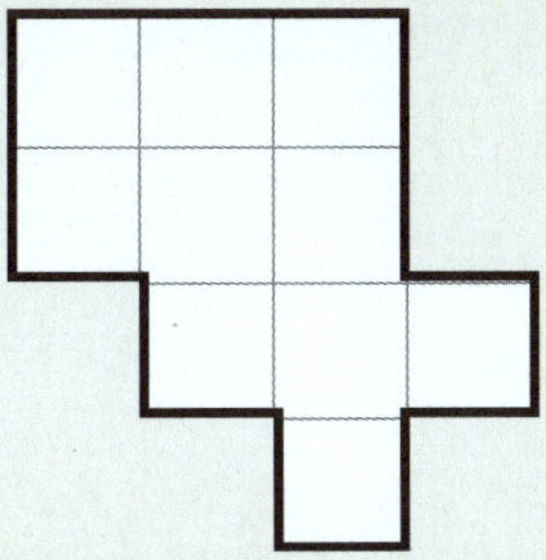

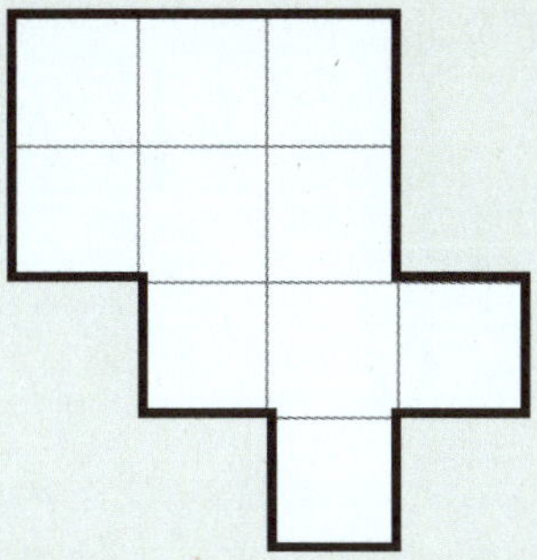

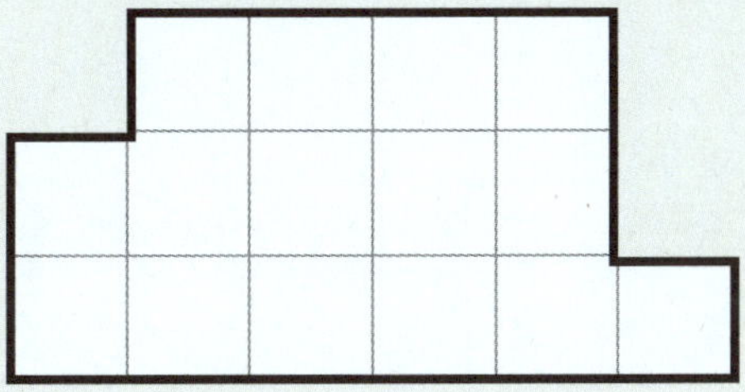

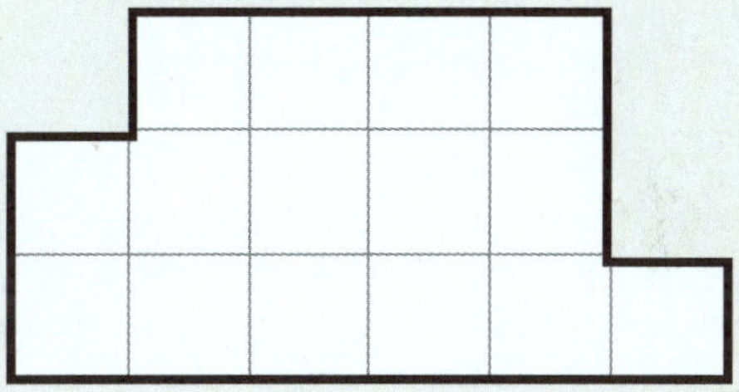

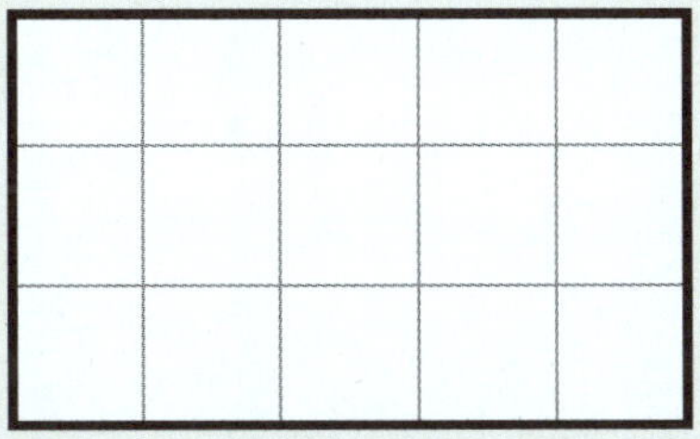

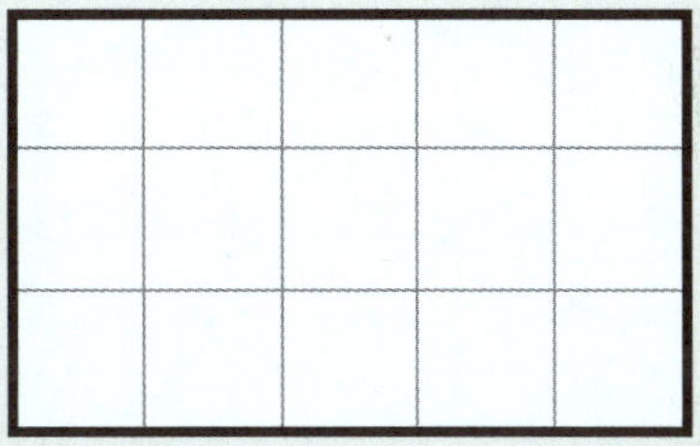

★ 

★ 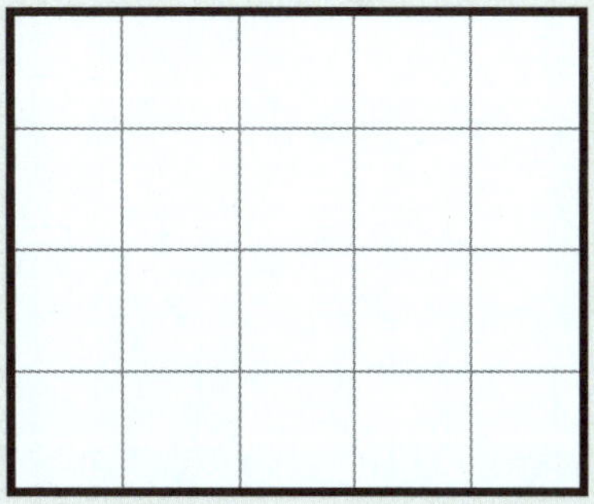

Review

Complete. Follow the steps.

1. Divide
2. Multiply
3. Subtract

$5\overline{)29}$ $4\overline{)29}$ $3\overline{)29}$ $6\overline{)29}$

Round to the nearest dollar.

\$9.99	\$5.55	\$7.77	\$3.33	\$4.44	\$1.11

Color the circles to match.

$2\frac{1}{4}$

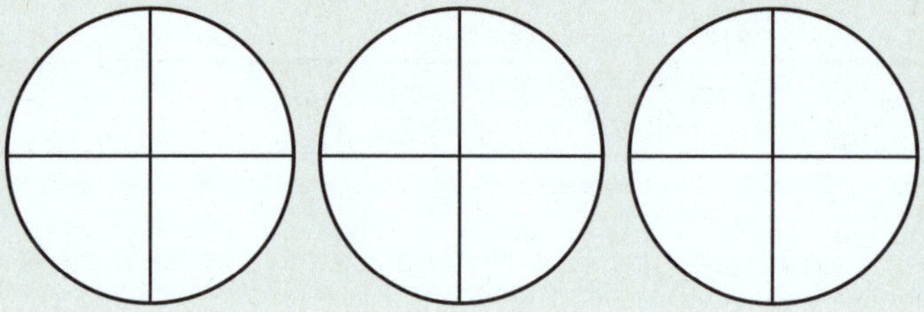

$1\frac{5}{6}$

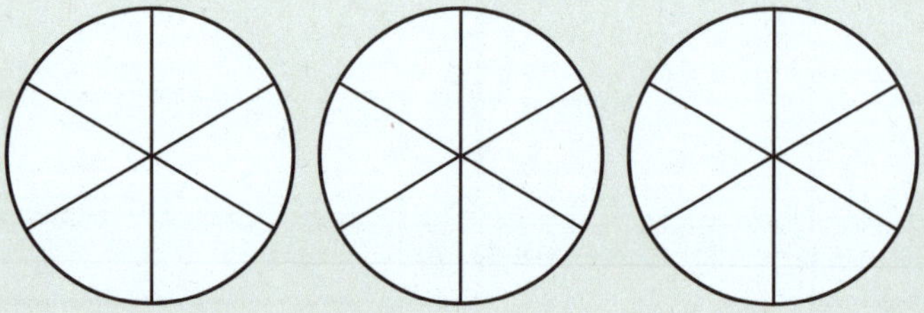

$\frac{7}{8}$

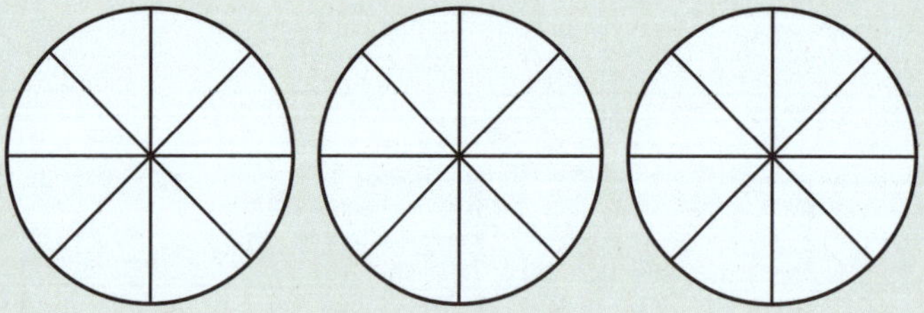

$2\frac{1}{2}$

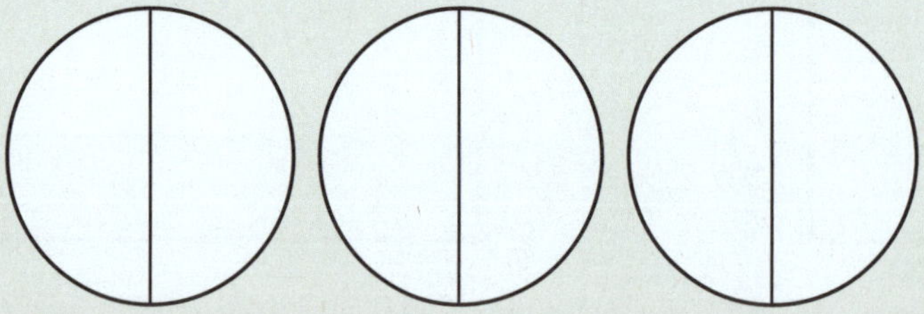

Complete with <, >, or =.

6 × 6 ◯ 35

8 × 7 ◯ 50

8 × 6 ◯ 50

7 × 7 ◯ 50

9 × 7 ◯ 60

9 × 9 ◯ 80

6 × 7 ◯ 40

8 × 8 ◯ 60

Lesson Activities

A

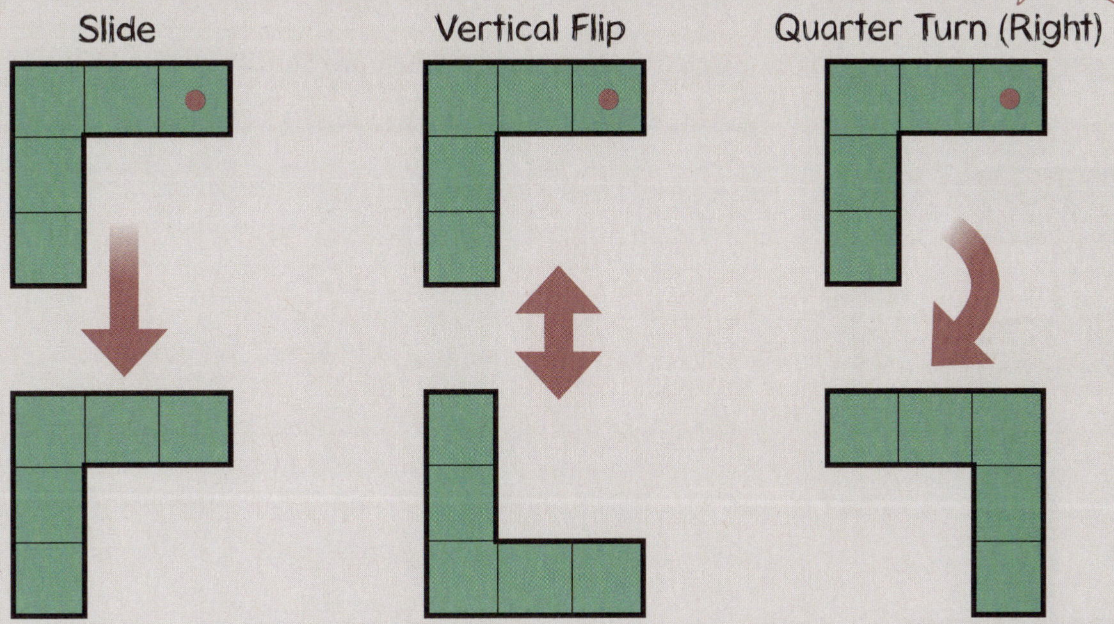

B

	Slide	Horizontal Flip (Right)	Quarter Turn (Right)
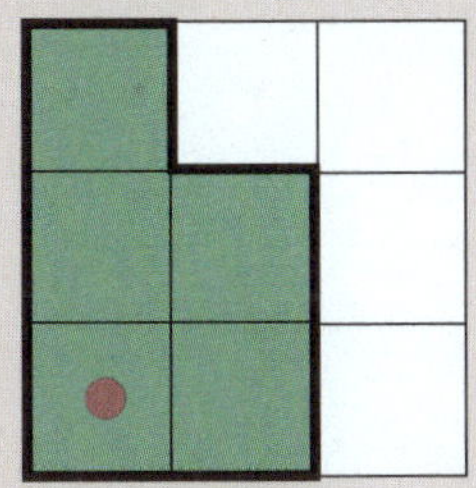			
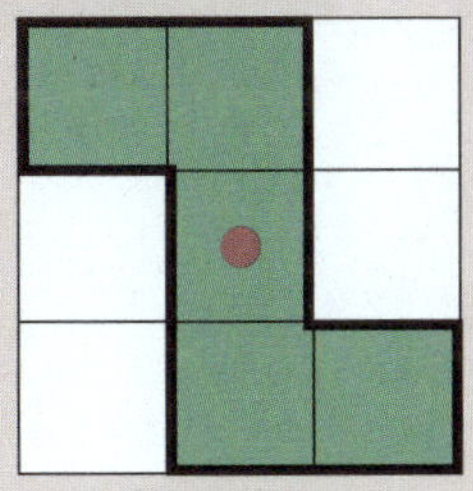			

13.4

Practice

Draw how each pentomino looks after a slide, horizontal flip to the right, and quarter turn to the right.

	Slide	Horizontal Flip (Right)	Quarter Turn (Right)
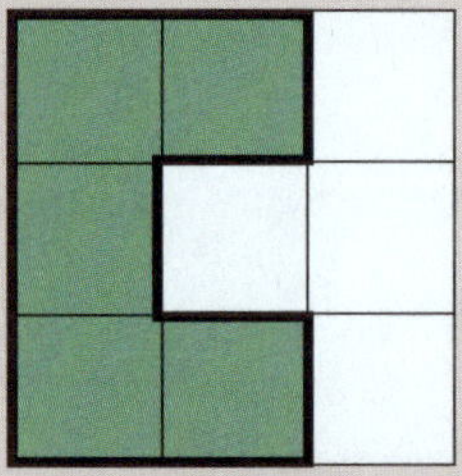			
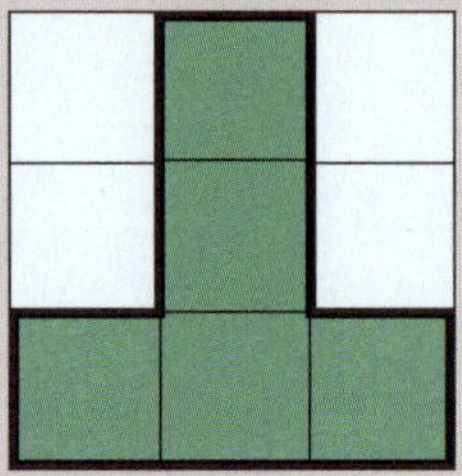			

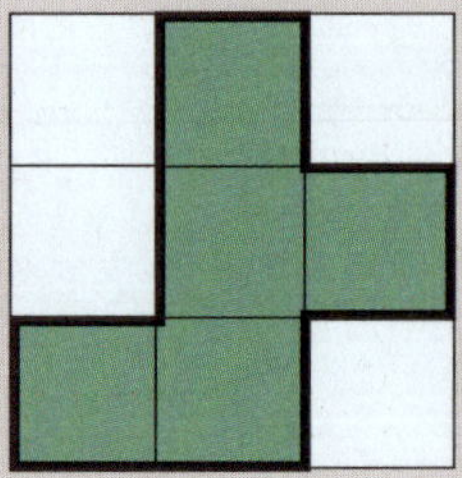			

Review

Write the time.

[:] [:] [:] [:]

Complete.

	÷ 3
18	
27	
24	
21	
30	

	÷ 4
40	
28	
32	
36	
24	

	÷ 6
60	
36	
48	
42	
54	

Complete.

2 more than 2,658 is [ ]

20 more than 2,658 is [ ]

200 more than 2,658 is [ ]

2,000 more than 2,658 is [ ]

2 less than 2,658 [ ]

20 less than 2,658 [ ]

200 less than 2,658 [ ]

2,000 less than 2,658 [ ]

Solve.

You pay the clerk $6.00.
How much change do you get?

Change
$

You pay the clerk $10.00.
How much change do you get?

Change
$

Lesson Activities

A

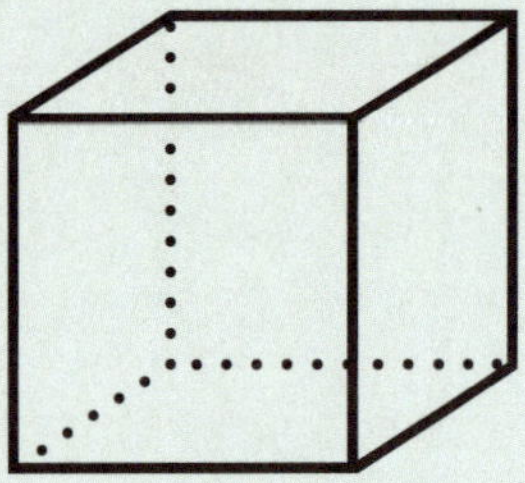

Cube

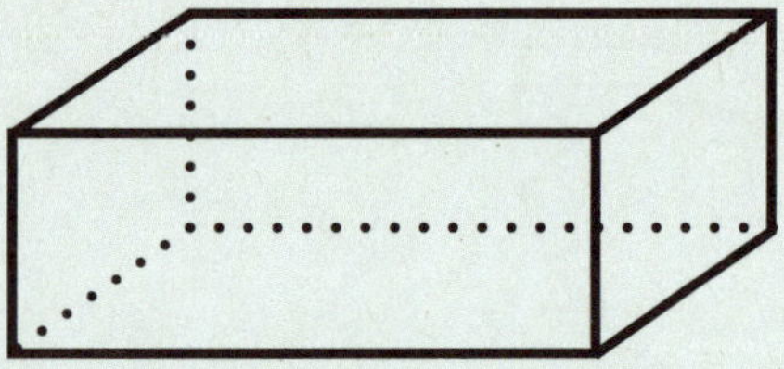

Rectangular prism

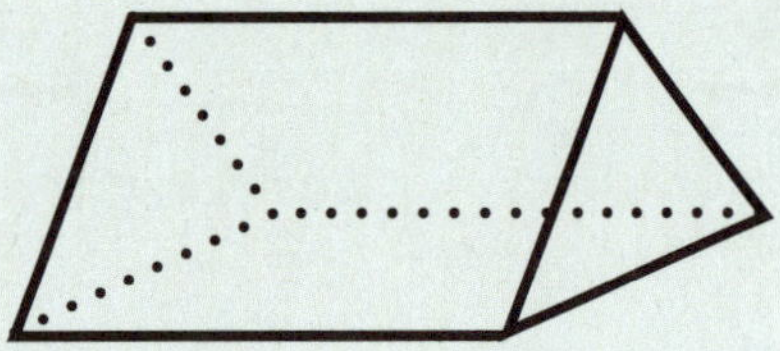

Triangular prism

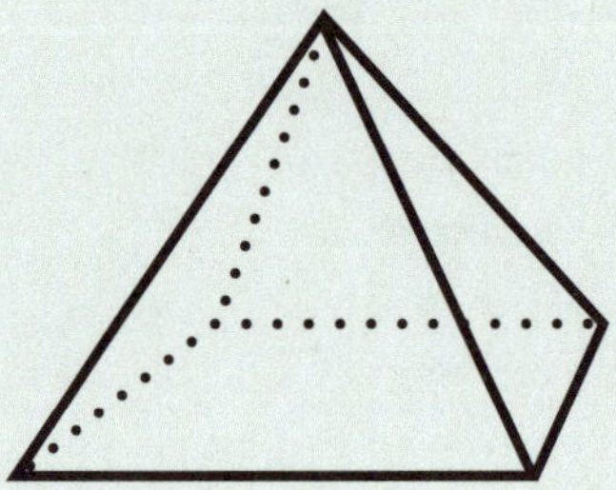

Pyramid

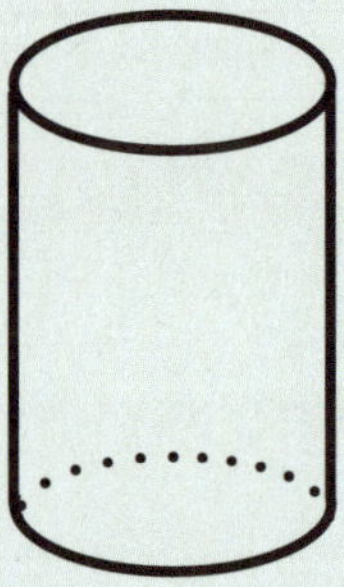

Cylinder

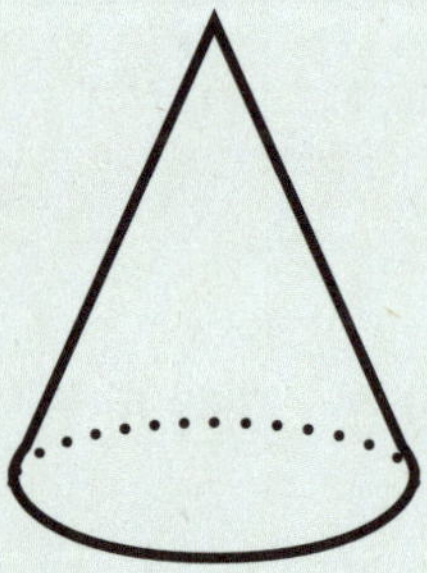

Cone

B

	Faces	Edges	Vertices
Cube			
Rectangular prism			
Triangular prism			
Pyramid			

Practice

Match each shape to its name.

Triangular prism	Cone	Cylinder	Rectangular prism	Cube

Find three things in your home that have each shape. Write their names.

Solid Shape Scavenger Hunt

Cube	Rectangular prism
Cone	Cylinder

Copy the shapes.

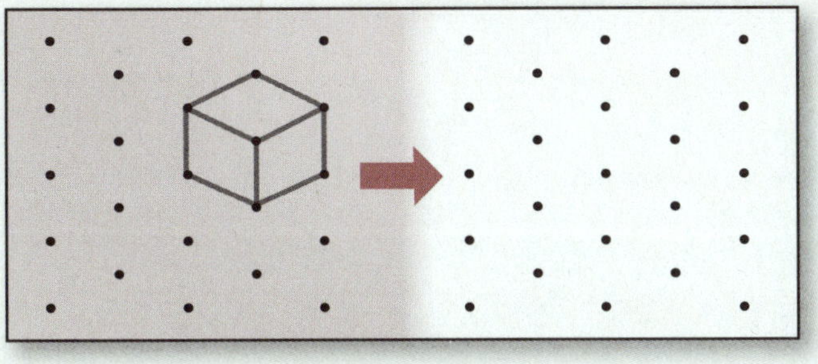

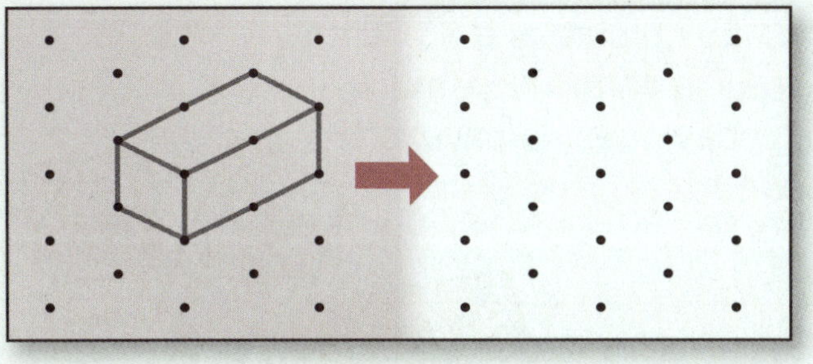

Review

Circle pairs that make 60.

55	35	36	24
5	25	34	46
15	45	26	14

Complete the sequences.

Count by 25s	4,550					4,675
Count by 50s	4,550					4,800

Complete.

$8 \times 9 = \square$ $\quad 6 \times 8 = \square$ $\quad 9 \times 9 = \square$

$7 \times 7 = \square$ $\quad 9 \times 7 = \square$ $\quad 7 \times 8 = \square$

$6 \times 9 = \square$ $\quad 8 \times 8 = \square$ $\quad 6 \times 7 = \square$

Solve. Write the equations you use.

Daniel has $8.00. He spends $1.25 on gum and $5.75 on trading cards. How much money does he have left?

Unit Wrap-Up

Circle the description that matches the highlighted angle.

Right angle
Smaller than a right angle
Larger than a right angle

Right angle
Smaller than a right angle
Larger than a right angle

Right angle
Smaller than a right angle
Larger than a right angle

Tell how many right angles each shape has.

☐ right angles

☐ right angles

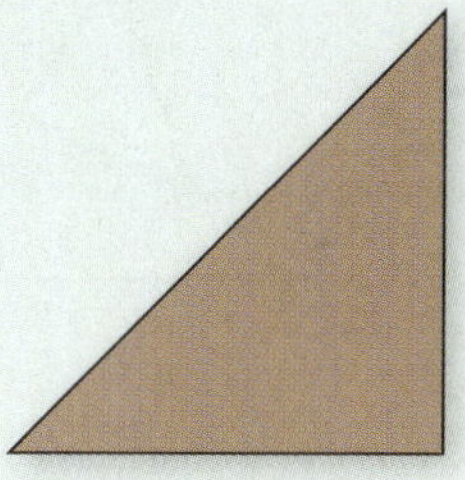

☐ right angles

Write the word that describes all the shapes in each group.

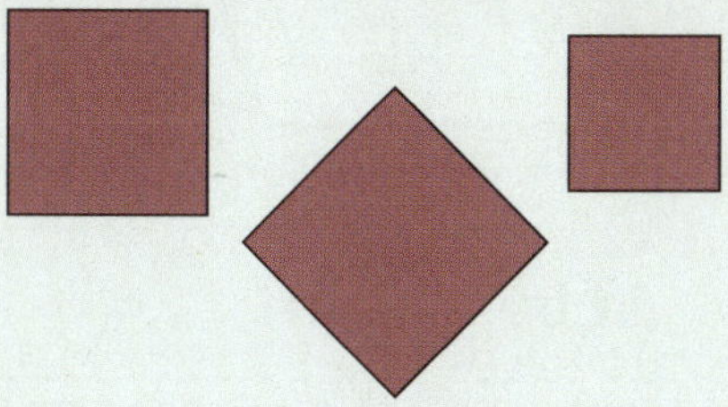

____

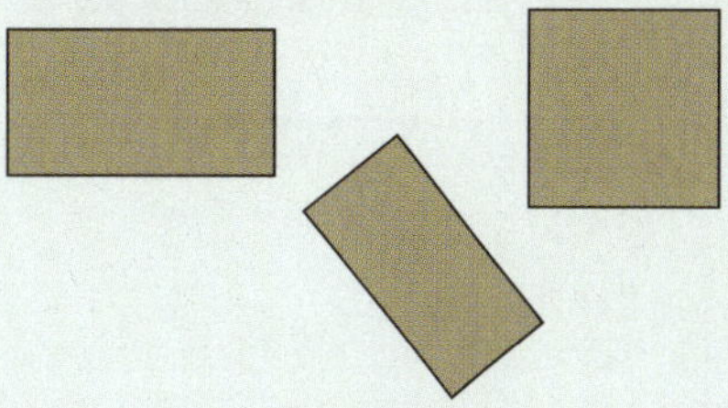

____

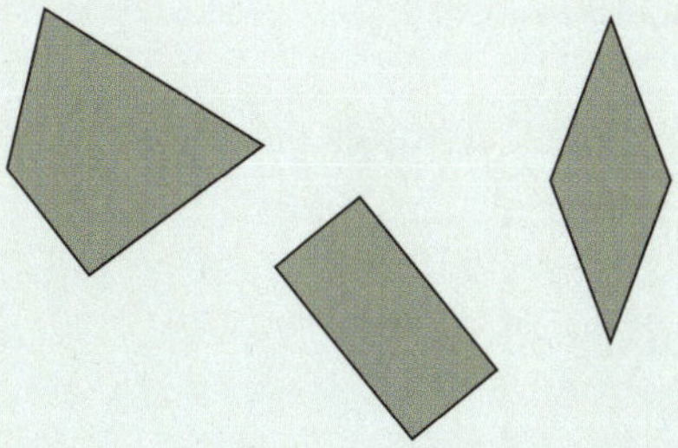

____

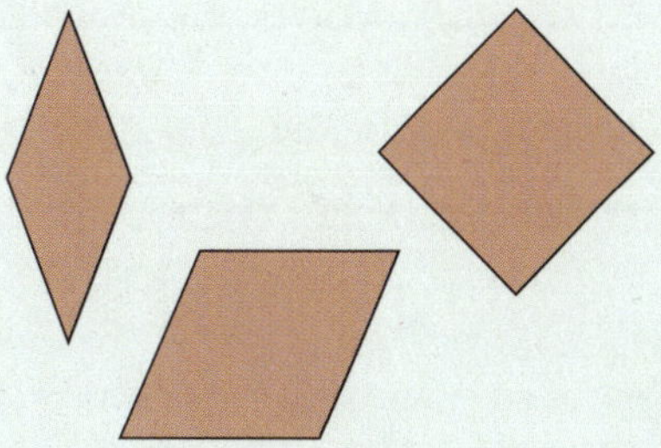

____

rhombuses • rectangles • quadrilaterals • squares

Unit Wrap-Up

Use the words in the word bank to label the shapes.

cube	rectangular prism	cylinder
cone	triangular prism	pyramid

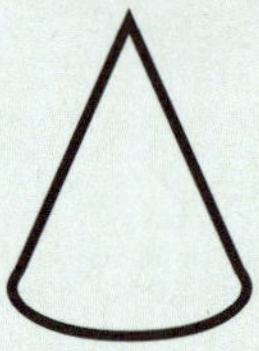

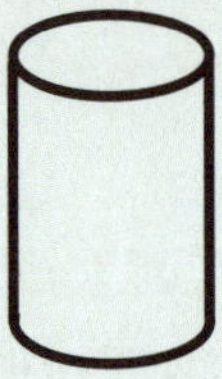

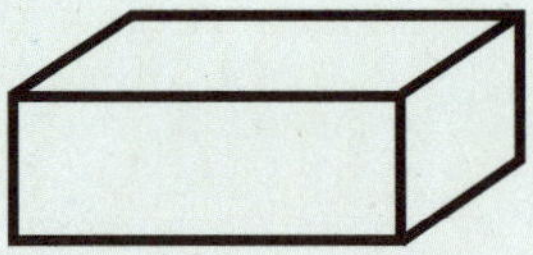

Complete the chart to match each shape.

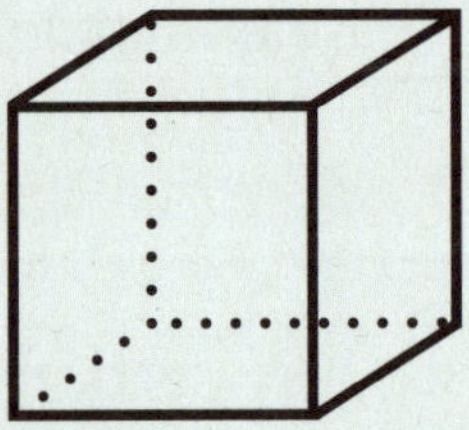

Faces	
Edges	
Vertices	

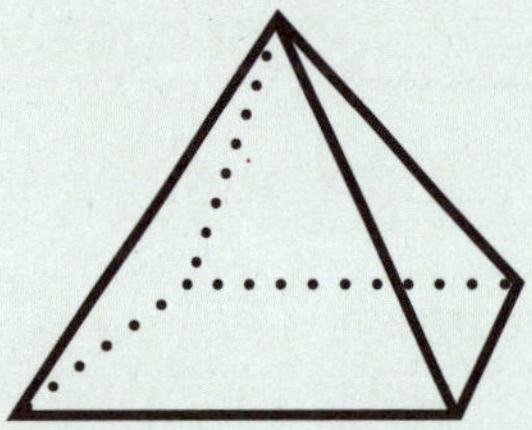

Faces	
Edges	
Vertices	

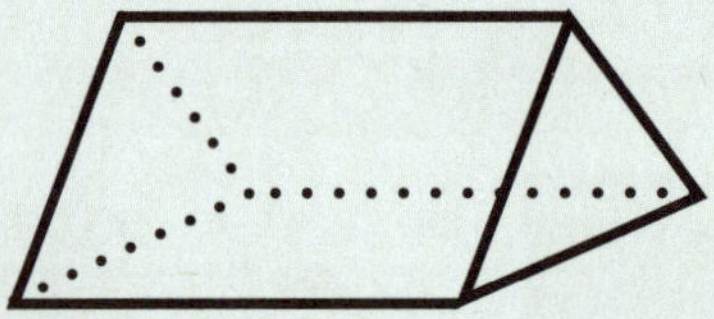

Faces	
Edges	
Vertices	

Cover the shape with pentominoes. Draw lines to show where you put each piece.

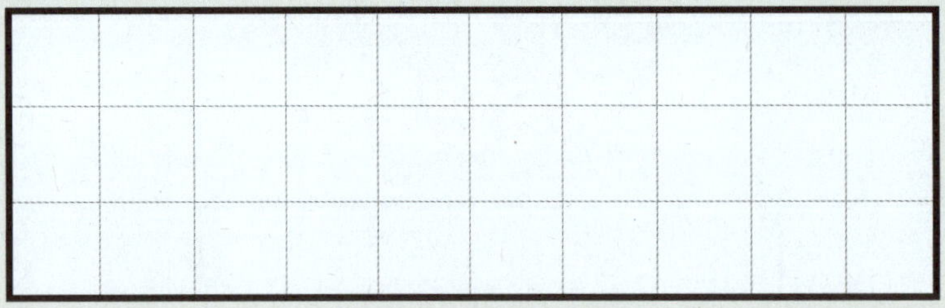

Lesson Activities

A

B

Science Museum Schedule

Tornado Vortex every 5 min.	Morning	9:25			
	Afternoon				3:05
Lightning every 10 min.	Morning	10:40			
	Afternoon				2:20
Chemistry Fun every 30 min.	Morning	9:20			
	Afternoon				1:30
Reptile Talk every 15 min.	Morning	10:45			
	Afternoon				4:30

Practice

Write the time.

:

:

:

:

:

:

:

:

Complete the sequences.

Review

Circle the shapes that have 4 right angles.
X the shapes that do not have 4 right angles.

Complete the multiplication table.

×	7	8	9	10
5				
6				
7				
8				
9				

Circle the greatest number in each row.

2,496	2,649	2,600
4,007	4,700	4,707
5,936	3,956	5,639
9,000	8,999	9,001

Solve. Write the equations you use to solve the problems.

Caleb helps his mother build a fence around a square garden. Each side of the garden is 9 feet long. What is the perimeter of the garden?

Mount Rainier is 4,392 meters tall. Mount Hood is 3,429 meters tall. How much taller is Mount Rainier than Mount Hood?

Lesson Activities

A

5 past 9		25 to 10	
10 past 9		20 to 10	
quarter past 9		quarter to 10	
20 past 9		10 to 10	
25 past 9		5 to 10	
half past 9		10 o'clock	

B

Time Riddles

4:20 3:40 3:55 3:35 3:50 4:05 3:45 4:30 4:25 3:30 4:10 4:15

Practice

Complete.

half past ☐

quarter past ☐

quarter to ☐

☐ past ☐

☐ past ☐

☐ to ☐

☐ to ☐

☐ past ☐

☐ to ☐

☐ o'clock

☐ to ☐

☐ past ☐

Review

Draw a shape to match each description.

Square

Rectangle

Rhombus

Complete.

$4\overline{)32}$ $3\overline{)21}$ $6\overline{)24}$ $4\overline{)20}$ $6\overline{)48}$

$3\overline{)30}$ $6\overline{)36}$ $5\overline{)35}$ $6\overline{)18}$ $4\overline{)40}$

$4\overline{)36}$ $5\overline{)45}$ $6\overline{)54}$ $4\overline{)24}$ $3\overline{)27}$

Solve. Write the equations you use to solve the problems.

The bathroom floor is a rectangle 9 feet long and 5 feet wide. What is the area of the floor?

Evan bought 4 hamburgers and 4 bags of chips. Each hamburger cost \$6, and each bag of chips cost \$2. How much did he pay?

Lesson Activities

A

Eleanor's Piano Practice Log

Day	Start Time	End Time	Number of Minutes
Monday	2:20		20
Tuesday	1:35		25
Thursday	3:55		15
Sunday	11:30		60
Monday	1:20	1:35	
Wednesday	2:40	3:00	
Friday	2:40	3:05	
Saturday	12:45	1:45	

B

Race to 2:00

Player 1	Player 2
12:00	12:00

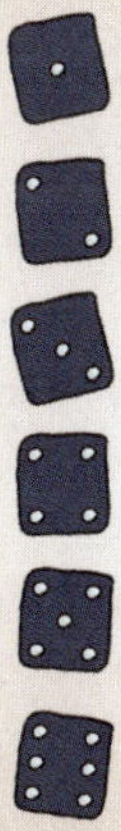

= 5 minutes

= 10 minutes

= 15 minutes

= 20 minutes

= 25 minutes

= 30 minutes

Practice

Complete.

Start	Time	End
5:45	10 min.	
5:45	15 min.	
5:45	30 min.	
5:45	60 min.	

Start	Time	End
12:50	10 min.	
12:50	20 min.	
12:50	25 min.	
12:50	42 min.	

Start	Time	End
3:55	min.	4:00
3:55	min.	4:15
3:55	min.	4:30
3:55	min.	4:55

Start	Time	End
1:20	min.	1:30
1:20	min.	2:00
1:20	min.	2:05
1:20	min.	2:07

Review

Match each word with its definition.

Square	Rhombus	Rectangle	Quadrilateral

4 equal sides	4 right angles and 4 equal sides	4 sides	4 right angles

Complete.

5 ⟌ 47

6 ⟌ 40

3 ⟌ 22

4 ⟌ 38

Complete.

	1	0
×		8

		9
×		8

		8
×		8

	1	0
×		7

		9
×		7

		8
×		7

Complete the sequences.

Count by 200s: 7,600, ___, ___, ___, ___, 8,600

Count by 250s: 3,500, ___, ___, ___, ___, 4,750

Lesson Activities

A

Gymnastics
- Monday at 2:30
- 20 min. drive
- Leave at ______

Library Story Hour
- Tuesday at 10:00
- 15 min. bike ride
- Leave at ______

Dentist Appointment
- Wednesday at 11:10
- 25 min. drive
- Leave at ______

Visit Aunt Claire
- Thursday at 1:30
- 1 hr. drive
- Leave at ______

Park Play Date
- Friday at 1:15
- 20 min. walk
- Leave at ______

B

Race to 12:00

Player 1	Player 2
2:00	2:00

 = 5 minutes

 = 10 minutes

 = 15 minutes

 = 20 minutes

 = 25 minutes

 = 30 minutes

Practice

Complete.

10:30	← 5 min.	10:35
	← 15 min.	10:35
	← 30 min.	10:35
	← 35 min.	10:35

	← 5 min.	4:05
	← 10 min.	4:05
	← 20 min.	4:05
	← 30 min.	4:05

	← 15 min.	1:15
	← 30 min.	1:15
	← 45 min.	1:15
	← 60 min.	1:15

4:30	← ___ min.	4:40
4:15	← ___ min.	4:40
4:00	← ___ min.	4:40
★ 3:58	← ___ min.	4:40

Review

Complete.

36 ÷ 4 =	15 ÷ 3 =	18 ÷ 3 =
24 ÷ 3 =	28 ÷ 4 =	48 ÷ 6 =
60 ÷ 6 =	30 ÷ 6 =	32 ÷ 4 =

Complete.

3,900 + 400 =	3,200 - 2,000 =
4,500 + 2,000 =	3,790 - 10 =
3,150 + 50 =	5,000 - 4,500 =
7,290 + 400 =	3,900 - 3,600 =

Solve. Write the equations you use to solve the problems.

Veronica is making bracelets.
She has 42 beads. If she puts 6 beads on each bracelet, how many bracelets can she make?

Veronica is making bracelets.
She has 42 beads. If she puts 10 beads on each bracelet, how many bracelets can she make?

Lesson Activities

A

Multiplication Undercover

Player 1	8	16	24	32	40	48	56	64	72	80
Player 2	8	16	24	32	40	48	56	64	72	80

B

Day Camp Schedule

Activity	Start Time	End Time
Outdoor Skills (1 hr. 10 min.)	8:00	
Capture the Flag (1 hr. 15 min.)		
Hike (1 hr. 45 min.)		
Lunch and Sing-along (50 min.)		
Afternoon Choice Time (3 hr. 30 min.)		

AFTERNOON ACTIVITY CHOICES

Activity	Start Time	End Time	Length of Activity
Swimming	1:00	4:00	
Canoeing	2:30	4:30	
Archery	2:00	3:40	
Crafts	1:30	2:45	
Rock Climbing	2:45	4:25	

Practice

Complete.

Start	Time passed	End
9:00	1 hr.	
9:00	2 hr.	
9:00	2 hr. 45 min.	
9:00	3 hr. 20 min.	

Start	Time passed	End
2:45	2 hr.	
2:45	2 hr. 10 min.	
2:45	2 hr. 15 min.	
2:45	2 hr. 25 min.	

Start	Time passed	End
6:00	☐ hr.	8:00
6:00	☐ hr. ☐ min.	8:30
6:00	☐ hr. ☐ min.	9:40
6:00	☐ hr.	12:00

Start	Time passed	End
4:50	☐ hr.	6:50
4:50	☐ hr. ☐ min.	7:00
★ 4:50	☐ hr. ☐ min.	7:15
★ 4:50	☐ hr. ☐ min.	8:05

Review

Round to the nearest thousand.

5,450	6,975	1,050	8,350	4,625	7,250

Match each shape to its name.

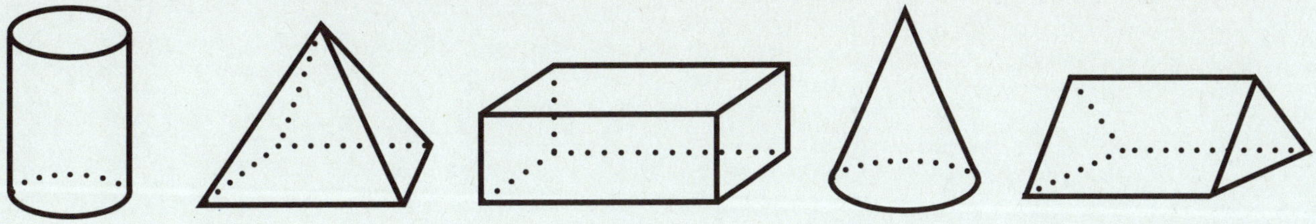

Pyramid | Triangular prism | Cylinder | Rectangular prism | Cone

Complete.

9	8	9	4	8
× 3	× 5	× 7	× 7	× 6

8	8	6	9	8
× 8	× 3	× 7	× 4	× 7

9	5	9	7	8
× 8	× 7	× 6	× 7	× 4

Lesson Activities

A

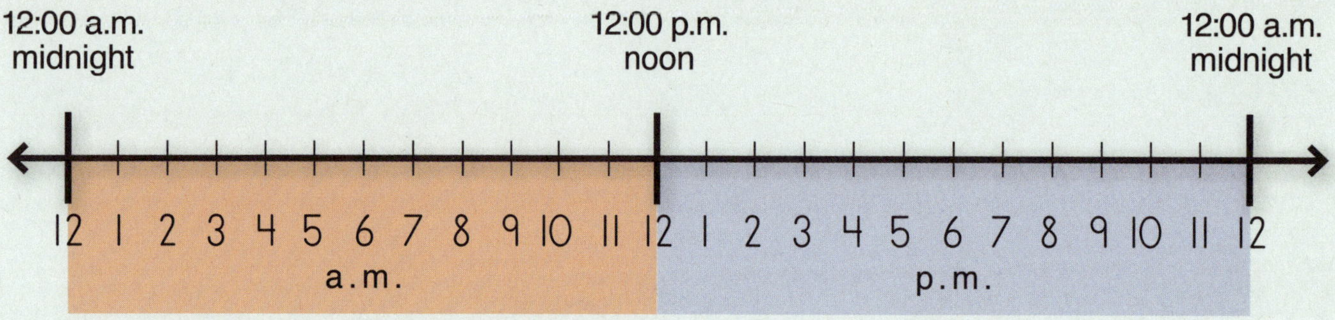

B

Time	How Long Until Midnight?
7:00 p.m.	
8:00 p.m.	
8:30 p.m.	
9:45 p.m.	
10:00 p.m.	
11:30 p.m.	

Time	How Long After Midnight?
12:30 a.m.	
1:00 a.m.	
1:45 a.m.	
2:00 a.m.	
2:45 a.m.	
3:30 a.m.	

Practice

Complete. Use the timeline to help.

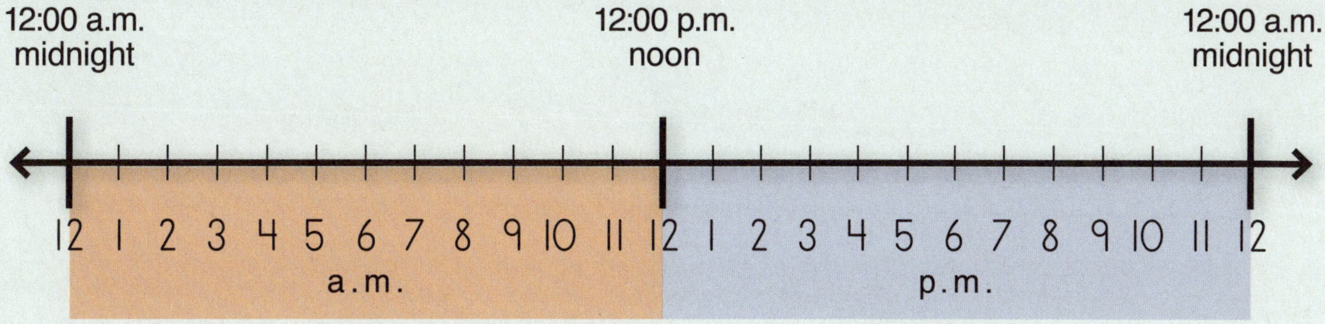

12:00 a.m. → **3 hr.** → ☐

12:00 a.m. → **5 hr.** → ☐

12:00 a.m. → **9 hr.** → ☐

11:00 a.m. → ☐ **hr.** → 12:00 p.m.

9:00 a.m. → ☐ **hr.** → 12:00 p.m.

7:00 a.m. → ☐ **hr.** → 12:00 p.m.

12:00 p.m. → **4 hr.** → ☐

12:00 p.m. → **4 hr. 30 min.** → ☐

12:00 p.m. → **12 hr.** → ☐

☐ ← **1 hr.** ← 12:00 p.m.

☐ ← **4 hr.** ← 12:00 p.m.

☐ ← **6 hr.** ← 12:00 p.m.

Review

Circle the description that matches the angle.

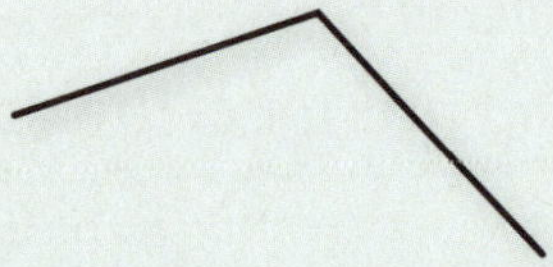

Right angle
Smaller than a right angle
Larger than a right angle

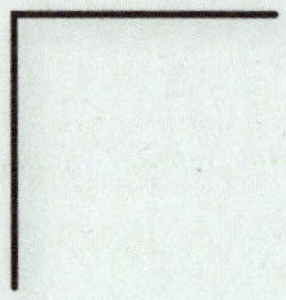

Right angle
Smaller than a right angle
Larger than a right angle

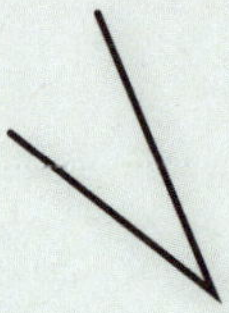

Right angle
Smaller than a right angle
Larger than a right angle

Complete.

6 weeks = ☐ days

7 weeks = ☐ days

8 weeks = ☐ days

6 weeks, 3 days = ☐ days

7 weeks, 1 day = ☐ days

8 weeks, 4 days = ☐ days

Complete.

	3,	0	0	0
-	1,	7	4	2

	5,	6	9	4
+		5	3	6

Complete.

$3\overline{)30}$	$6\overline{)42}$	$4\overline{)28}$	$4\overline{)20}$	$3\overline{)27}$
$6\overline{)60}$	$3\overline{)21}$	$6\overline{)48}$	$3\overline{)18}$	$4\overline{)36}$
$4\overline{)24}$	$6\overline{)54}$	$3\overline{)24}$	$4\overline{)40}$	$6\overline{)36}$

Lesson Activities

A

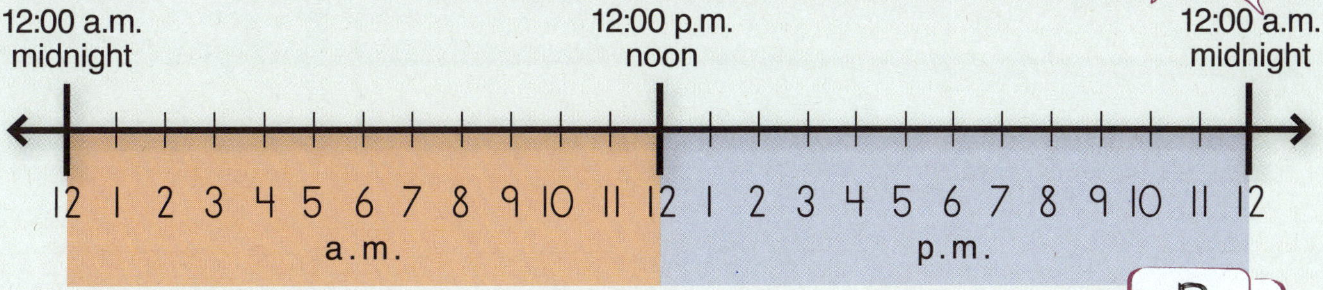

B

Animal Shelter Volunteer Log

Start Time	End Time	Elapsed Time
11:00 a.m.		2 hr. 45 min.
11:30 a.m.	2:00 p.m.	
	3:45 p.m.	2 hr. 15 min.
12:00 p.m.		4 hr. 20 min.
3:30 p.m.	7:15 p.m.	
	6:05 p.m.	2 hr. 30 min.
8:00 p.m.	8:00 a.m.	
9:30 p.m.		9 hr. 45 min.

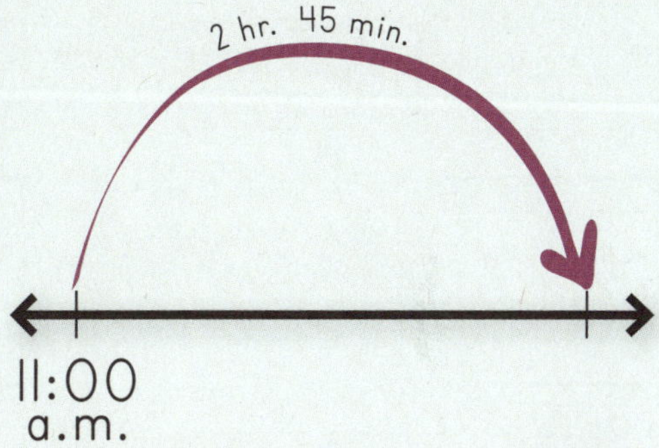

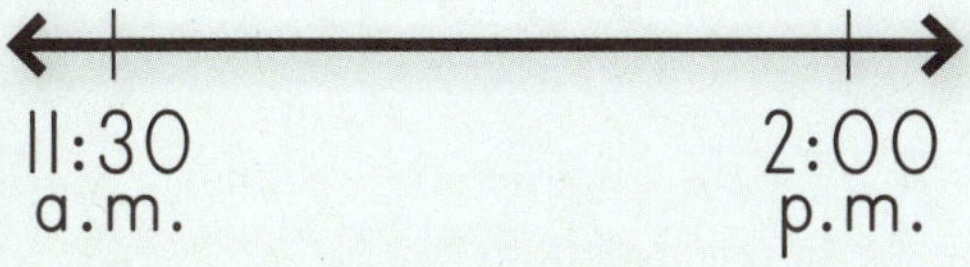

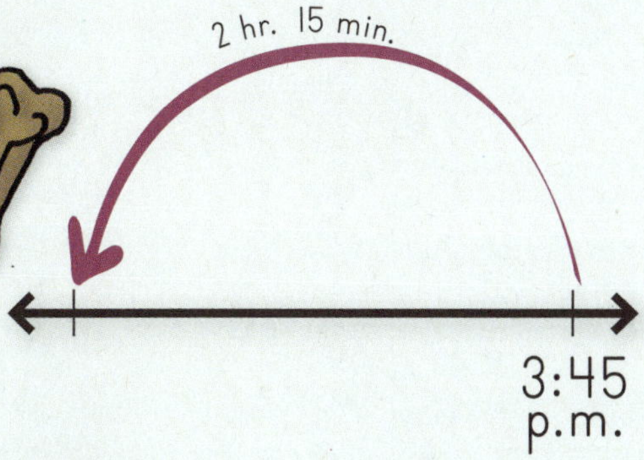

Practice

Complete. Use the timelines to help.

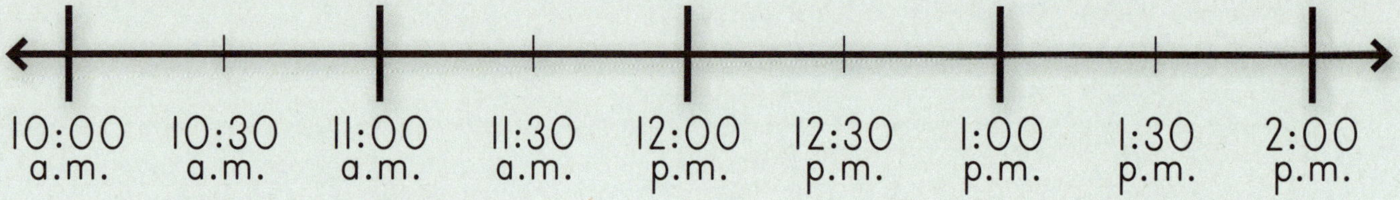

Start	Elapsed	End
11:00 a.m.	2 hr. →	☐
11:00 a.m.	2 hr. 30 min. →	☐
11:30 a.m.	2 hr. →	☐
11:30 a.m.	2 hr. 30 min. →	☐

Start	Elapsed	End
12:00 p.m.	☐ hr. →	1:00 p.m.
10:00 a.m.	☐ hr. →	1:00 p.m.
10:00 a.m.	☐ hr. ☐ min. →	1:30 p.m.
10:30 a.m.	☐ hr. ☐ min. →	1:00 p.m.

Start	Elapsed	End
☐	← 1 hr. 30 min.	3:00 p.m.
☐	← 2 hr. 15 min.	4:30 p.m.
☐	← 2 hr. 45 min.	5:00 p.m.
☐	← 1 hr. 45 min.	4:15 p.m.

Start	Elapsed	End
1:15 p.m.	☐ hr. ☐ min. →	3:30 p.m.
2:30 p.m.	☐ hr. ☐ min. →	5:00 p.m.
1:45 p.m.	☐ hr. ☐ min. →	3:15 p.m.
1:15 p.m.	☐ hr. ☐ min. →	4:30 p.m.

Review

Complete. Follow the steps.

1. Divide
2. Multiply
3. Subtract

5) 31   4) 25   3) 19   10) 61

Complete.

360 ÷ 60 = ☐

480 ÷ 60 = ☐

600 − 60 = ☐

7 × 60 = ☐

8 × 60 = ☐

9 × 60 = ☐

Complete the charts to match the shapes.

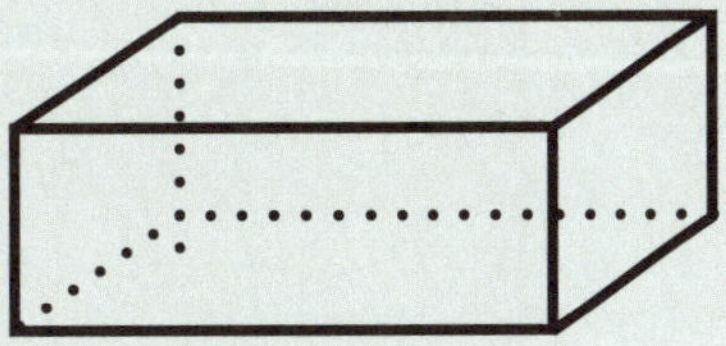

Faces	
Edges	
Vertices	

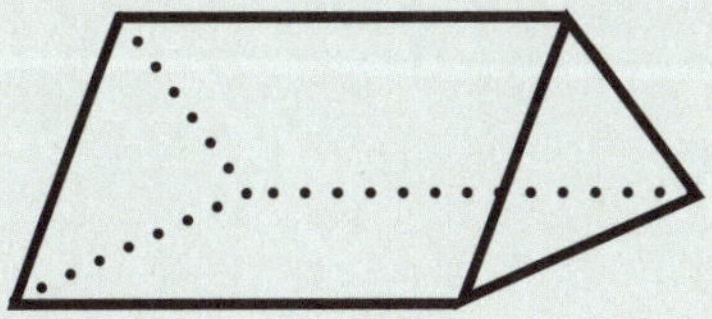

Faces	
Edges	
Vertices	

Solve. Write the equations you use to solve the problems.

Arjun helps his parents plant 90 carrot seeds. They plant 9 rows.
How many seeds are in each row?

Arjun helps his parents plant flowers, too.
They plant 6 rows.
They plant 20 flowers in each row.
How many flowers do they plant?

Lesson Activities

A

Elapsed Time Tic-Tac-Toe

Start	End
7:00	9:30
7:15	9:45
7:30	10:00
7:45	10:15
8:00	10:30
8:15	10:45

All times are a.m.

2 hr. 45 min.	3 hr. 15 min.	1 hr. 30 min.	2 hr. 30 min.
3 hr.	2 hr.	2 hr. 45 min.	3 hr. 30 min.
2 hr. 30 min.	1 hr. 45 min.	2 hr.	1 hr. 15 min.
3 hr. 45 min.	2 hr. 15 min.	3 hr.	2 hr. 15 min.

B

Ruby starts watching a movie at 1:45 p.m.
The movie is 2 hours and 20 minutes long.
When will the movie be over?

The baby naps from 12:50 p.m. until 2:40 p.m. How long does the baby nap?

Jayden's family is making a ham. They want the ham to be done at 1:15 p.m. The ham takes 2 hours and 40 minutes to bake. When should they put the ham in the oven?

Practice

Complete. Use the timeline sketches to help.

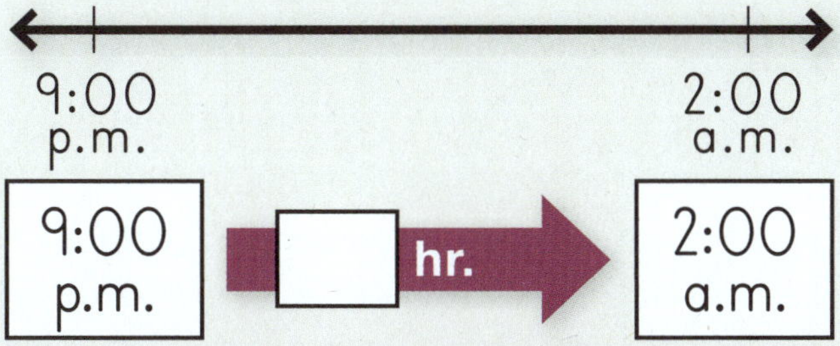

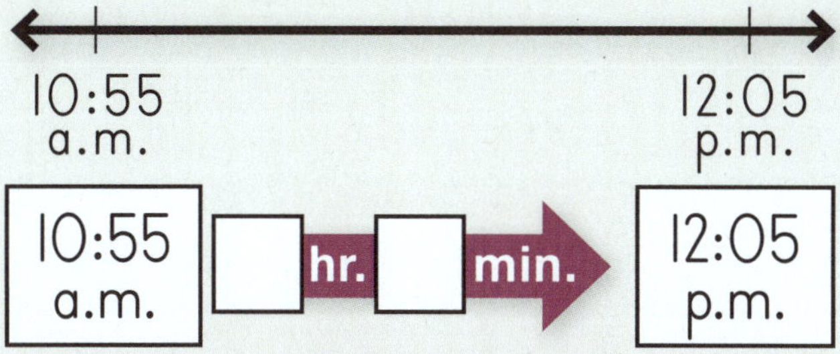

Solve.

The plane takes off at 9:30 a.m. and lands at 1:15 p.m. How long is the flight?

It takes 2 hours and 35 minutes to get to Charlie's cousins' house. If his family starts driving at 3:45 p.m., when will they arrive?

Quinn's baseball game lasted 1 hour and 40 minutes. It ended at 8:20 p.m. When did the game begin?

★ Brynn wants to get 10 hours of sleep. If she goes to bed at 8:30 p.m., when should she wake up?

Review

Use the numbers to complete the blanks.
You will use each number once.

1	2	3	4	5	6	7	8	9

☐ × 7 = 14	7 × ☐ = 28	7 × ☐ = 49
☐ × 7 = 56	7 × ☐ = 7	7 × ☐ = 21
☐ × 7 = 35	7 × ☐ = 63	7 × ☐ = 42

Complete.

$ ______

$ ______

Complete.

	2.	8	3
+	4.	9	6
$			

	9.	1	5
-	5.	4	7
$			

Complete the sequences.

Start

6,250 + 1,000 = ______

6,250 + 1,250 = ______

★ 6,250 + 1,275 = ______

4,700 - 1,000 = ______

4,700 - 1,200 = ______

★ 4,700 - 1,250 = ______

Unit Wrap-Up

Write the time.

:

:

:

:

Match.

quarter to 8	7:45
quarter past 8	7:50
10 to 8	8:10
10 past 8	8:15
half past 8	8:30

Write a.m. or p.m. for each meal.

Meal	Time	a.m. or p.m.
Breakfast	7:30	
Morning Snack	10:15	
Lunch	12:00	
Afternoon Snack	3:45	
Dinner	6:15	
Midnight Snack	12:00	

Complete.

Start	→	End
7:25	20 min. →	
7:25	35 min. →	
7:25	2 hr. →	
7:25	2 hr. 30 min. →	

	←	
	← 10 min.	8:15
	← 20 min.	8:15
	← 3 hr.	8:15
	← 3 hr. 20 min.	8:15

Unit Wrap-Up

Complete. Make sure to write a.m. or p.m. for each time.

Start	Elapsed time	End
6:30 a.m.	☐ hr. →	9:30 a.m.
6:30 a.m.	☐ hr. ☐ min. →	9:50 a.m.
6:30 a.m.	☐ hr. ☐ min. →	10:10 a.m.

Start	Elapsed time	End
12:00 a.m.	☐ hr. →	7:00 a.m.
7:00 a.m.	☐ hr. →	12:00 p.m.
12:00 p.m.	☐ hr. ☐ min. →	3:30 p.m.

Start	Elapsed time	End
10:30 a.m.	4 hr. →	☐
10:30 a.m.	4 hr. 30 min. →	☐
10:30 a.m.	4 hr. 35 min. →	☐

Start	Elapsed time	End
☐	← 2 hr.	1:00 a.m.
☐	← 2 hr. 15 min.	1:00 a.m.
☐	← 2 hr. 45 min.	1:00 a.m.

Solve.

Karate class is 50 minutes long. It ends at 4:30 p.m. When does karate class begin?

Ramona played outside from 2:30 p.m. to 4:40 p.m. How long did she play outside?

The movie was 2 hours and 5 minutes long. It ended at 1:25 p.m. When did the movie begin?

Xavier's grandparents are coming to visit. At 9:25 a.m., they called to say they have 1 hour and 50 minutes left to drive. When will they arrive?

Lesson Activities

A

56 ÷ 7 = ☐

☐ × 7 = 56

14 ÷ 7 = ☐	28 ÷ 7 = ☐	35 ÷ 7 = ☐
42 ÷ 7 = ☐	7 ÷ 7 = ☐	49 ÷ 7 = ☐
21 ÷ 7 = ☐	70 ÷ 7 = ☐	63 ÷ 7 = ☐

B

Dice Tic-Tac-Toe

21 ÷ 7	63 ÷ 7	42 ÷ 7	7 ÷ 7	56 ÷ 7
14 ÷ 7	35 ÷ 7	70 ÷ 7	14 ÷ 7	35 ÷ 7
42 ÷ 7	56 ÷ 7	35 ÷ 7	42 ÷ 7	49 ÷ 7
63 ÷ 7	7 ÷ 7	49 ÷ 7	21 ÷ 7	63 ÷ 7
28 ÷ 7	49 ÷ 7	56 ÷ 7	28 ÷ 7	70 ÷ 7

Practice

Complete and match the equations.

☐ × 7 = 14	42 ÷ 7 = ☐
☐ × 7 = 28	49 ÷ 7 = ☐
☐ × 7 = 42	14 ÷ 7 = ☐
☐ × 7 = 35	70 ÷ 7 = ☐
☐ × 7 = 49	28 ÷ 7 = ☐
☐ × 7 = 7	35 ÷ 7 = ☐
☐ × 7 = 70	7 ÷ 7 = ☐
☐ × 7 = 63	56 ÷ 7 = ☐
☐ × 7 = 21	63 ÷ 7 = ☐
☐ × 7 = 56	21 ÷ 7 = ☐

Review

Complete the two missing sides for each square.

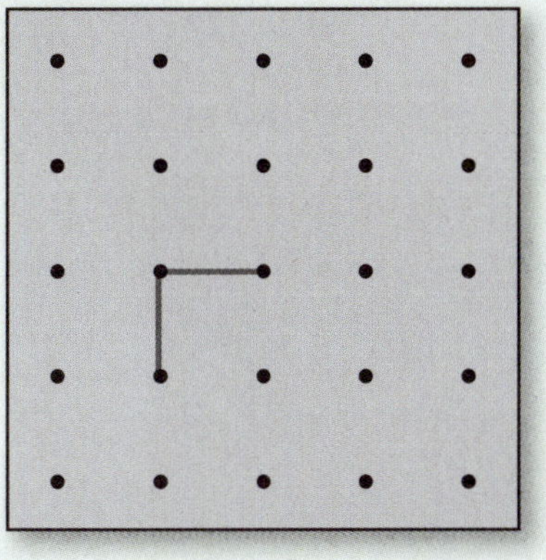

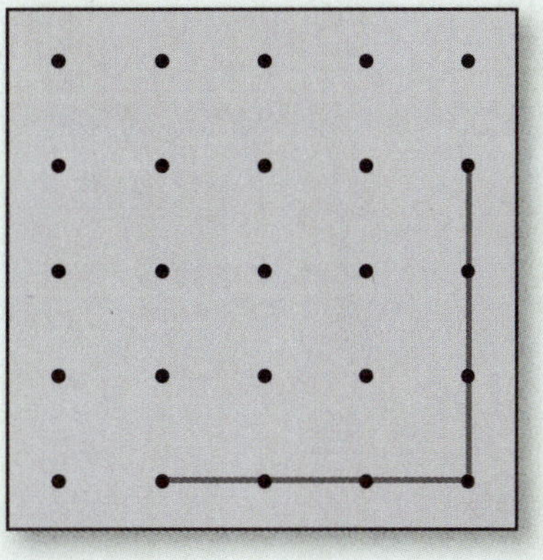

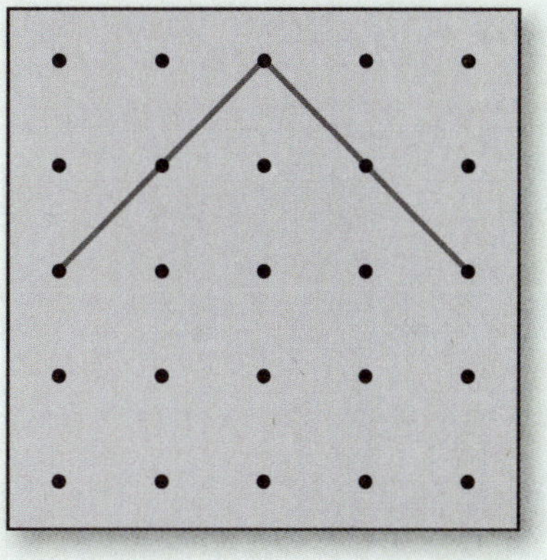

Complete.

24 ÷ 3 = ☐

25 ÷ 3 = ☐

26 ÷ 3 = ☐

27 ÷ 3 = ☐

Complete.

4 weeks = ☐ days

4 weeks, 2 days = ☐ days

7 weeks = ☐ days

7 weeks, 6 days = ☐ days

Use logical thinking to label the missing sides.

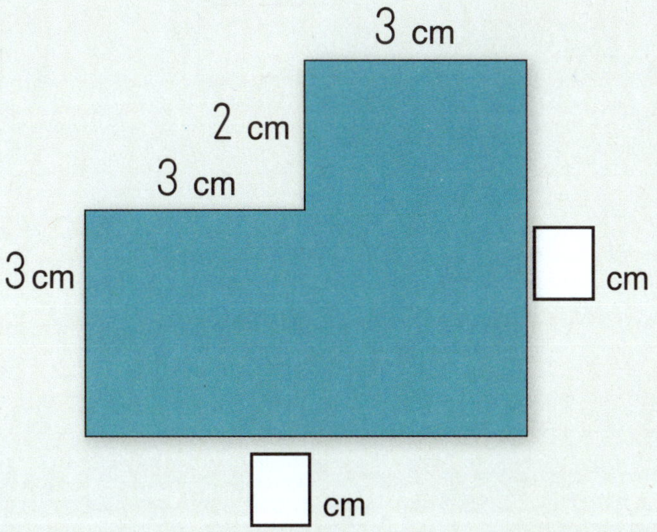

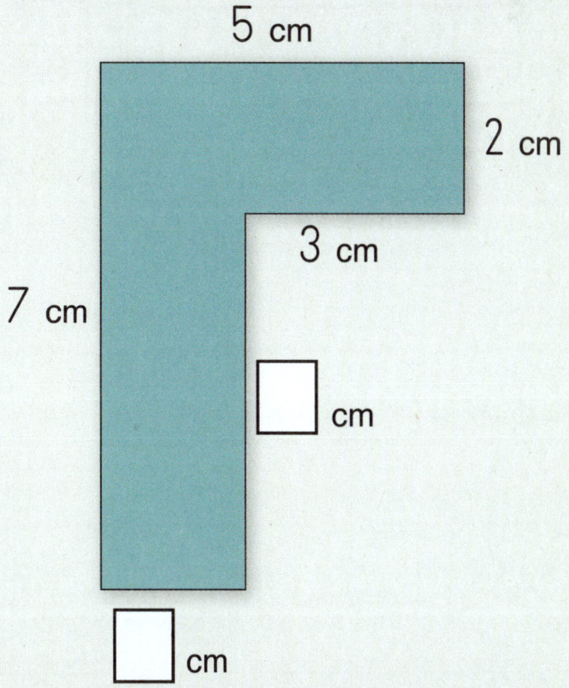

Lesson Activities

A

Division Bingo (÷7)

B	I	N	G	O
35	28	56	14	63
70	49	42	21	42
7	63	70	28	56
49	21	42	49	70
56	35	14	63	7

B	I	N	G	O
14	7	49	63	70
42	35	56	28	7
70	63	21	42	49
42	56	14	28	70
21	49	63	56	35

B

28 days = ☐ weeks

$28 \div 7 =$ ☐

30 days = ☐ weeks, ☐ days

$30 \div 7 =$ ☐

14 days = ☐ weeks

17 days = ☐ weeks, ☐ days

49 days = ☐ weeks

50 days = ☐ weeks, ☐ days

Practice

Complete.

7)70	7)63	7)28	7)56	7)21
7)14	7)49	7)35	7)42	7)7
5)40	6)48	4)32	3)24	2)16
3)27	5)45	2)18	6)54	4)36

Complete.

21 days = ☐ weeks

27 days = ☐ weeks, ☐ days

70 days = ☐ weeks

71 days = ☐ weeks, ☐ days

35 days = ☐ weeks

40 days = ☐ weeks, ☐ days

★ 77 days = ☐ weeks

80 days = ☐ weeks, ☐ days

Review

Color the multiples in order from Start to End.

Multiples of 8

50	54	56	64	72
45	49	48	63	80 END
14	10	40	42	81
12	20	32	36	28
Start 8	16	24	35	21

Complete.

$30 \times 5 =$ ☐

$20 \times 7 =$ ☐

$50 \times 6 =$ ☐

$90 \times 2 =$ ☐

$18 \times 10 =$ ☐

Complete. Use the timeline sketches to help.

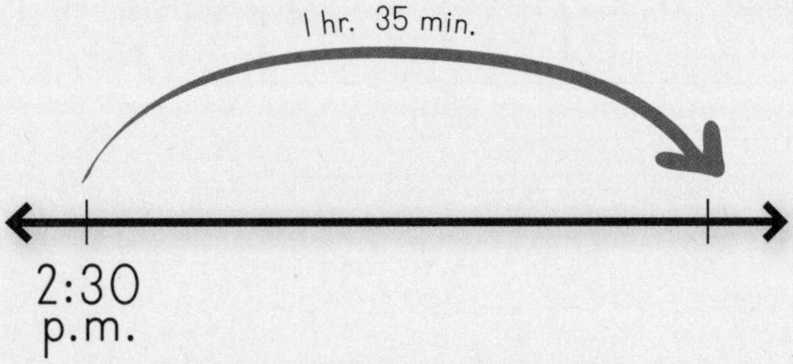

2:30 p.m. → 1 hr. 35 min. → ☐

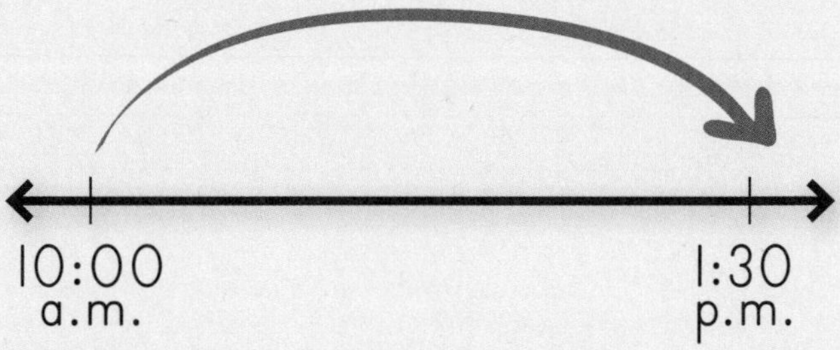

10:00 a.m. → ☐ hr. ☐ min. → 1:30 p.m.

Complete the two missing sides for each rhombus.

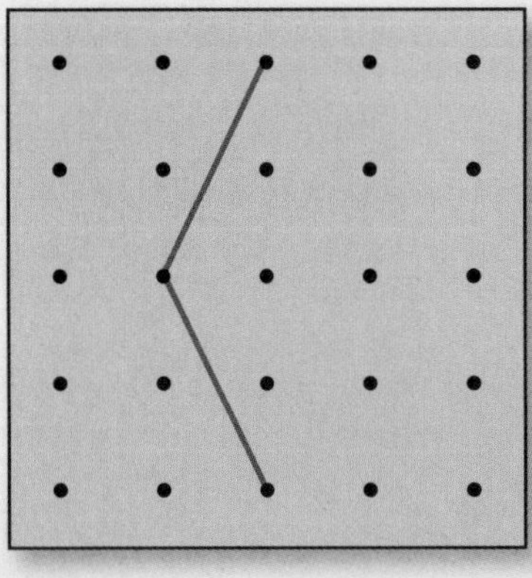

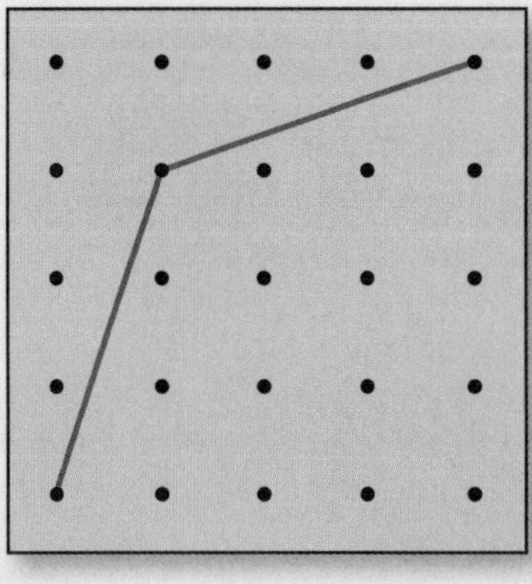

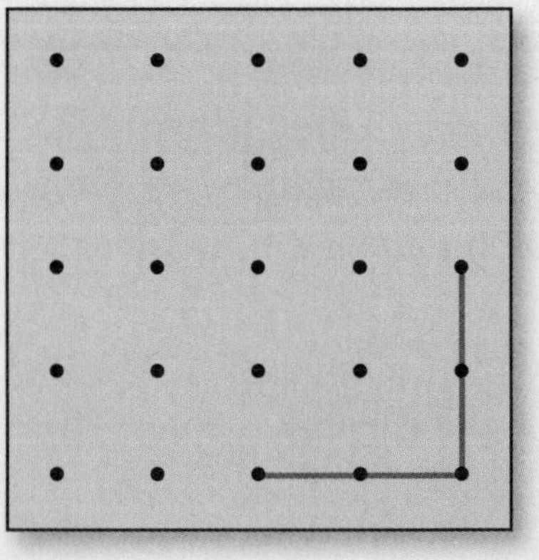

Lesson Activities

A

64 ÷ 8 = ☐

☐ × 8 = 64

24 ÷ 8 = ☐	32 ÷ 8 = ☐	80 ÷ 8 = ☐
56 ÷ 8 = ☐	16 ÷ 8 = ☐	72 ÷ 8 = ☐
40 ÷ 8 = ☐	48 ÷ 8 = ☐	8 ÷ 8 = ☐

B

Climb and Slide

Practice

Complete and match the equations.

$\square \times 8 = 24$	$24 \div 8 = \square$
$\square \times 8 = 40$	$80 \div 8 = \square$
$\square \times 8 = 32$	$8 \div 8 = \square$
$\square \times 8 = 8$	$32 \div 8 = \square$
$\square \times 8 = 48$	$40 \div 8 = \square$
$\square \times 8 = 80$	$56 \div 8 = \square$
$\square \times 8 = 56$	$72 \div 8 = \square$
$\square \times 8 = 64$	$64 \div 8 = \square$
$\square \times 8 = 72$	$16 \div 8 = \square$
$\square \times 8 = 16$	$48 \div 8 = \square$

Review

Find the perimeter of each shape.

Each side is 5 ft. long.

Perimeter: ______

Each side is 3 m long.

Perimeter: ______

Each side is 4 yd. long.

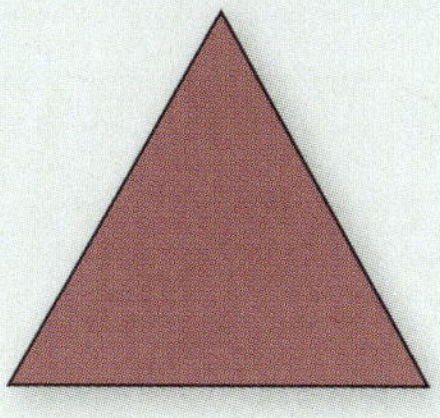

Perimeter: ______

Complete the sequences.

Solve.

Daniela played with blocks for 1 hour and 20 minutes. She started at 3:50 p.m. When did she end?

Daniela stacked the blocks to make a wall. She used 36 blocks and arranged them in 4 equal rows. How many blocks were in each row?

Lesson Activities

A

Division Crash (÷8)

$8\overline{)80}$	$8\overline{)56}$	$8\overline{)16}$	$8\overline{)40}$	$8\overline{)64}$
$8\overline{)24}$	$8\overline{)72}$	$8\overline{)8}$	$8\overline{)48}$	$8\overline{)32}$

B

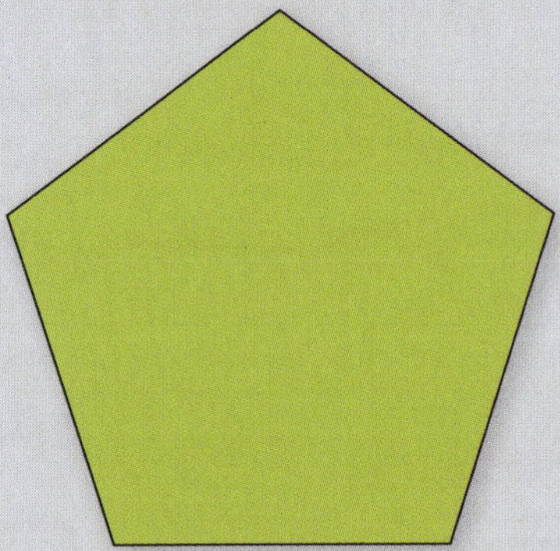

All sides are equal.

Perimeter: 15 cm

Length of each side: ______

Perimeter: 20 yd.

Length of each side: ______

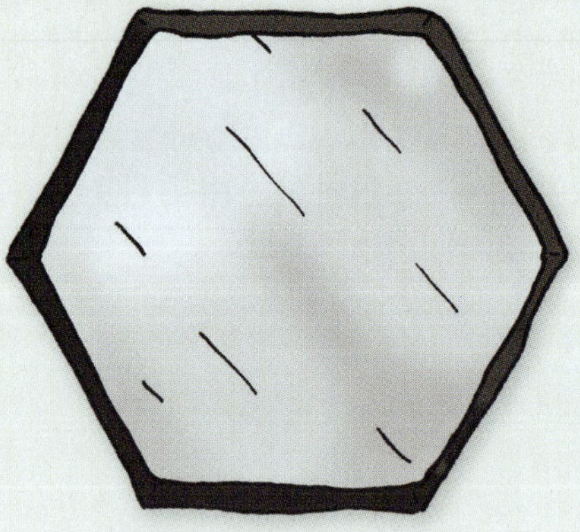

Perimeter: 54 in.

Length of each side: ______

Practice

Complete.

$40 \div 8 = \square$	$48 \div 8 = \square$	$16 \div 8 = \square$
$24 \div 8 = \square$	$64 \div 8 = \square$	$56 \div 8 = \square$
$72 \div 8 = \square$	$80 \div 8 = \square$	$32 \div 8 = \square$
$56 \div 7 = \square$	$32 \div 4 = \square$	$48 \div 6 = \square$

Complete. The sides of each shape are the same length.

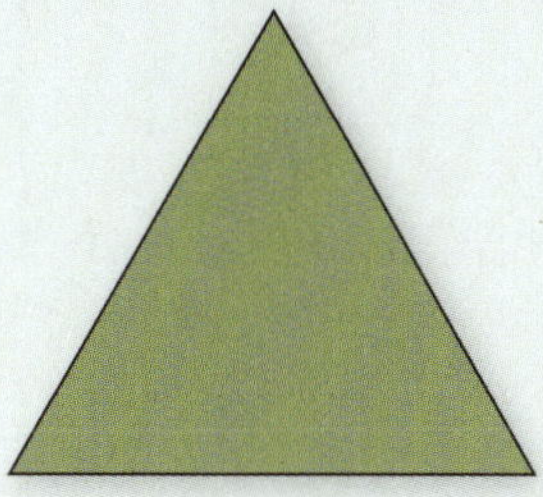

Perimeter: 27 in.

Length of each side: $\square$

Perimeter: 28 m

Length of each side: $\square$

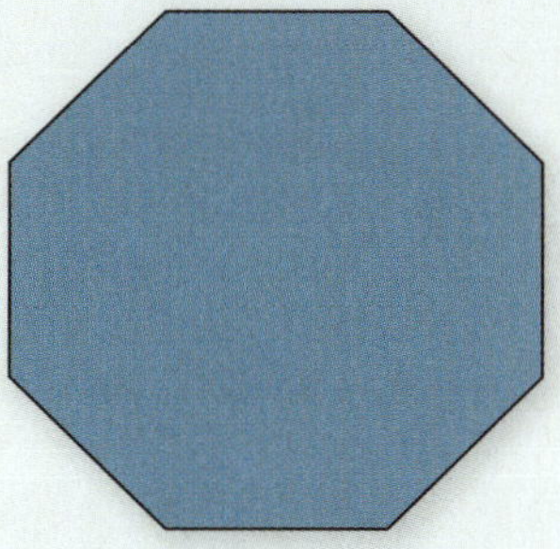

Perimeter: 80 cm

Length of each side: $\square$

Perimeter: 40 ft.

Length of each side: $\square$

15.4

Review

Circle the more sensible unit for each item.

Area of a computer screen

150 sq. ft. | 150 sq. in.

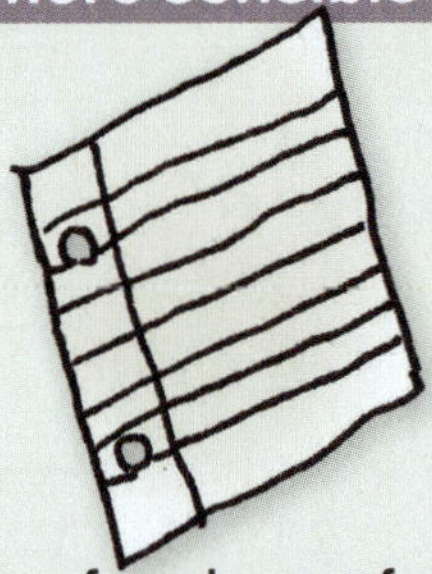

Area of a piece of paper

600 sq. m | 600 sq. cm

Area of a poster

1 sq. mi. | 1 sq. yd.

Color the multiples in order from Start to End.

Multiples of 9

Start →

9	18	25	30	49
12	27	36	42	48
15	21	45	54	56
20	28	40	63	90
24	32	64	72	81

END

Complete.

$10 \times 5 + 3 =$ ☐

$7 \times 4 + 2 =$ ☐

$9 \times 3 + 6 =$ ☐

$5 \times 8 + 4 =$ ☐

$6 \times 4 + 1 =$ ☐

Complete. Use the timeline sketch to help.

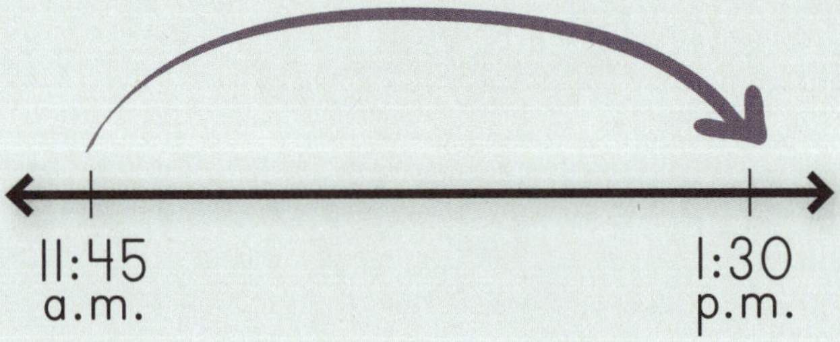

11:45 a.m. → ☐ hr. ☐ min. → 1:30 p.m.

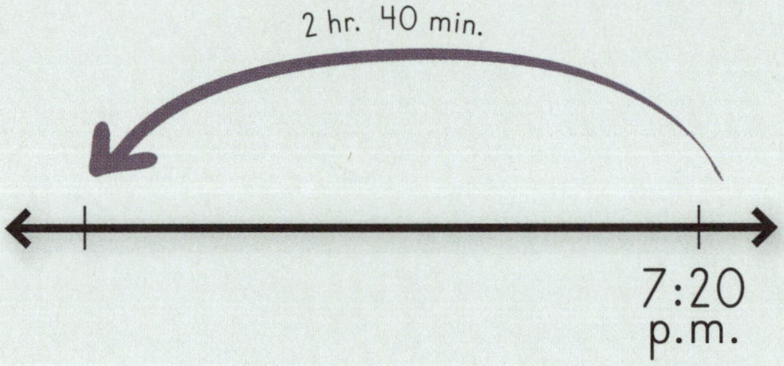

☐ ← 2 hr. 40 min. ← 7:20 p.m.

Lesson Activities

A

$36 \div 9 = \square$

$\square \times 9 = 36$

$18 \div 9 = \square$	$90 \div 9 = \square$	$72 \div 9 = \square$
$81 \div 9 = \square$	$9 \div 9 = \square$	$63 \div 9 = \square$
$27 \div 9 = \square$	$45 \div 9 = \square$	$54 \div 9 = \square$

B

Practice

Complete and match the equations.

$\square \times 9 = 9$	$90 \div 9 = \square$
$\square \times 9 = 90$	$81 \div 9 = \square$
$\square \times 9 = 81$	$45 \div 9 = \square$
$\square \times 9 = 18$	$9 \div 9 = \square$
$\square \times 9 = 45$	$72 \div 9 = \square$
$\square \times 9 = 72$	$18 \div 9 = \square$
$\square \times 9 = 54$	$36 \div 9 = \square$
$\square \times 9 = 27$	$54 \div 9 = \square$
$\square \times 9 = 36$	$27 \div 9 = \square$
$\square \times 9 = 63$	$63 \div 9 = \square$

Review

Write a fact family to match the array.

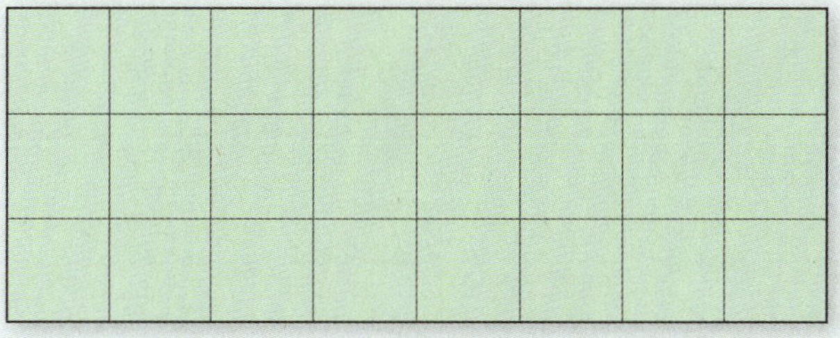

3	×	8	=	
	×		=	
	÷		=	
	÷		=	

Find the area.

6 m

4 m 

Area:

2 ft.

3 ft. 

Area:

10 in.

10 in. 

Area:

Complete.

Start		End
12:05 p.m.	1 hr. 5 min. →	
12:00 p.m.	1 hr. 5 min. →	
11:55 a.m.	1 hr. 5 min. →	
11:50 a.m.	1 hr. 5 min. →	

	← 3 hr.	7:00 p.m.
	← 3 hr.	7:20 p.m.
	← 3 hr.	1:00 a.m.
	← 3 hr.	1:15 a.m.

Lesson Activities

A

PLAYER 1 45 START	63	81	54	PLAYER 2 72 END
81	54	72	45	63
72	45	63	81	54
PLAYER 2 63 START	81	54	72	PLAYER 1 45 END

B

☐ cm

3 cm

Area: 24 sq. cm

☐ cm

2 cm

Area: 14 sq. cm

5 cm

☐ cm

Area: 20 sq. cm

Practice

Complete.

$90 \div 9 = \square$	$81 \div 9 = \square$	$45 \div 9 = \square$
$54 \div 9 = \square$	$18 \div 9 = \square$	$72 \div 9 = \square$
$36 \div 9 = \square$	$63 \div 9 = \square$	$27 \div 9 = \square$
$63 \div 7 = \square$	$72 \div 8 = \square$	$54 \div 6 = \square$

Complete.

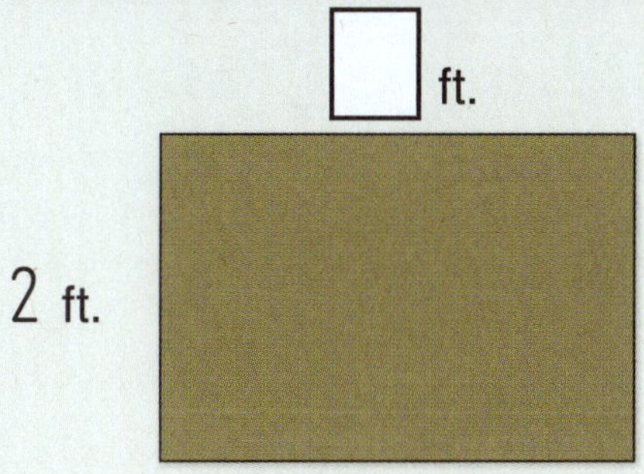

Area: 6 sq. ft.

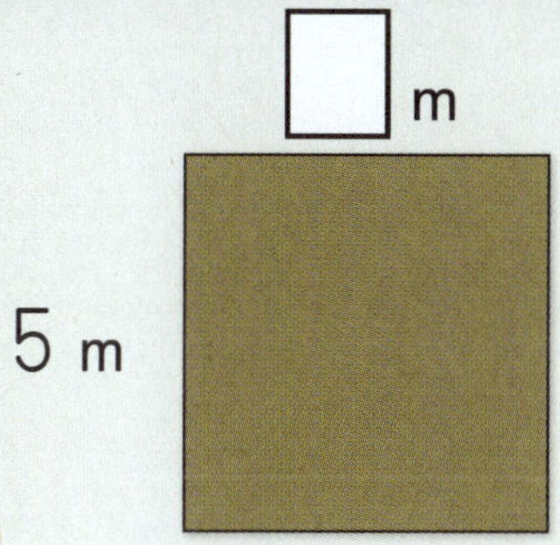

Area: 25 sq. m

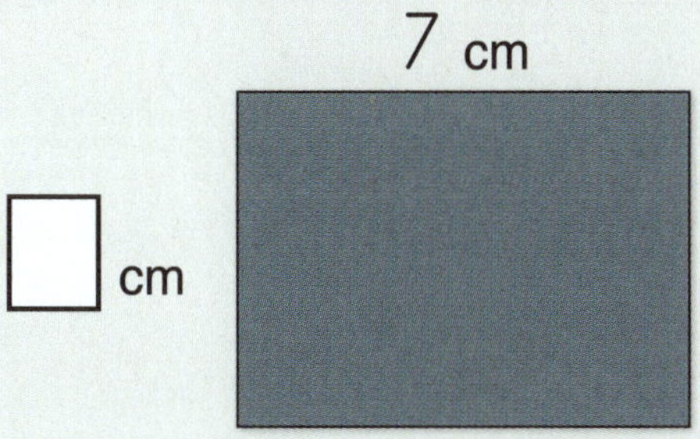

Area: 35 sq. cm

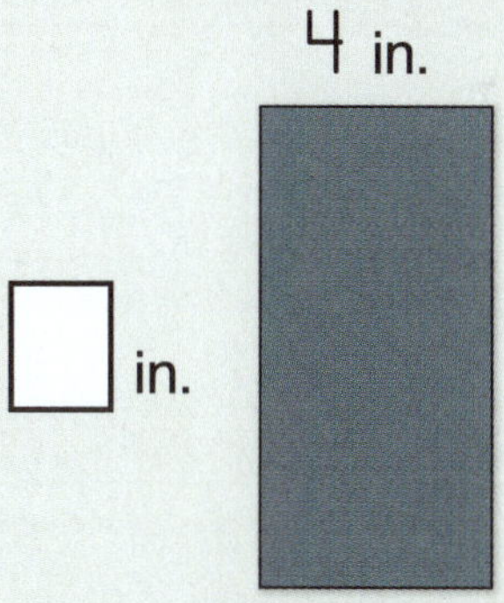

Area: 32 sq. in.

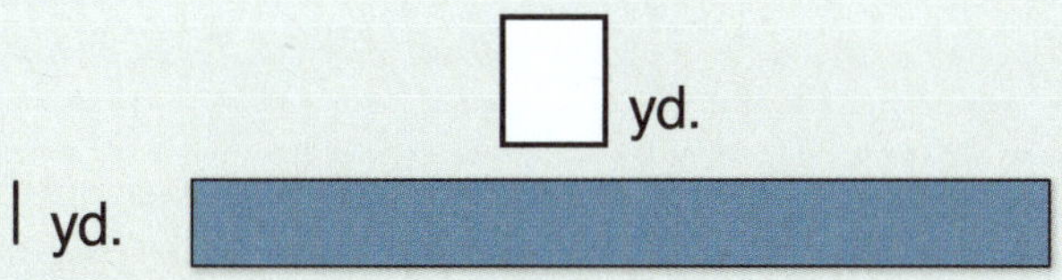

Area: 9 sq. yd.

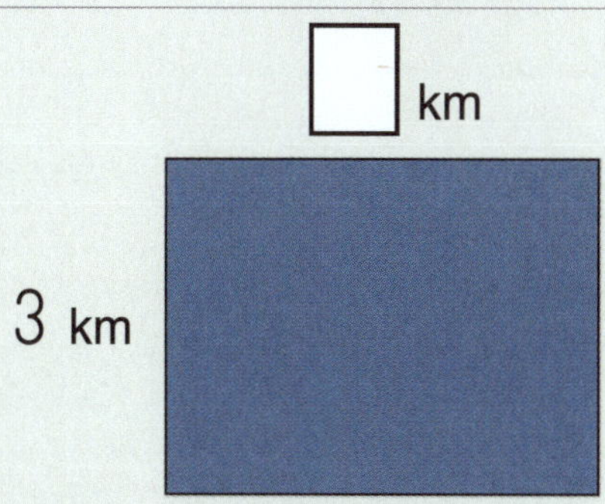

Area: 12 sq. km

Review

Complete.

☐ past ☐

☐ to ☐

quarter to ☐

Use a ruler to measure each line to the nearest quarter inch.

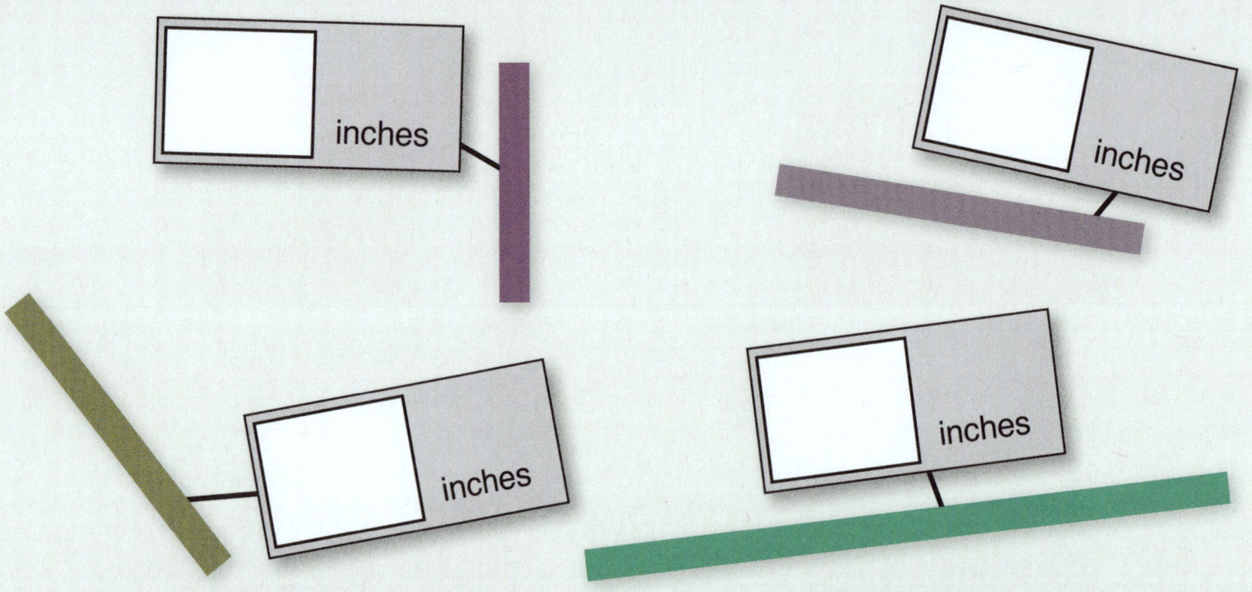

Solve.

David's family arrived at the fair at 10:45 a.m. They left at 2:05 p.m. How long did they spend at the fair?

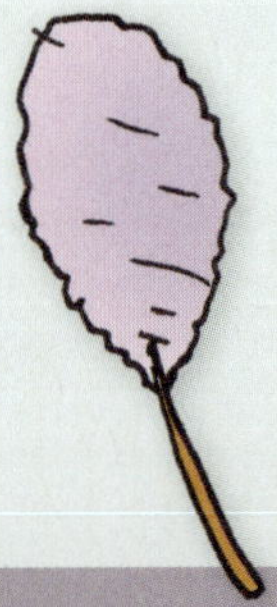

David's family bought 6 sandwiches for $8 each. They bought 6 ice cream cones for $3 each. How much more did they spend on sandwiches than ice cream cones?

Unit Wrap-Up

Complete.

7)70	8)32	9)45	8)56	7)56
8)48	7)63	9)63	8)40	7)49
9)54	8)80	7)35	9)72	8)72
9)90	9)81	8)64	7)42	9)27

Complete.

14 days = ☐ weeks

20 days = ☐ weeks, ☐ days

28 days = ☐ weeks

31 days = ☐ weeks, ☐ days

42 days = ☐ weeks

45 days = ☐ weeks, ☐ days

56 days = ☐ weeks

61 days = ☐ weeks, ☐ days

Unit Wrap-Up

Complete.

All sides are equal.

Perimeter: 32 ft.

Length of each side: ☐

All sides are equal.

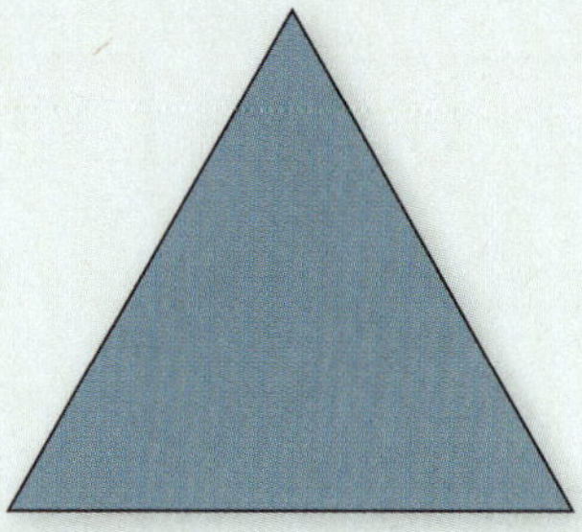

Perimeter: 24 m

Length of each side: ☐

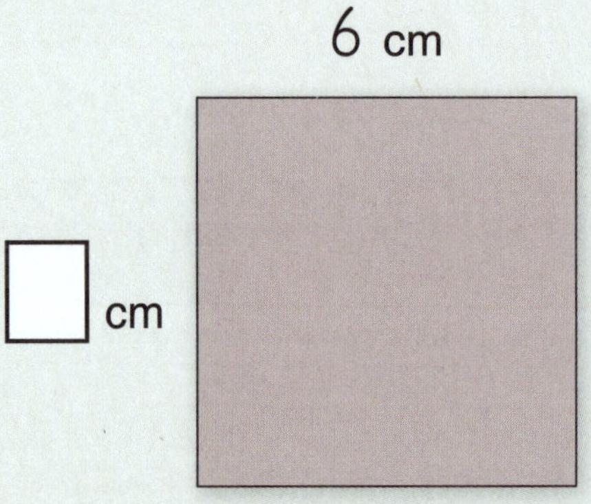

Area: 36 sq. cm

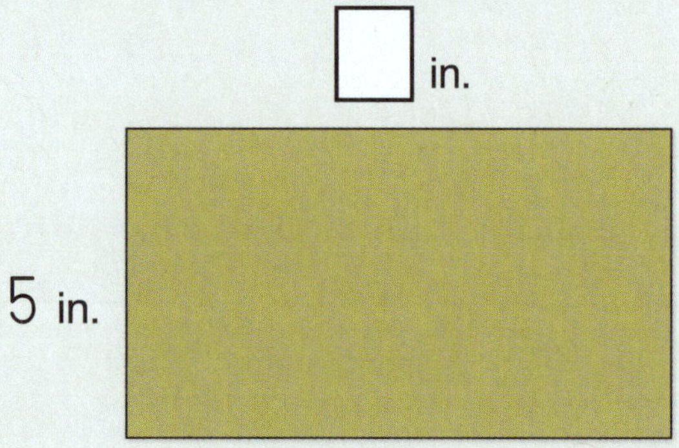

Area: 45 sq. in.

Solve. Write the equations you use to solve the problems.

RJ arranges his rock collection in bins. He has 72 rocks. 9 rocks fit in each bin. How many bins does he fill?

Audrey organizes her stuffed animals on shelves. She has 56 stuffed animals and 8 shelves. She puts the same number on each shelf. How many stuffed animals are on each shelf?

Lesson Activities

A

1 ounce (oz.)

16 ounces = 1 pound

1 pound (lb.)

B

C

Item	Estimated Weight	Actual Weight

16.1

Practice

Choose the more sensible unit for each item.

Weight of a dumbbell

5 oz.	5 lb.

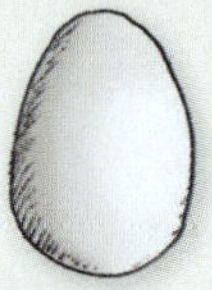

Weight of an egg

2 oz.	2 lb.

Weight of a new baby

8 oz.	8 lb.

Find the weight of each item. Include the correct unit.

Solve. Write the equations you use to solve the problems.

Bella's grandma needs 32 oz. of tomatoes for a recipe. Each tomato weighs about 4 oz. How many tomatoes does she need?

The mother elephant at the zoo weighs 6,507 lb. Her baby weighs 237 lb. How much more does the mother elephant weigh than her baby?

Caleb has 48 oz. of modeling clay. He splits the clay equally into 8 balls. How much does each ball weigh?

Oliver weighs 72 lb. His little sister weighs 34 lb. less than him. How much does his sister weigh?

Review

Match.

90 ÷ 9	6	72 ÷ 8
72 ÷ 9	7	56 ÷ 8
54 ÷ 9	8	48 ÷ 8
81 ÷ 9	9	80 ÷ 8
63 ÷ 9	10	64 ÷ 8

Complete.

	7.	4	2
−	3.	8	7
$			

	4.	2	9
+	3.	7	8
$			

	5.	0	5
+	4.	3	8
$			

Complete. Use long division.

$9\overline{)67}$ $8\overline{)70}$ $7\overline{)73}$

Complete.

$ ______

$ ______

16.2

Lesson Activities

A

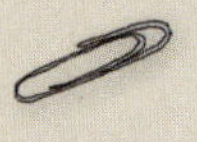

1 gram (g)

1,000 grams = 1 kilogram

1 kilogram (kg)

B

C

Item	Estimated Weight	Actual Weight

Practice

Choose the more sensible unit for each item.

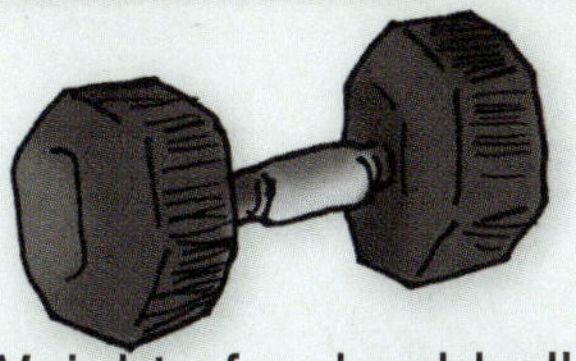

Weight of a dumbbell

2 g	2 kg

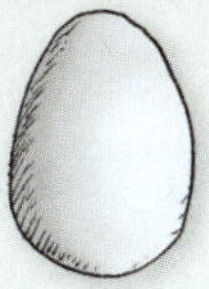

Weight of an egg

60 g	60 kg

Weight of a new baby

4 g	4 kg

Find the weight of each item. Include the correct unit.

Solve. Write the equations you use to solve the problems.

Eve weighs 29 kg.
Her brother weighs 16 kg more than her.
How much does her brother weigh?

The baby horse weighs 48 kg.
Its mother weighs 512 kg. How much less does the baby weigh than its mother?

Ana has 7 balls of modeling clay.
Each ball weighs 80 g. If she puts the clay together into one big ball, how much will the ball weigh?

The bread recipe calls for 275 g of white flour and 175 g of whole wheat flour. How many total grams of flour are in the recipe?

Review

Match.

70 ÷ 7	6	48 ÷ 6
42 ÷ 7	7	36 ÷ 6
63 ÷ 7	8	60 ÷ 6
49 ÷ 7	9	42 ÷ 6
56 ÷ 7	10	54 ÷ 6

Complete.

All sides are equal.

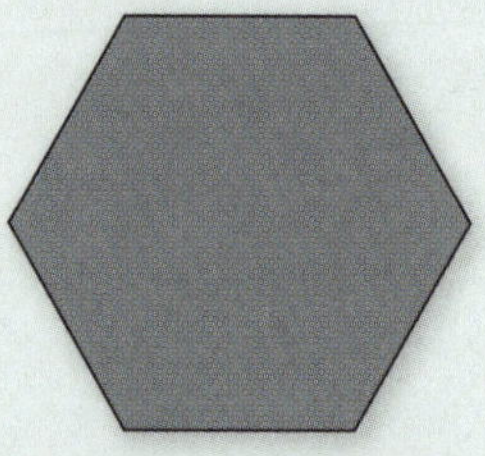

Perimeter: 42 m

Length of each side: ______

All sides are equal.

Perimeter: 36 in.

Length of each side: ______

Complete.

Start		End
4:45	15 min. →	
2:55	25 min. →	
3:05	30 min. →	
10:40	40 min. →	

Start		End
	← 35 min.	6:30
	← 20 min.	7:10
	← 30 min.	8:45
	← 25 min.	9:05

Lesson Activities

A

1 cup (c.) | 1 pint (pt.) | 1 quart (qt.) | 1 gallon (gal.)

B

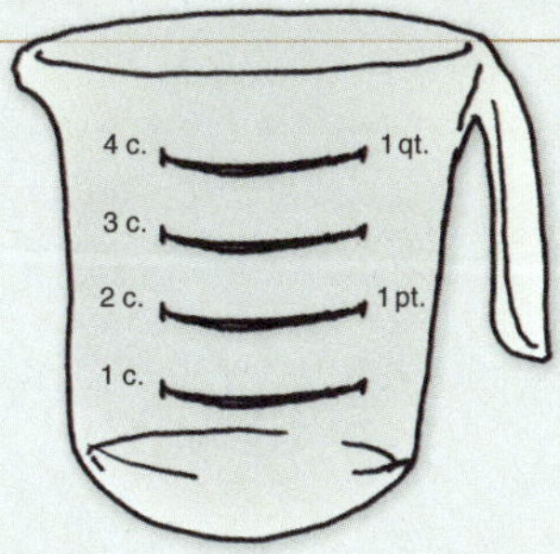

☐ c. = 1 pt.

☐ c. = 1 qt.

☐ pt. = 1 qt.

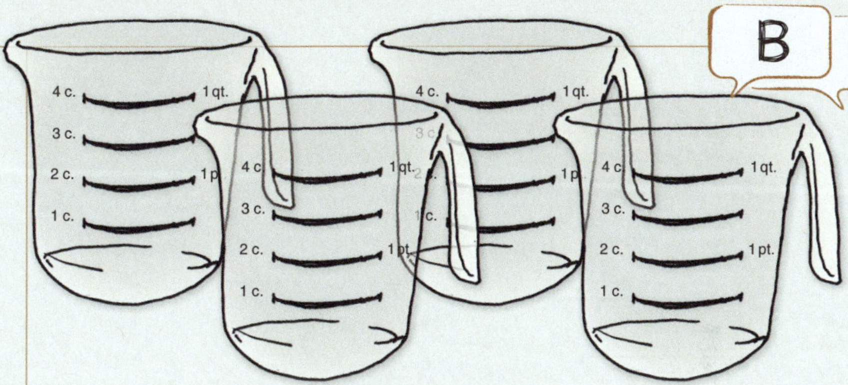

4 qt. = 1 gal.

★ ☐ c. = 1 gal.

★ ☐ pt. = 1 gal.

C

Capacity Scavenger Hunt

Holds less than 1 cup	Holds more than 1 cup and less than 1 pint	Holds more than 1 pint and less than 1 quart
Holds more than 1 quart and less than 1 gallon	Holds more than 1 gallon	

Practice

Choose the more sensible unit for each item.

Capacity of a bathtub

42 c.	42 gal.

Capacity of a teapot

3 c.	3 gal.

Capacity of an aquarium

10 c.	10 gal.

Complete with <, >, or =.

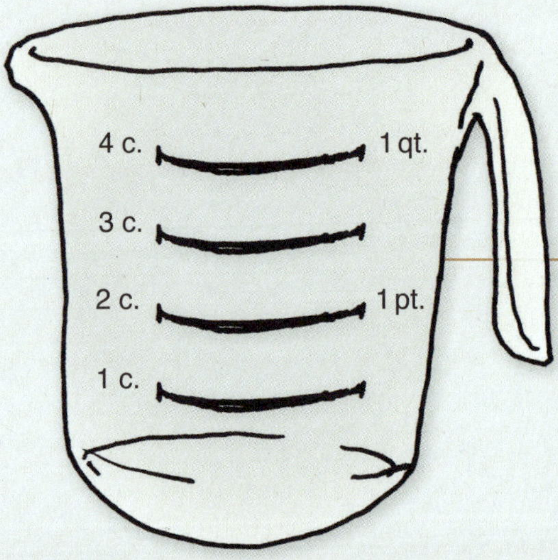

1 c. ◯ 1 pt.

2 c. ◯ 1 pt.

3 c. ◯ 1 pt.

2 c. ◯ 1 qt.

3 c. ◯ 1 qt.

4 c. ◯ 1 qt.

1 pt. ◯ 1 qt.

2 pt. ◯ 1 qt.

3 pt. ◯ 1 qt.

★ 5 c. ◯ 1 qt.

★ 3 qt. ◯ 12 c.

★ 8 pt. ◯ 5 qt.

Solve. Write the equations you use to solve the problems.

Alisha and her dad make a big batch of tomato sauce. They put 4 cups of sauce in each jar, and they fill 6 jars. How many cups of sauce do they make?

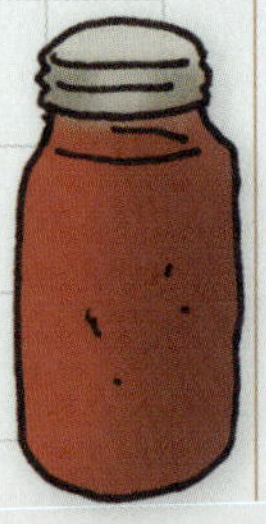

The swimming pool holds 8,800 gallons of water. The hot tub holds 500 gallons of water. How much water does it take to fill both?

Review

Color the problems that match the number in the star.

7	6	9	8
49 ÷ 7	54 ÷ 9	72 ÷ 8	72 ÷ 8
56 ÷ 8	56 ÷ 7	81 ÷ 9	56 ÷ 7
90 ÷ 9	48 ÷ 8	56 ÷ 7	72 ÷ 9

5	4	2	3
35 ÷ 7	45 ÷ 9	16 ÷ 8	24 ÷ 8
32 ÷ 8	28 ÷ 7	27 ÷ 9	28 ÷ 7
45 ÷ 9	32 ÷ 8	14 ÷ 7	27 ÷ 9

Complete.

6 weeks = ☐ days

4 weeks = ☐ days

☐ weeks = 21 days

☐ weeks = 63 days

950¢ = $ ☐

137¢ = $ ☐

☐ ¢ = $2.45

☐ ¢ = $7.06

Complete.

40 × 8 = ☐

30 × 9 = ☐

50 × 6 = ☐

80 × 8 = ☐

48 × 2 = ☐

54 × 2 = ☐

64 × 2 = ☐

72 × 2 = ☐

Lesson Activities

A

1 milliliter (mL)

1,000 mL = 1 L

1 liter (L)

B

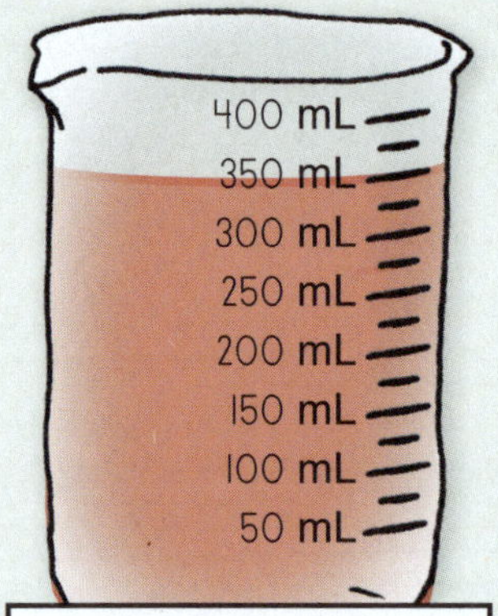

Red:

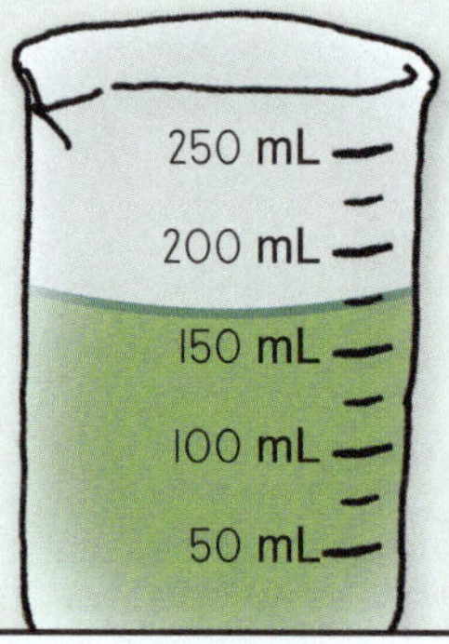

Green:

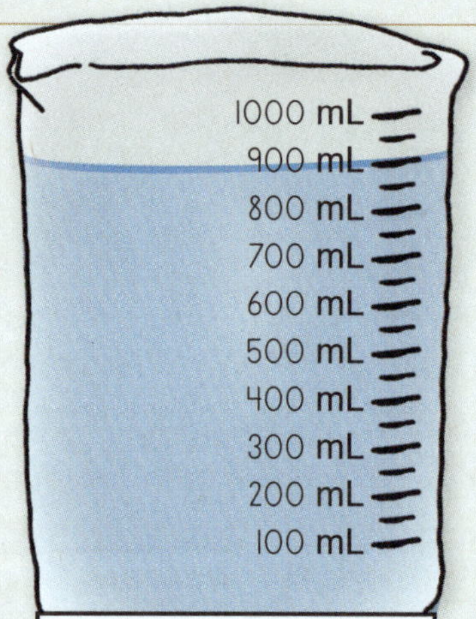

Blue:

C

Capacity Scavenger Hunt

less than 100 mL	100-249 mL	250-499 mL
500-749 mL	750-999 mL	more than 1 L

Practice

Choose the more sensible unit for each item.

Capacity of a watering can

8 mL | 8 L

Capacity of a soda bottle

2 mL | 2 L

Capacity of a medicine bottle

60 mL | 60 L

Write how much liquid is in each beaker. Then, use the beakers to answer the questions.

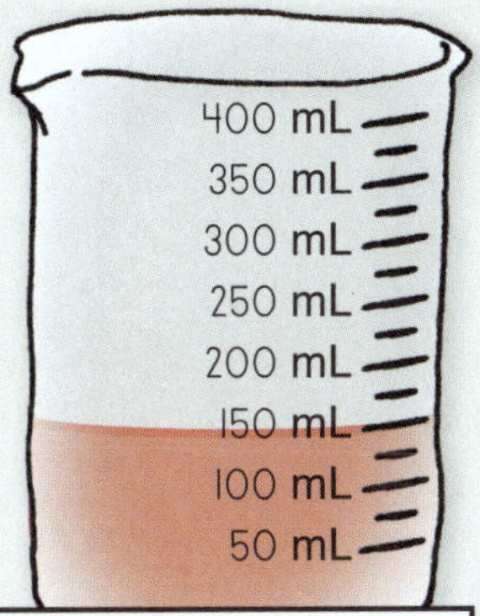

Red:

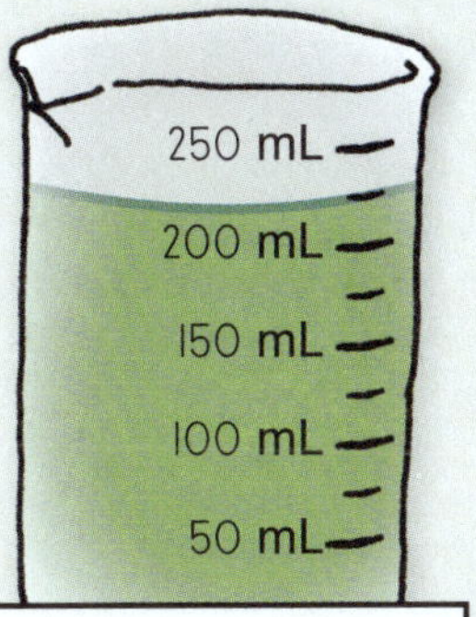

Green:

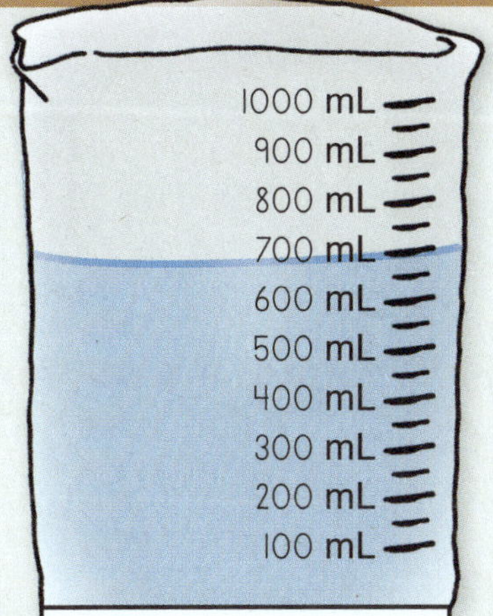

Blue:

How much less red liquid than green liquid is there?

If you pour the red and green liquid into the same beaker, how much liquid will be in the beaker?

If you remove 80 ml of blue liquid from the large beaker, how much liquid will be left?

★ If you split the blue liquid equally into 2 beakers, how much liquid will be in each beaker?

Review

Complete.

$9\overline{)90}$	$7\overline{)49}$	$8\overline{)56}$	$7\overline{)63}$	$9\overline{)54}$
$8\overline{)72}$	$9\overline{)81}$	$7\overline{)70}$	$9\overline{)63}$	$8\overline{)48}$
$7\overline{)42}$	$8\overline{)64}$	$9\overline{)72}$	$7\overline{)56}$	$8\overline{)80}$

Complete.

☐ ft.

5 ft.

Area: 35 sq. ft.

☐ m

8 m

Area: 48 sq. m

☐ in.

9 in.

Area: 81 sq. in.

Complete.

Start		End
11:30 a.m.	1 hr. →	☐
11:15 a.m.	1 hr. 10 min. →	☐
10:30 p.m.	2 hr. →	☐

☐	← 1 hr. 15 min.	1:00 p.m.
☐	← 2 hr. 30 min.	12:00 a.m.
☐	← 12 hr.	5:00 p.m.

Unit Wrap-Up

Choose the more sensible unit for each item.

Weight of a suitcase

46 lb.	46 oz.

Weight of a purse

3 kg	3 g

Weight of a wallet

100 lb.	100 g

Capacity of a bathtub

190 L	190 mL

Capacity of a wading pool

26 gal.	26 c.

Capacity of a tea cup

1 L	1 c.

Capacity of a salad dressing bottle

355 mL	355 qt.

Weight of a dolphin

500 lb.	500 L

Capacity of a pitcher

2 kg	2 qt.

Use the numbers to complete the boxes.

2	2	4	16	1,000	1,000

1 lb. = ☐ oz.

1 kg = ☐ g

1 L = ☐ mL

1 pt. = ☐ c.

1 qt. = ☐ pt.

1 gal. = ☐ qt.

Unit Wrap-Up

Complete. Include the correct units.

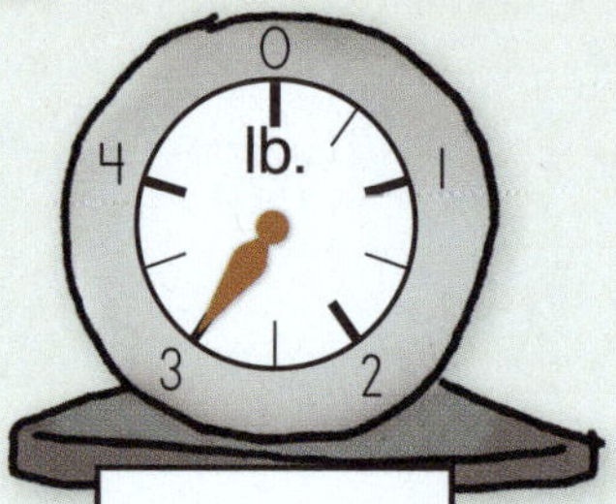

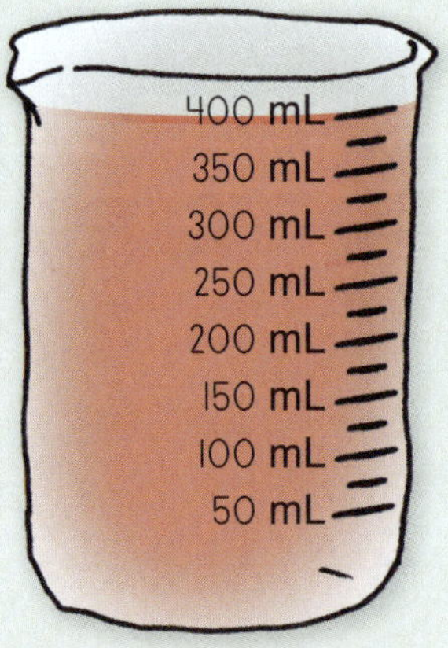

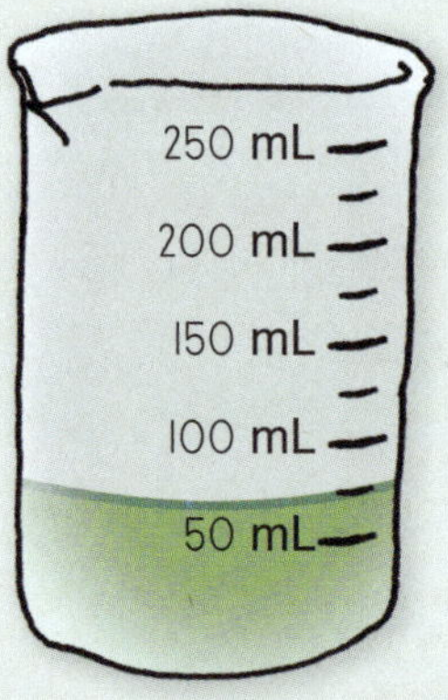

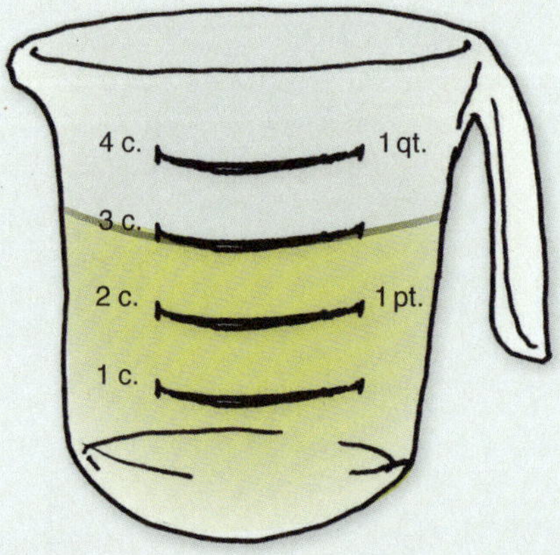

Solve. Write the equations you use to solve the problems.

Sara's guinea pig weighs 890 g. Her hamster weighs 120 g. How much less does her hamster weigh than her guinea pig?

There are 450 mL of water in the water bottle. If you drink 225 mL, how much water is left?

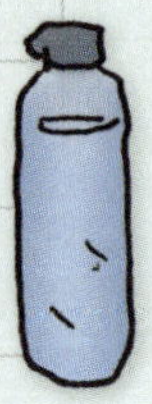

Each bag of mulch weighs 20 lb. How much do 7 bags weigh?

Aman's family fills 6 pitchers with punch for a party. Each pitcher holds 8 cups. How many cups of punch do they have?

Lesson Activities

A

Make Your Own Math Game

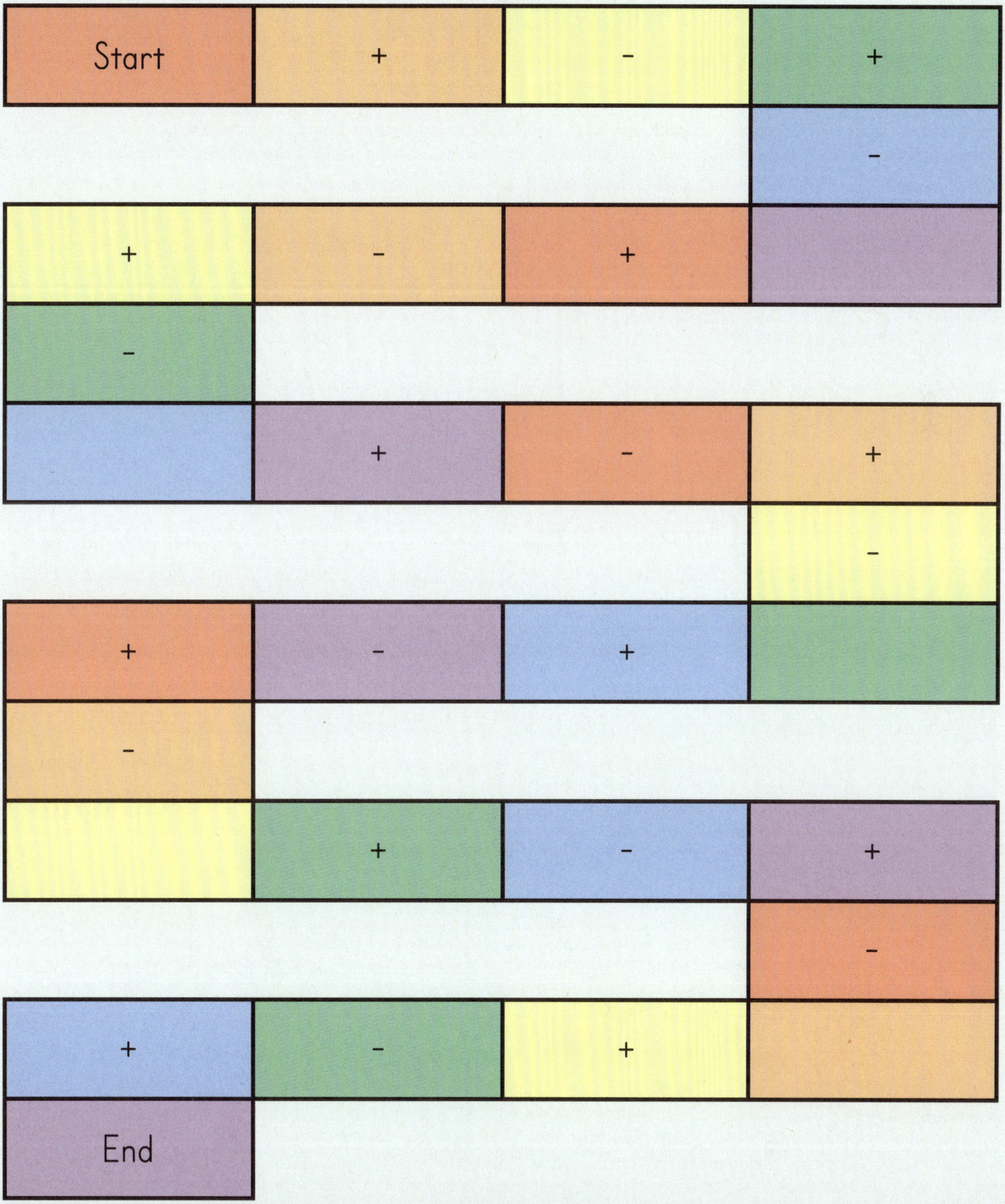

16.6

Practice

Complete.

	5,	4	8	1
+	2,	6	0	9

	4,	2	8	6
−	2,	7	4	5

	5.	5	0
−	3.	6	4
$			

Round to the nearest thousand.

4,960	
8,007	
5,531	
2,399	
788	

Complete.

Expanded Form	Number
700 + 90 + 4	
2,000 + 600 + 8	
	5,902
	4,075

Complete.

$ ______

$ ______

Complete with <, >, or =.

2,000 + 5 ◯ 2,000 + 50

500 + 500 ◯ 700 + 300

4,200 − 400 ◯ 4,300 − 600

580 + 50 ◯ 570 + 60

7,800 + 600 ◯ 7,900 + 500

730 + 80 ◯ 750 + 50

Review

Complete the sequences.

Solve. Write the equations you use to solve the problems.

Mom is 36 years old. Carlos is 28 years younger than Mom. Grandma is 53 years older than Carlos. How old is Grandma?

A cup of cocoa costs $1.79. A muffin costs $1.35 more than cocoa. How much does it cost to buy cocoa and a muffin?

The sum of 3 numbers is 100.
One number is 35. Another number is 15.
What is the last number?

Julia spends $4.25 on a hot dog and $1.50 on a drink. She gives the clerk $10.00.
How much change does she get?

Lesson Activities

A

Multiples of 1

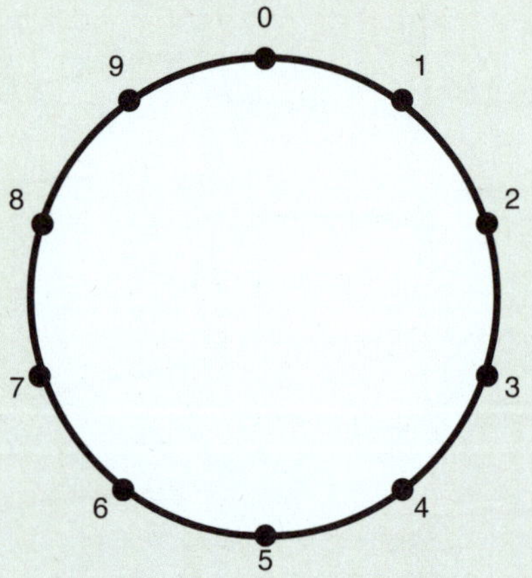

Multiples of 2

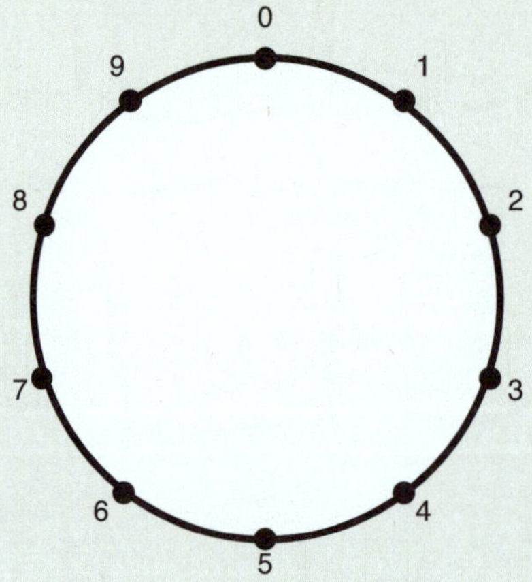

Multiples of 3

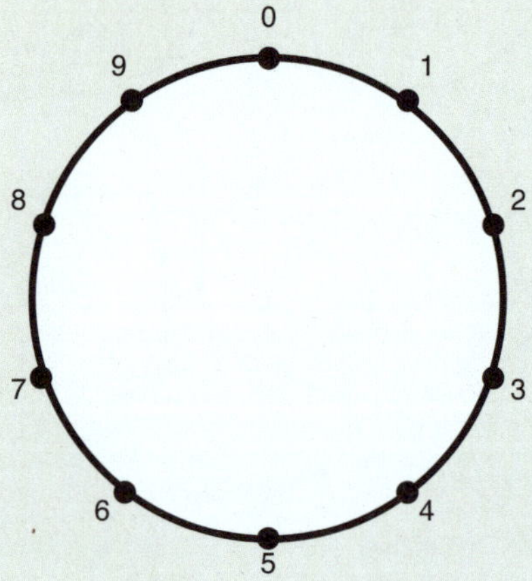

Multiples of 4

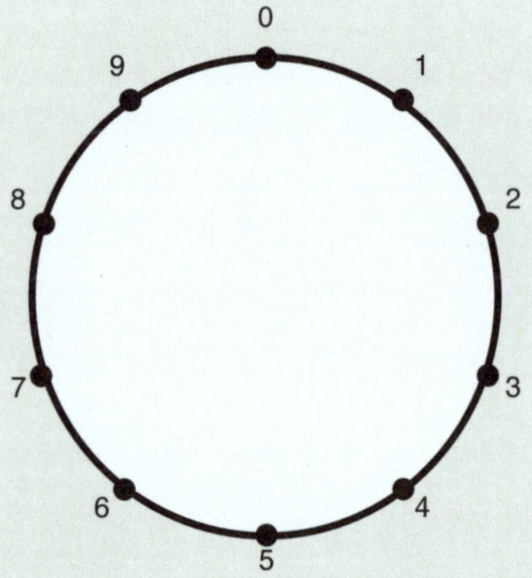

Multiples of 5

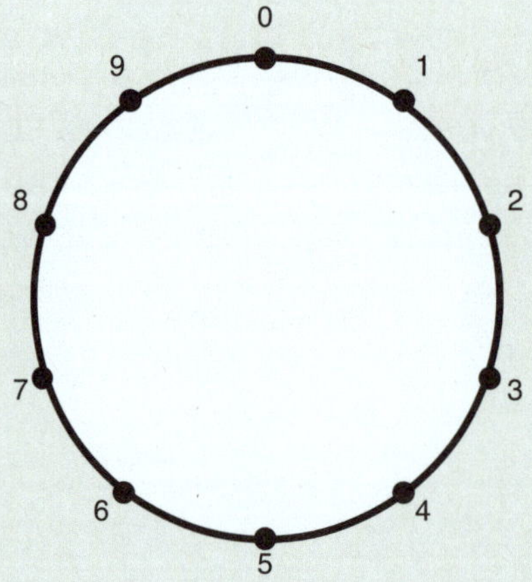

Multiples of 6

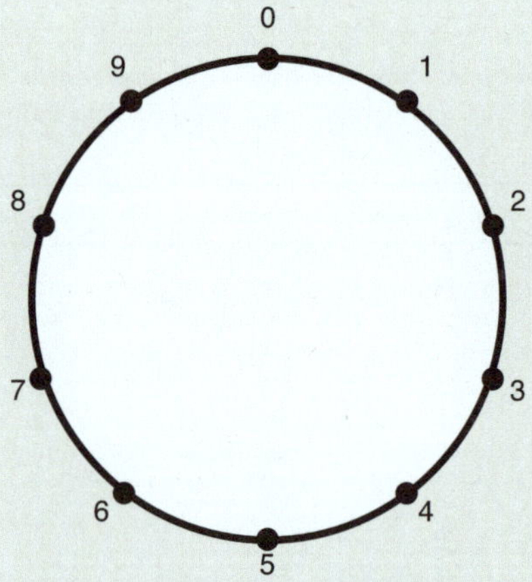

Multiples of 7

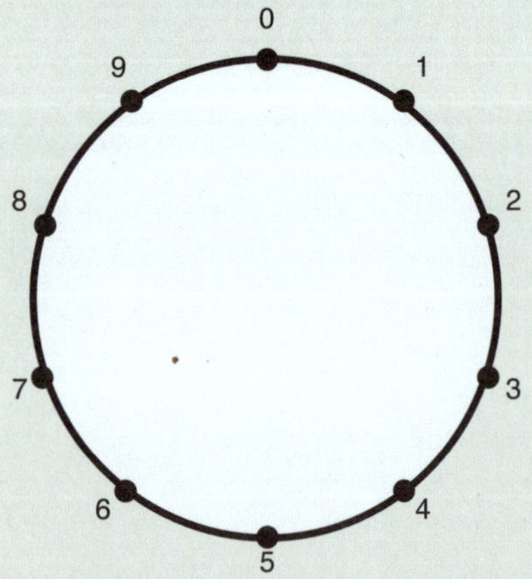

Multiples of 8

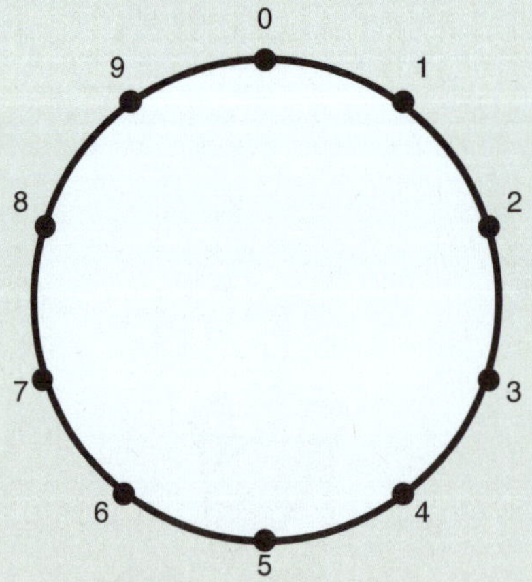

Multiples of 9

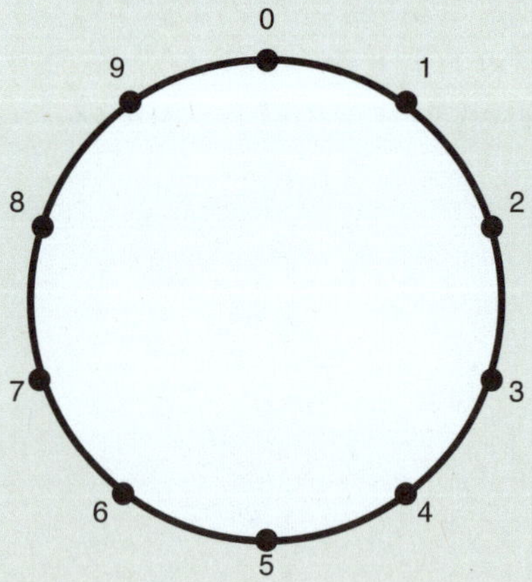

Practice

Complete the fact family to match the array.

☐ × ☐ = ☐

☐ × ☐ = ☐

☐ ÷ ☐ = ☐

☐ ÷ ☐ = ☐

Complete.

$4 \times 3 =$ ☐	$9 \times 6 =$ ☐	$10 \times 8 =$ ☐
$7 \times 7 =$ ☐	$9 \times 8 =$ ☐	$6 \times 7 =$ ☐
$4 \times 8 =$ ☐	$6 \times 4 =$ ☐	$4 \times 9 =$ ☐
$8 \times 6 =$ ☐	$5 \times 10 =$ ☐	$7 \times 4 =$ ☐
$5 \times 9 =$ ☐	$8 \times 7 =$ ☐	$6 \times 7 =$ ☐

Complete.

$4 \times 8 + 3 =$ ☐

$9 \times 6 + 1 =$ ☐

$35 \times 2 =$ ☐

$47 \times 2 =$ ☐

$90 \times 3 =$ ☐

$50 \times 6 =$ ☐

Solve. Write the equations you use.

Ruth earns $9 for mowing the lawn. If she mows the lawn 7 times, how much money will she earn?

Review

Complete.

18 ÷ 2 = ☐	28 ÷ 7 = ☐	40 ÷ 5 = ☐
36 ÷ 6 = ☐	27 ÷ 3 = ☐	35 ÷ 7 = ☐
54 ÷ 9 = ☐	90 ÷ 10 = ☐	72 ÷ 9 = ☐
48 ÷ 6 = ☐	64 ÷ 8 = ☐	36 ÷ 4 = ☐
49 ÷ 7 = ☐	56 ÷ 8 = ☐	63 ÷ 9 = ☐

Complete. Use long division.

$4\overline{)33}$ $3\overline{)28}$ $5\overline{)42}$

Complete.

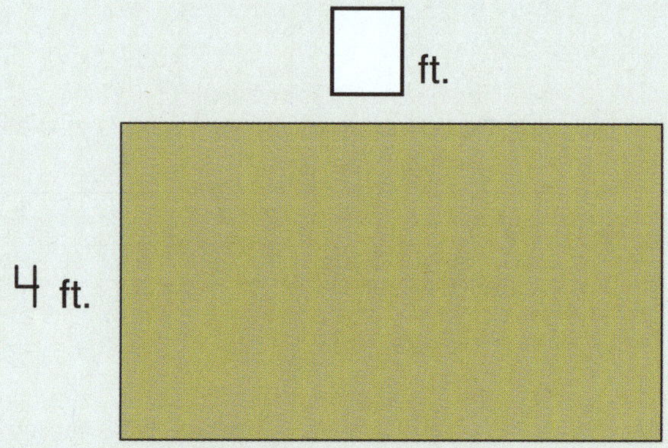

Area: 28 sq. ft.

Solve. Write the equations you use.

Oscar has 38 ft. of string.
He cuts the string into 6-foot-long pieces.
How much string is left over?

Mira's family buys 3 pizzas.
Each pizza has 8 slices. If they eat 17 slices, how many slices are left?

Lesson Activities

A

in.	lb.	km	sq. mi.
g	sq. yd.	m	sq. ft.
L	oz.	pt.	yd.
cm	ft.	mL	c.
qt.	gal.	sq. cm	min.
sq. km	sq. in.	kg	sq. m
	hr.	mi.	

	U.S.	Metric
Length		
Area		
Weight		
Capacity		
Time		

Practice

Choose the more sensible unit for each item.

Area of a window

1 sq. cm	1 sq. m

Area of a rug

35 sq. in.	35 sq. ft.

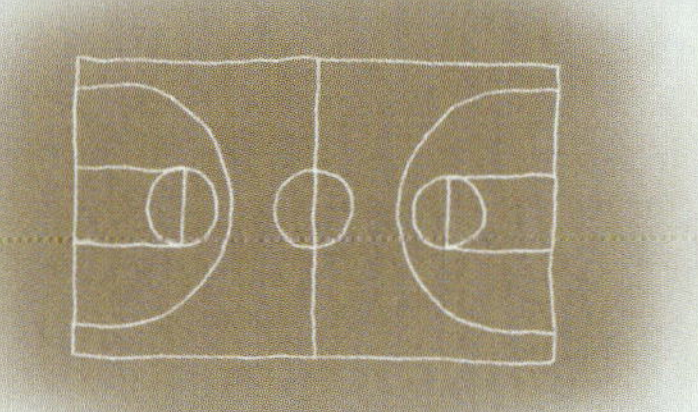

Area of a basketball court

600 sq. yd.	600 sq. mi.

Capacity of a drink can

355 mL	355 L

Capacity of a large pot

3 pt.	3 gal.

Weight of a small dog

9 g	9 kg

Find the perimeter and area.

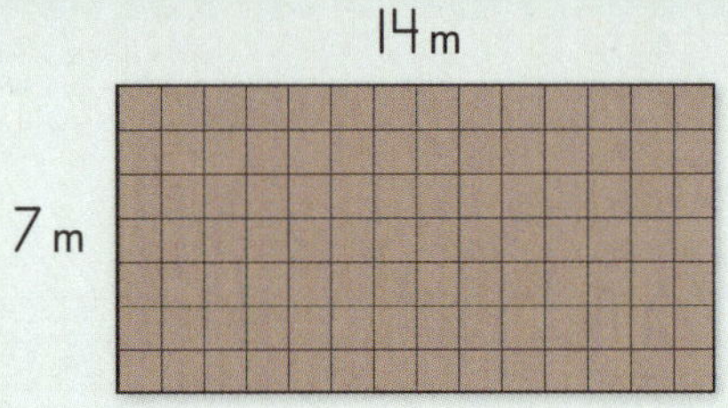

Perimeter:

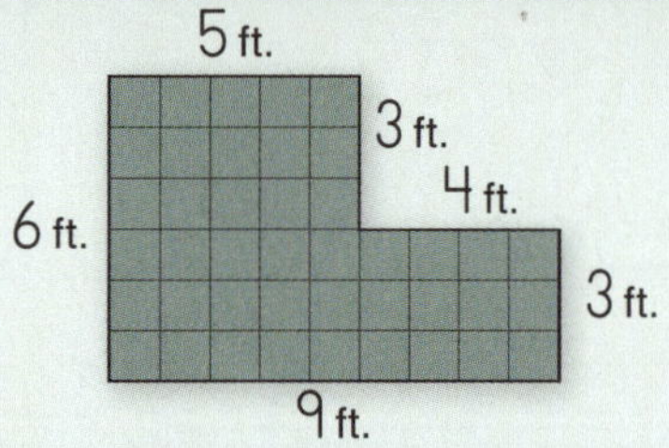

Perimeter:

Solve. Write the equations you use.

The shorter side of the rug is 5 feet long. The other side is 3 feet longer. What is the area of the rug?

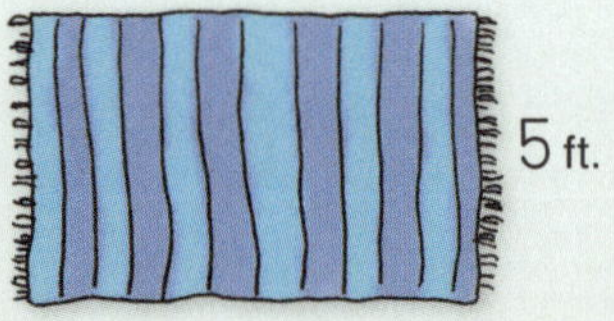

Cody and his mom use 24 m of fence to enclose this garden. How long is the unlabeled side of the garden?

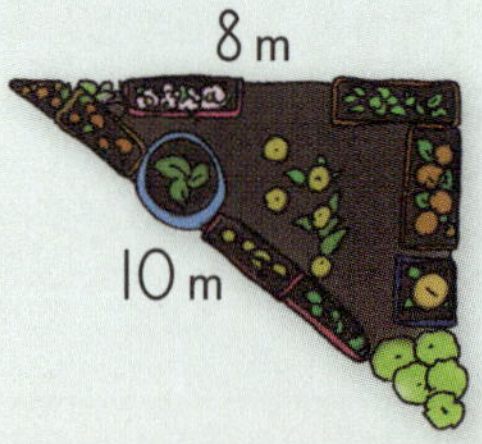

Review

Write the time.

Complete the chart.

Start Time	End Time	Elapsed Time
10:30 a.m.	11:15 a.m.	
11:45 a.m.		40 min.
	1:00 p.m.	3 hr.
2:30 p.m.		2 hr. 30 min.
4:45 p.m.	6:20 p.m.	
	12:00 a.m.	1 hr. 50 min.

Solve.

Tim played outside from 11:30 a.m. to 12:20 p.m. How long did he play outside?

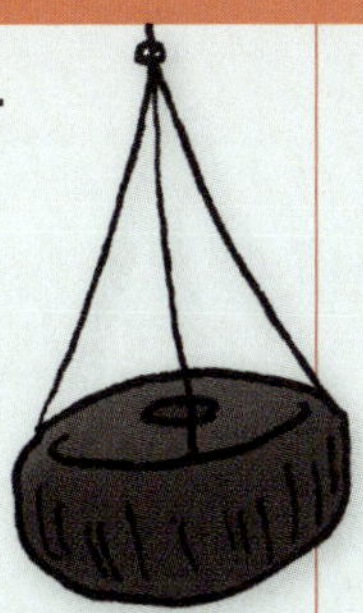

Josie starts watching a movie at 6:25 p.m. The movie is 1 hour and 50 minutes long. When will the movie be over?

Lesson Activities

A

Elements to Include

- Right angle
- Angle larger than a right angle
- Angle smaller than a right angle
- Square
- Rectangle
- Rhombus

B

What was your favorite math activity this year?	What math topic was most interesting to you this year?
What math skill did you work hardest to learn this year?	What do you hope to learn in math next year?

Practice

Complete.

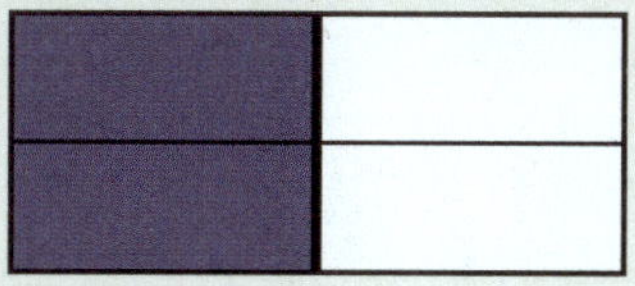

$\frac{1}{2} = \frac{\square}{4}$

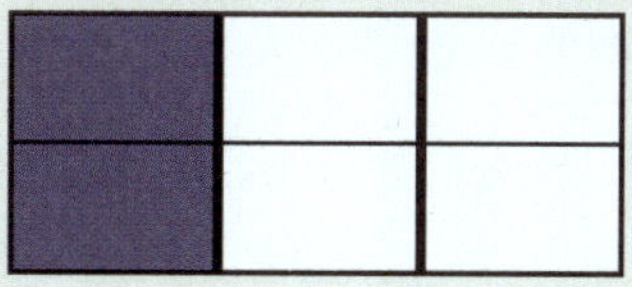

$\frac{1}{3} = \frac{\square}{6}$

$\frac{3}{4} = \frac{\square}{8}$

Write <, >, or =.

$\frac{1}{3} \bigcirc \frac{2}{3}$

$\frac{4}{8} \bigcirc \frac{1}{2}$

$\frac{2}{3} \bigcirc \frac{2}{8}$

$\frac{2}{2} \bigcirc \frac{7}{8}$

Complete.

$\frac{4}{8} + \frac{3}{8} = \frac{\square}{\square}$

$\frac{5}{6} - \frac{2}{6} = \frac{\square}{\square}$

$\frac{1}{3} + \frac{2}{3} = \frac{\square}{\square}$

$\frac{4}{4} - \frac{1}{4} = \frac{\square}{\square}$

Draw a shape to match each description.

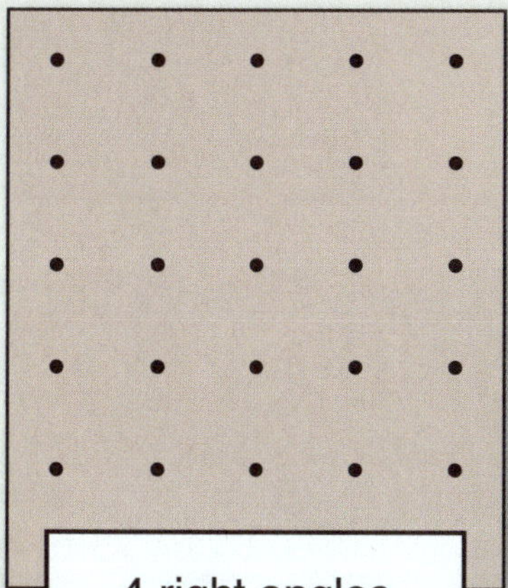

4 right angles

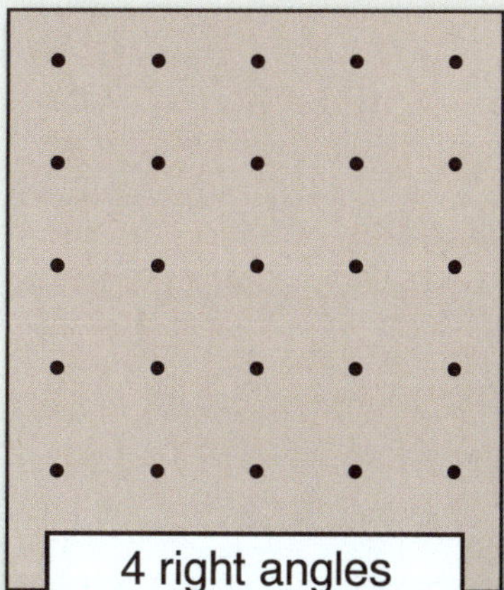

4 right angles and 4 equal sides

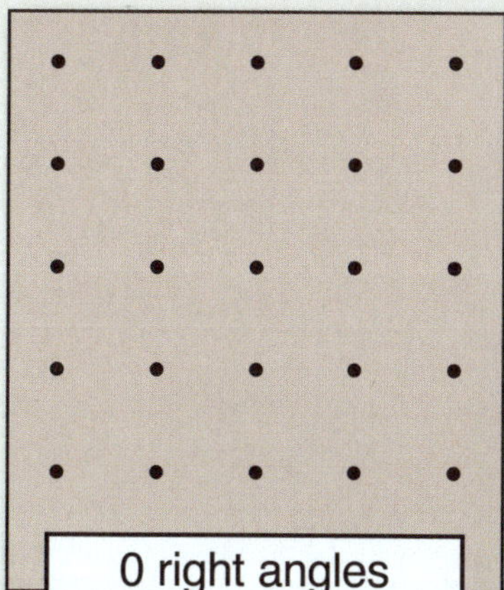

0 right angles and 4 equal sides

CONGRATULATIONS!

Presented to

____

for successfully completing

Third Grade Math with Confidence

____________________ Date

____________________ Signature